Upheaval

In *Upheaval* journalists do something they normally avoid. They turn the spotlight on themselves and their industry. They narrate a brutal transition at a critical moment in the media. This oral history documents the culture of Australian journalism before the internet – extemporising, sexist, booze-fuelled and brash – and reveals the private pain of the digital dislocation for many journalism lifers who had to reshape their professional identities. *Upheaval* puts readers in the newsroom as the rivers of gold dried up.

Katharine Murphy, political editor,
Guardian Australia

Essential reading for those who care about journalism and its struggle to survive. This book captures the essence of what it is to be a reporter amid tectonic shifts in the media and in the world that we strive to make sense of for our audiences. Anyone who follows the news and politics will be absorbed by *Upheaval*.

Nick McKenzie, investigative journalist,
The Age and *The Sydney Morning Herald*

Few occupations have gone through such a rapid transformation as journalism. Important and original, *Upheaval* illuminates aspects of contemporary journalism that few, if any, other books have achieved.

Rodney Tiffen, emeritus professor, University of Sydney

To journalists who seek light, not heat.

Upheaval
Disrupted lives in journalism

EDITED BY
ANDREW DODD &
MATTHEW RICKETSON

UNSW PRESS

A UNSW Press book

Published by
NewSouth Publishing
University of New South Wales Press Ltd
University of New South Wales
Sydney NSW 2052
AUSTRALIA
newsouthpublishing.com

© Andrew Dodd and Matthew Ricketson 2021
First published 2021

10 9 8 7 6 5 4 3 2 1

This book is copyright. While copyright of the work as a whole is vested in the editors, copyright of individual chapters is retained by the chapter authors. Apart from any fair dealing for the purpose of private study, research, criticism or review, as permitted under the *Copyright Act*, no part of this book may be reproduced by any process without written permission. Inquiries should be addressed to the publisher.

ISBN   9781742237275 (paperback)
        9781742245287 (ebook)
        9781742249841 (ePDF)

 A catalogue record for this book is available from the National Library of Australia

Design Josephine Pajor-Markus
Cover design Luke Causby, Blue Cork

All reasonable efforts were taken to obtain permission to use copyright material reproduced in this book, but in some cases copyright could not be traced. The editors welcome information in this regard.

Contents

1. **The precede** — 1
   Andrew Dodd and Matthew Ricketson

2. **Where do journalists come from?** — 12
   Lawrie Zion

3. **Many roads to journalism** — 29
   Andrew Dodd

4. **The first byline: Early careers** — 46
   Lawrie Zion

5. **Copy copy copy! Newsroom culture** — 62
   Andrew Dodd, Matthew Ricketson and Penny O'Donnell

   Profile: Amanda Meade — 77
   Penny O'Donnell and Matthew Ricketson

6. **The constant undercurrent: Sexual harassment and discrimination** — 89
   Penny O'Donnell, Merryn Sherwood and Brad Buller

7. **The thrill of the chase: Memorable stories** — 102
   Andrew Dodd

8. **Errors and regrets** — 117
   Matthew Ricketson

9. **Knocking on grass: Reporting trauma** — 131
   Merryn Sherwood and Matthew Ricketson

10. **Work-life imbalance** — 145
    Brad Buller

    Profile: David Marr — 156
    Matthew Ricketson

11.	**Chasing clicks: Changing technology** Merryn Sherwood and Andrew Dodd	168
12.	**Should I stay or should I go now?** Matthew Ricketson and Timothy Marjoribanks	184
13.	**Pickets and payouts: Unions in the newsroom** Penny O'Donnell, Brad Buller and Matthew Ricketson	199
14.	**Mate, this gives me absolutely no pleasure, but …** Andrew Dodd and Timothy Marjoribanks	215
15.	**The walk to the lift: Last days at work** Andrew Dodd	228
	Profile: Flip Prior Penny O'Donnell and Lawrie Zion	243
16.	**What just happened? The days after redundancy** Penny O'Donnell and Timothy Marjoribanks	254
17.	**Resilience and reinvention** Penny O'Donnell	264
18.	**The wrap** Andrew Dodd and Matthew Ricketson	277

The roll call	283
The redundancy timeline: Media coverage of job losses	312
Contributors	327
Acknowledgments	330
Notes	335
Bibliography	347
Index	349

CHAPTER 1
The precede

Andrew Dodd
Matthew Ricketson

Once *The Age* required an entire building. Now everything fits on one floor. To reach it, you go to the Melbourne headquarters of the Nine Entertainment Company. It's an office tower, with glass panels and polished surfaces and only a few traces of Nine's past. The workers rush past the old tripod-mounted TV camera on display and the monitors screening network shows on the wall. They wave staff cards above the turnstiles before heading to different sets of lifts where they diverge one way for insurance offices and telecommunication companies, or another way for the television newsroom.

The lift opens on a dimly lit corridor on the seventh floor, the new home of the Fairfax Media newspapers that Nine acquired after the last of the longstanding media ownership rules were dismantled in 2017. Turn right for *The Age* or left for *The Australian Financial Review*. Either way, you'll end up in the same horseshoe-shaped newsroom. Look around the floor and you can see the newsroom, all its sections, the library, editorial conference rooms, graphic department, podcast and video studios and the staff kitchens. You can also see *The Fin Review*'s own cluster of desks. On the walls are references to the 180-year heritage of the Fairfax empire, including an excerpt from *The Fin Review*'s first editorial and a quote from *The Age*'s revered editor Graham Perkin reminding staff the newspaper 'does certain things differently' because it has 'a responsibility to our readers and to society in general'.

Less than two decades ago, Fairfax, along with the rest of the Australian media, had boundless optimism about the future. In 2003 new presses were built at a $220 million printing plant near Tullamarine Airport. The facility featured a sculptured desert rock garden and a tall statue, which was described mockingly by author Rachel Buchanan as a 'luminous half-furled copy of *The Age* that rose 32-metres high … made of 542 glass panels attached to a steel frame, each one shaped by computer modelling'. Journalist David Marr would often pass the facility on the freeway from the airport, on his regular visits to Melbourne. He described it as an 'extravagant triumphalist building'. But on one visit he noticed the presses had gone, and the site was 'desperately for sale, or for lease or for anything'. There were fewer pages to print so the work could be done at Fairfax's press in Ballarat in regional Victoria.[1]

In 2007 the Howard Coalition government succeeded in watering down Paul Keating's cross-media ownership rules, which had prevented any company owning more than one of the major mediums of radio, TV or print in the same market. The new rules allowed companies to own two of the three mediums, prompting a complex deal that resulted in the owners of *The Age* also owning Southern Cross's influential metropolitan radio station 3AW.

Within two years, the former rivals occupied the same building, the purpose-built, stylishly modern Media House just 300 metres away from Nine's current location and two city blocks from *The Age*'s longstanding home on Lonsdale Street. Rising up on the corner of Collins and Spencer streets, Media House reflected how confidence persisted before journalism's business model collapsed and disruption swept away thousands of jobs. Soon the effects were visible inside the building, with *The Age* reduced to occupying just the second floor. The library and *The Fin Review* moved on to the same level too, along with sales and marketing and management.

The precede

And then came the Turnbull government's changes in 2017, allowing companies to own all three mediums in the same market. The owners of Nine were free to also own *The Age* and 3AW and they soon swooped, prompting the move one city block across to Nine's headquarters. 3AW remained at Media House, due to its technical studio requirements, but nothing is stopping the three former rivals cohabiting – a clear sign of the deregulation of the industry and of Australia's diminishing media diversity.

In *The Age*'s new foyer, sometimes a video plays on loop with footage of the newspaper's production plant. Perhaps it's to reassure visitors the newspaper is still printed, while reminding them of publishing's noisy and grimy history. The video also inevitably indicates how much has changed. Not so long ago, the printing presses shuddered to life each night in the old building, churning out hundreds of thousands of copies.

This contraction and consolidation enabled further concentration of the media, but it did not solve the commercial problem posed by digital disruption. It did, however, have real effects on people's lives. In the decade to the end of 2020, an estimated 4000 to 5000 journalism jobs, once considered safe for life, have simply disappeared, along with mastheads, outlets and production houses.[2]

Ways of working have gone too. Old industrialised and demarcated modes of creating stories have given way to quicker, cheaper methods. Newsrooms – the engine rooms of reporting in the second half of the 20th century – have shrunk, or disappeared.

And that was all before the Covid-19 pandemic of 2020, which accelerated or worsened what was already happening.

It's the task of this book to bear witness to all this change through the personal stories of the workers who have experienced both the old order of legacy media, as well as the upheaval that mostly occurred before Covid-19 struck. These stories take us into newsrooms and chronicle how journalists once worked and how the industry's disruption affected them, as well as the journalism they produced. In this book we place emphasis on the stories of career-long journalists because most have gone untold and collectively they reveal so much. But we have generally resisted the temptation to theorise or prescribe conclusions about what those stories mean. We don't see that as our role. We do, however, ask questions about where the journalists, and journalism, are heading.

*

Joel Deane, a poet and former speechwriter for political leaders, began his working life as a journalist. In 1987 he was a cadet at *The Sun News-Pictorial,* then and for many years before, the biggest-selling metropolitan daily newspaper in Australia. In a 2020 article for *Meanjin* he describes journalism then as a 'scruffy, sexist, self-serving semi-profession' and recalls the atmosphere in the linoleum-floored newsroom in the Flinders Street, Melbourne, headquarters of The Herald and Weekly Times:

> Although overwhelmingly Anglo, the reporters and sub-editors were an eclectic mix of broken toys – alcoholics and dreamers, rebels and soldiers of fortune, cranks and bleeding hearts, ex-cons and drug addicts, evangelists and thieves ... *The Sun* was primarily the happy hunting ground of white blokes. And the holy trinity of news for those beetroot-faced blokes was yarns, pics and booze; you had to get the story first, you had to get the best photo, and you had to hold your beer. Alcohol was everywhere. It was the stimulant, the salute, the salve, the release.[3]

Another ex-reporter, Jan McGuinness, recalls her time in the same building, but at a different masthead, the afternoon newspaper, *The Herald.*[4] She describes entering the 'big, brass-framed, plate-glass doors beyond which lies *The Herald* newsroom' in the 1960s and being 'confronted by a sea of desks where journos, most with a cigarette dangling from their lips, pound furiously at typewriters which are bolted to the desks'. She describes the artificial light where 'the jangle of dozens of ringing telephones fills the air heavy with the smell of printers' ink and cigarette smoke'. Despite its blokey culture and its many rough and gruff characters, she asserts there was 'an overarching culture of family. But that said, it was a boot camp out of which life long bonds and friendships were born.'

McGuinness's and Deane's vivid snapshots capture key elements of a dominant journalistic culture. But different shades and emphases could be found at each publication, even within the same media company, and in different parts of the industry. The rhythms of weekly suburban newspapers differed, as they did in country publications where there were fewer staff, but where the editor could be a significant local force. Metropolitan radio and television newsrooms also had small teams and relied on the big city newspapers' stories for many of their news leads, but they could break news by the hour and, in the case of television, their journalists learnt the power of moving images to shape events and perceptions of them in ways that far exceeded even *The Sun News-Pictorial*.

The mass media consolidated its power and influence in the 20th century. Newspaper was the first mass medium, followed by radio, and then television. The last decades of the last century were the highwater mark of the media in Australia. It was a profitable industry for most companies and a highly profitable one for commercial television stations, which could charge many thousands of dollars for an individual 30-second advertisement.

Metropolitan daily newspapers expanded the range and style of their coverage between the 1970s and the 1990s. They created supplements, about television or food or music or education or personal finance – one for each day of the week – and on weekends they began publishing magazines on glossy stock filled with ads and what were known in the industry as long reads. To give an idea of the scale of growth, by 1996 *The Age* published as many pages each weekday as it had on a Saturday four decades before, and its weekend edition routinely exceeded a whopping 250 pages.[5] Around this time, too, the big Saturday editions of *The Sydney Morning Herald* and *The Age* were making a profit of $1 million each week. Though not as well paid as lawyers or doctors, journalists had social cachet. To say you worked at *The Australian* or the Nine Network opened doors across the country and in the highest offices. Media companies had money to spend on pursuing stories. Simon Mann, when he was European correspondent for *The Age* and *The Sydney Morning Herald*, recalls how his bosses did not even blink when a £7000 mobile phone bill arrived after two months reporting in Kosovo.

*

In late 2011, the chief executives of the nation's biggest media companies fronted an inquiry into the media set up by the Gillard Labor government, telling its head, Ray Finkelstein QC, that whatever may have been happening to the media overseas, things were going well in Australia, and there was no need for government support as the industry moved from an analogue to a digital world.[6] (Disclosure: one of this book's editors assisted Finkelstein in the inquiry.) Just four months after the retired Federal Court judge delivered his report to government in early 2012, Fairfax Media announced the biggest round of redundancies in its history, shedding 1900 jobs throughout the company, 20 per cent of them journalists.[7]

Fairfax had, for several years, tried desperately to convince shareholders that its strategy for making the shift from print to digital was working. The so-called 'rivers of gold' revenue from advertising, especially classifieds, were drying up. A succession of websites emerged in the first decade of the 21st century offering ads for all the major categories – houses, jobs and cars. They were easily searched and free. But Fairfax was slow to adapt and missed several key opportunities to invest in online classified advertising start-ups. Not that they were alone. Rupert Murdoch, one of the world's most astute media businesspeople, was similarly slow to adapt, and made missteps too.

The ABC was free from commercial pressures, but still faced the costs of switching from analogue to digital technology. It was certainly freer to experiment with new media. Which it did, creating in 2008 a world-class online catch-up service for television, ABC iview.[8] The ABC's problem in this period was the hostility of the federal Coalition government, which regained power in 2013 and promptly began cutting the corporation's funding.[9]

Where did all these journalists go after they took redundancy? Some were fortunate enough to walk straight into another job in the media, while others took longer to find journalistic work elsewhere. Some moved to the so-called dark side of public relations, and some decided to change careers altogether, ranging from academia to driving a truck. Finally, some nearing retirement happily took the payout, which depending on length of service could be more than two years' salary. The full range of redundancy experiences is found among the interviewees for this book.

*

In 2021, we still haven't solved the problem of who will pay for journalism, and the legacy media has fewer resources to combat the growth of fake news, populism, and online trolls. The media now operates in a world where 'everyone is entitled to their own facts', and where opaque algorithms are designed to offer up a reality based on the beliefs and searches of users.[10]

What can the lives of previous generations of journalists tell us about how to deal with the problems facing journalism – and society – today? A lot actually. Journalists deal with ethical and legal and storytelling challenges every day. Over time the industry has created a body of practical wisdom, or what Aristotle called phronesis,[11] from which individual reporters can draw ideas and strategies to help them solve problems. This wisdom is sometimes written down, in codes of ethics or style guides, but usually it resides in the people in the newsroom, who have dealt with all manner of challenges over their careers, and offer advice to one another, sometimes yelled across partitions or confided in a chat by the photocopier. This book is a distillation of that practical wisdom about the industry, much of which has resonance for the future of journalism, even in the upheaval of digital disruption.

Now is a good time to hear from a generation of journalists who, for the past half-century, have been telling us what has been happening out in the world and under our noses. These journalists, some of whom became household names while others honoured journalism's anonymous crafts, such as sub-editing, covered the biggest stories, as well as the many smaller ones that shaped the country's self-image and fed the national conversation. They learned their craft in predominantly male newsrooms where few had a tertiary education, but many became highly qualified at finding out what really happens within society's centres of power.

Crucially, this generation of journalists witnessed the upheaval in their own workplaces. They lived the disruption around them. They watched it draining the resources they needed to tell stories. They saw it sapping confidence and creating anxiety among newsroom colleagues. Most did not report on this as it was happening – an interesting phenomenon in its own right – but in this book they are doing just that, and doing so with the observational and storytelling skills they developed as working journalists. Importantly they are sharing their doubts and vulnerabilities, which journalists rarely do in public.

*

The precede

This book includes material from interviews with 57 journalists who, with one exception, experienced redundancy between 2012 and 2016. As with the industry overall, some are still working in the media. Many moved on to jobs in new fields. Others are unemployed or choosing to work less, and some have opted for retirement. These whole-of-life interviews were recorded in association with the National Library of Australia (NLA) and cover regional, rural and metropolitan journalists from radio, television, online and print media. The interviewees include sub-editors, as well as veteran journalists, photographers, cartoonists, magazine writers and section editors. There are reporters covering almost every round, including sport, business, politics, arts and crime. That said, this breadth differs slightly from the actual group of journalists who took redundancy packages in 2012, and the years immediately afterward, which is when the bulk of job losses occurred. Redundancies were mainly drawn from the two major media companies – Fairfax and News Corporation – and there were relatively few redundancies in commercial broadcast media. Also they were skewed older and male. We have aimed for a 50/50 gender balance. Achieving greater cultural and ethnic diversity among the interviewees has been more difficult because of the lack of diversity historically in Australian newsrooms, though we've witnessed slow, but growing, improvement since.

The interviews ranged in length from four to eight hours and overall generated 4885 pages of transcript. The interviews can be found in the NLA's catalogue and are available for public access now or, in some cases, at a future date. Where a quote appears from a journalist in the book, unless otherwise noted, it is from their interview for this project. Note, though, that some quotes have been edited for clarity and brevity. They have also all been checked with the interviewees. Sadly, one of the interviewees, Rosslyn Beeby, died as this book was going to press.

*

Common to most of the interviewees was a loss of professional identity, which they experienced deeply and in ways shared with other jobs but also in ways particular to journalism and the industry in which it is practiced. It is important to give readers a fuller sense of journalists' lives before charting the industry's response to digital disruption and how that led to wholesale job loss. We did this partly to flesh out the kind of people who become journalists and partly because we need to show the extent to which journalists define themselves by their professional identity so readers can see what it means when that identity is taken away or, at the least, threatened by redundancy. To that end, the book is structured chronologically and thematically. It begins with how journalists became journalists, their early mentors and big stories. It then discusses how women experienced discrimination in newsrooms, and the ethical binds that journalists encountered. We then look more closely at how journalists faced the seismic changes in their industry and how they made the decision to take redundancy – or had it made for them. We go inside newsrooms across the nation as people experience their final days at work, and then what they did after walking away.

Because so many different voices appear in the text we have provided resources to help navigate the material. Alongside the standard academic apparatus – endnotes and bibliography – you'll find pocket biographies of each of the 57 journalists interviewed for the book, as well as a timeline of the media coverage of redundancies in Australian newsrooms, beginning with Fairfax Media's shock announcement in June 2012, and continuing through to the end of 2020.

To provide a sense of the overall shape of a journalist's career since the 1970s, we have included profiles of three individuals. We could have chosen almost any of the 57 interviewees, such is the richness of their working lives and the stories they have to tell. We opted for three people whose careers illustrated a range of experiences in and out of newsrooms, but who interestingly all returned to the media in one way or other following redundancy. We placed their profiles, which are edited transcripts of their NLA interviews, after chapters five, ten and fifteen. The first profile is of Amanda Meade who reported on her own industry throughout this period of intensive change. The second profile is of David Marr whose career began during the peak of the print media's influence and includes roles in radio and television as well as books. The third profile is of Flip Prior whose working life began like that of many others, in regional and metropolitan newspapers, before redundancy prompted her to create a second career. Since taking a package in 2012 she has worked in communications for the journalists' union, has trained politicians and journalists in how to use twitter, devised social media strategy for the ABC and more recently worked on the national broadcaster's 50/50 project aimed at improving women's representation in the news.

Finally, a note on company names: we use the current name of media companies, but in the period covered by this book several names have changed, not least because of the effects of digital disruption. For example, News Limited became News Corporation Australia in 2013 and Fairfax Media became part of the Nine Entertainment Company in 2018.

CHAPTER 2

Where do journalists come from?

Lawrie Zion

On 21 August 1991, *Herald Sun* journalist Ross Brundrett was told to go to West Melbourne to 'do some colour' about a fire at the massive oil storage tanks at Coode Island. Luckily, he already knew the local area, having grown up in the western suburbs. He had also recently purchased a beige anorak and, for reasons that evade him to this day, decided to take a clipboard on the job, along with the newsroom's two-way radio.

He and photographer Brett Faulkner drove to Footscray, with Brundrett giving directions down the side streets he knew so well. They avoided the police roadblocks and found a place to park, just 100 metres from the fire. Brundrett believes he must have looked like some sort of government official, because no one stopped them.

'So, I've got my clipboard, I've got my two-way radio, I've got my anorak, and a photographer, and we've just walked up to the fire like you would to a Sunday picnic.'

They stood around next to the firemen who were fighting what had by then become an inferno.

'We're next to them saying howdy doody. It's quite surreal,' says Brundrett.

He was able to get more than colour. Brundrett had what journalists always want: a backstage access-all-areas pass, even though it was unofficial and placed him directly under a cloud of burning benzene particles. After about 45 minutes he used the radio to call his chief of staff, Keith Moor.

> I said, 'Keith, we're in.' He goes, 'You're kidding.' I go, 'Yeah. What do you want us to do?' 'Stay there! See what you can do.' So, we're watching a fire and we go back a bit from the heat, and there's blokes behind a fire truck and they're all lighting up, having a cigarette, as you do when you're fighting a toxic fire. There's no one with face masks or anything, and we're chatting away. We're going great guns, getting some good quotes.

Of course, it didn't last. Eventually, someone with a helmet came up and asked them whether they were from the Department of Health. Brundrett told him they were reporters from the *Herald Sun*.

'Well, I can't say what he said,' Brundrett recalls. 'But he said, "Get the effing out of here."'

Brundrett remembers it was 'slightly disturbing' when they were sent nearly 500 metres away and everyone was wearing a face mask. In fact, they kept seeing people with face masks on the drive back to the newsroom. 'This is not a good sign,' they said to each other.

Brundrett's coverage of the story, which he still remembers proudly, echoed the reporting of another disaster two decades earlier, which first opened his young eyes to the power of being on the spot when a big story is breaking.

On 15 October 1970, when he was just 13, Melbourne's West Gate Bridge, which was still under construction, collapsed into the muddy reaches of the Yarra below, resulting in the deaths of 35 workers, many of whom were lunching in the workers' huts beneath the bridge.[1]

'I think that was probably the one story that I never forgot, and absorbed,' says Brundrett, who grew up a few kilometres away in Yarraville, and recalls seeing the dust in the air from their home after the tragedy. He also recalls being captivated by how journalists reported on the disaster, especially a story by *The Herald*'s Bruce Wilson.

'For years I could remember whole slabs of that story because I just absorbed the whole thing. I must've read it two or three times, which you don't usually do with a newspaper story.' What particularly struck him was the power of the eyewitness accounts:

> The actual access that you got to those stories back then was so much more than you would now, where it would be all cordoned off in a matter of hours ... There, people were walking through discovering survivors. Journalists were talking to people before they'd even been seen by ambulance men and women. So, you had these very vivid accounts from people that actually did survive after coming down that 30 or 40 metres with the bridge.

He acknowledges the survivors interviewed were in a state of shock and perhaps shouldn't have been reported on, but 'it was such a raw and immediate story, and so close to home'.

Many forces prompt people to work in the news media. Some people were always going to become journalists. They were the first to volunteer to edit their school newspaper or they wrote letters to their local paper when only 10 years old. Some enjoyed performing in plays and could see themselves in front of the television camera, while others were natural stickybeaks, always asking questions and wanting to know what was going on around them. Perhaps journalism just ran in the family? For some, journalism was not a natural choice until a parent or role model nudged them towards the media. Conversely, a false start in one career pushed some in the direction of journalism. Regardless of their motivations, formative experiences, like Brundrett's exposure to the West Gate Bridge tragedy, had long-lasting effects, even shaping their later work in journalism.[2]

Jo Roberts came to see the power of journalism long before entertaining any idea of a career as a reporter. Growing up on Victoria's Mornington Peninsula, she was like lots of kids her age. She enjoyed watching cartoons and *Get Smart* on TV, and when she was home sick from school she got to watch the variety program, *The Mike Walsh Show*, at midday. She still remembers all the ladies in the audience with their blue and mauve hair. She and her brothers were into music, especially the Rolling Stones, Deep Purple, and Black Sabbath, as well as the Beatles, of course. Her family's media habits were not unusual. She says she came from 'a *Sun* family', meaning her parents received *The Sun News-Pictorial* in the morning and *The Herald* in the afternoon, but not *The Age*, where she would eventually work as a journalist for 14 years.

Roberts developed an early appreciation of the local *Southern Peninsula Gazette*, in Rosebud on the Peninsula. 'The local paper was really big back then,' she says. 'I'd ride past the office of the *Gazette* on Ninth Avenue and dream about working there.'

She used to deliver the *Gazette* to homes around Rosebud, getting to know the local mix of sport, council news and crime. 'There were so many papers that my back tyre would be just about flat with the weight of them all,' she recalls. She soon recognised the role the paper played, at a time well before social media. 'That's how you found out stuff in your local community. That's when the local paper was a big deal. Because unless somebody had died, local stories didn't rate in the metropolitan news.'

Roberts' own family became the subject of one of these local stories. While she was still in primary school, her father, a police sergeant, experienced mental health issues that destroyed both his career and family life. He had stockpiled canisters of petrol and threatened to burn the house down if her mother didn't move the family back to Melbourne. Luckily they were staying elsewhere the night Roberts' father followed through on his threat. A local fire is a big suburban story, and she recalls it was covered by the *Gazette*.

'I remember seeing a picture of our burned house in the local paper a week later. Isn't that bizarre?' Roberts remembers she was initially more interested in a career in public relations.

> Maybe because of what was going on at home I was a pretty reclusive kid, you know. I didn't have a lot of friends. I remember being quite lonely in primary school and quite a lot of high school. It was funny, actually, that was one of the reasons I ended up becoming a journalist. Because I wanted to not be so shy.

But with no public relations courses on offer, she opted to study journalism first, as a stepping-stone to public relations. Soon after, she began working in suburban newspapers where she found herself drawn to stories that could make a positive impact on a local community. 'You wanted to be the voice of the little guy,' she recalls, protecting community groups trying to build new sporting grounds against councils pushing new, more lucrative housing developments.

For Rocco Fazzari, who would become one of the country's best-known cartoonists and illustrators at *The Sydney Morning Herald*, engagement with the news became hardwired during his days as a newspaper boy in Adelaide.

> I used to go and pick up a bundle of newspapers and I remember the smell … and the ink and standing on a corner. I must have been about 13 and selling the paper and I just remember some of the headlines, you know, Nixon says more bombing in Vietnam … and thinking, my God what's going on in the world? And that's when I first became aware of real issues in the world, because I used to sit there and read them.

In the pre-internet era, newspapers presented themselves as journals of record, and headlines were burned into the collective consciousness. Phil Kafcaloudes, who would go on to become a journalist and program host at the ABC, says he still remembers stories that 'really touched' him.

'I remember my life through newspaper headlines. I remember [Winston] Churchill dying and that was in 1965 through a newspaper headline.'

Rocco Fazzari recalls that his father encouraged him to keep newspapers that recorded momentous events.

> We had copies of the newspaper when Neil Armstrong landed on the moon for years and years. I think it instilled in me how important it is to record historical events and newsworthy events and how important they were to people.

Other would-be journalists whose careers began in the last quarter of the 20th century came from families where the media was an ingrained part of life.

'The ABC was always on and reading *The Weekend Australian* was a Saturday ritual,' recalls Sophie Tedmanson, who joined *The Australian* at the age of 18. 'The more I got interested in news and current affairs, the more time I would spend sitting at the table and reading with them as well,' she recalls.

In her case, having a mother engaged in politics provided access not only to the news, but to newsmakers. On one occasion her mother, Deirdre – who was later a South Australian Labor Senate candidate and member of the party's National Executive – took her to Trades Hall in Adelaide.

'I remember a big mood in the room and all this kerfuffle, and then Mum was like, "You have to come with me, you're going to meet someone really important."'

After being taken down to the basement she noticed a swarm of men in suits and a cloud of smoke – it was the mid-80s.

> And suddenly, literally, the crowd parted and there was this little man with grey hair and he turned around and it was Bob Hawke, who was the prime minister. And I remember him, because he had a cigar in his hand. The minute he saw me he actually put the cigar behind his hand and he put his other hand out to shake my hand. He said, 'Hello little girl', and I didn't say anything except I was trying to look at what he was hiding and I said, 'What are you hiding?' and the whole crowd laughed because of course I was an eight-year-old asking the prime minister what he was hiding and he was just trying to protect me from this cigar. Mum just was mortified, but thought it was really funny that I had the audacity to say that to the prime minister.

Asking a PM what sounded like a gotcha question didn't set Tedmanson on a direct path to journalism, but the political milieu she was brought up in certainly played a key role in her career aspirations. She remembers that as a little girl, if the family went out to a restaurant, she would always take a 'baby notebook' in the pocket of her jeans. When the family began talking about politics and she was bored, she would 'look at other tables and I would find a couple or a mum or dad, and I'd imagine who they were, what their conversation was, and I would write it all down in the book'.

Michael Sainsbury, who would eventually work in the same Sydney newsroom of *The Australian* as Tedmanson, also grew up with politics in the foreground. He was just 11 when his father, Murray, became the Liberal member of parliament for the rural New South Wales seat of Eden-Monaro, and grew up in Goulburn 'up to my neck in newsprint' and watching ABC news and the current affairs program *This Day Tonight*. Not surprisingly dinner conversations revolved entirely around politics.

'That's what we lived,' he explains. 'Quite a lot of people who've had parents in politics end up in journalism, I've found. There's a group of us ... I think you just grow up with the news cycle. We had five papers delivered to our house every day.'

There were no politicians in Matthew Franklin's immediate family, but the journalist who eventually became a Canberra-based political correspondent for *The Australian* does fondly recall poring over *The Courier-Mail* with his father in Brisbane.

> I think I learnt to read out of newspapers, I was reading them at a very young age. It was a good way to hang out with Dad. Like, we'd sit at the table over breakfast and he'd read one part and we'd hand it back and forth. He was really interested in current events, politics and social justice, but to my memory most of my siblings weren't.

George Megalogenis, whose parents were Greek immigrants, recalls that his father was an avid media consumer, reading the papers and listening to everything from the BBC and the Voice of America and Radio Moscow on shortwave radio. His quest was reliable information about events on the other side of the world. With Greece under military rule, the suspicion was that mail from Greece was being censored, so the challenge was to verify what was actually happening.

> It's interesting he would go to both capitalist and communist sources for information ... partly to figure out what's going on in Greece. Can you imagine his circumstance? Young teenager migrates to Australia, doesn't know anybody on arrival, does a number of odd jobs before he settles into a career in the

> Victorian Railways as a signalman. Reads intensively. Didn't complete primary school, but self-taught.

Megalogenis, who went on to become one of the nation's leading political journalists, sees this cosmopolitan media diet as a formative component of his upbringing in suburban Melbourne.

> You absorb these things as a child and you don't realise what you've absorbed until many years later when it becomes your profession and you realise that I've almost been prepped for this particular life by quite a curious father.

Of course, newspapers weren't just disseminators of news, they also provided entertainment, especially in households where there was no television, such as Tom Hyland's. He would make his name as a foreign correspondent in Asia and the UK, but his early years were spent in regional Tasmania, where he grew up in small purpose-built towns that housed the workers who built the state's hydro-electric scheme.

> There was a newspaper delivered to the house every day, which in my case was the *Mercury* which was published in Hobart. Later on, when we moved to the north of Tasmania, it was *The Examiner* and maybe *The Advocate*, which was produced out at Burnie. But there was always a newspaper delivered to the house. I remember as a child, even in the bush in Tasmania, every Saturday Dad would buy *The Herald*, which was shipped in from Melbourne. The distribution network must've been incredible. It worked so that on Saturday he could get a copy of that day's Melbourne *Herald*. And he used to buy *The Herald* because it had a crossword competition and the prize was £10 000 or whatever, and Dad used to do it every Saturday in the hope that he would win.

As well as crosswords and comics, there was sport. For a young Tony Walker, whose early career as a journalist included covering the dismissal of the Whitlam government in 1975, sport was a good reason to scour the papers every day while growing up at boarding school in Geelong.

> We must have got *The Sun News-Pictorial* at the school, *The Age* of course, and *The Argus*. Now I don't remember clearly looking at the news every day, but I do remember being aware of sports coverage particularly, and I do remember *The Argus*'s colour presentations of the Olympic Games in 1956. I think it was the first time colour was used in the world for newspapers. And *The Argus*, sadly, folded soon after.

School figured in the development of both media habits and the political consciousness of many proto-journalists. At Sophie Tedmanson's primary school, and many others around the country, students watched *Behind the News*, a long-running ABC program launched in 1968 to provide children with an appreciation of events outside their own lives.

'I just remember being fascinated by what that show was about and by the news, which obviously I'd seen at home, but seeing it in that school context gave it a different perspective to me.'

While *Behind the News* provided insights into the role of news, few teachers explicitly exhorted their charges to become journalists. But Stephen Corby's Year 5 teacher, Mrs Anderson, was a notable exception.

'She drove us into the ground,' recalls the future editor of *Top Gear Australia* and *Wheels* magazines. 'But she was also the most influential teacher in my whole life. And she sat me down at some point in the year and said, "This is what you're going to do – you're going to be a journalist. This is what you will do with your life."

'From that day on, I never really countenanced being anything else,' says Corby, who nonetheless had to look up the word 'journalist'.

'She was so convincing ... And it's funny, my son's in Year 5 now, and I say, "Just be careful what your Year 5 teacher tells you. If she says "journalist", let's talk!'

Antoinette Lattouf admits that she 'was the type of kid who the teacher had to say, "Does anyone else have an answer?"' She wanted to become a journalist, but faced resistance at home and school.

> I was really clear about what I wanted to do and I was furious that my careers advisor would suggest that the best thing I could do was go to TAFE and get some credit points to go to Western Sydney University when I'd said I want to go to UTS, because I believe they offer the best Comms degree for what I want to do. So, I realised that wasn't the right environment for me. So, I left and went to a new school.

The move was supported by her mother, but not her father.

> He was like, 'Well what kind of career is that?' I recall having a huge fight with him in Year 12 because he didn't want me to study journalism. My mum was backing me. And he was like, 'No. You don't need to. What for?' His favourite quote –
> I always say it back to him and he laughs, 'Education has ruined women.'

In other cases, future journalists weren't highly rated or inspired by their high school teachers. Ross Brundrett, who applied to teachers' college after completing high school, recalls a Year 12 English teacher who was especially uninspiring.

'I still remember what she wrote in my comments about English, because I only got a 56 for English in Year 12.'

Years later, when his daughter saw his results she said, 'My God, jobs must've been easy to get ... you got 56, your lowest mark in Year 12. How could you ever be a journalist?'

Brundrett replied, 'Because she was the deadliest boring teacher, and I used to just fall asleep in the class.'

On his final appraisal, his teacher wrote, 'Ross has a sleepy approach to English', which he says 'was about the wittiest thing she ever wrote'.

For Campbell Cooney, a career as a reporter simply wasn't on the radar when growing up on properties in western Queensland, or attending a rural training school in Longreach. But the experiences gleaned from that upbringing and a range of early career jobs – including stock and station agent and shed hand – provided invaluable background knowledge for his eventual role as a rural radio broadcaster at the ABC.

> I'm one of the few people in the media in Australia who actually knows how to mules a sheep, which is a very unpopular thing to know how to do nowadays. But those were the skills that we learnt, along with how to class wool, how to grade beef or cattle, basic husbandry.

For others, journalism seemed like it might be an option, if not an actual ambition. Sophie Morris recalls, 'I had this idea I wanted to do journalism without knowing anything about it, without really knowing any journalists.'

She also considered whether to follow in the footsteps of her parents, who were both doctors, but decided she wanted to do her 'own thing'.

Morris, like many others who went on to be journalists, cites a love of reading, writing, and telling stories as reasons for considering the profession.

> My first experience of being paid for writing was winning a number of writing competitions when I was at high school. I'd sussed out that there were various competitions for essays, short stories which no one entered so there was prize money there to be had, so it seemed an easier way to earn money than working at McDonald's at that stage.

By the time she finished school, Morris had won several competitions and a trip to Japan.

For Michael Shmith, letter writing was the primary form of communication with his mother, Patricia 'Bambi' née Tuckwell, a violinist and fashion model who moved to the UK when Michael was just four years old, where she met and eventually married the Queen's cousin, the Earl of Harewood, in 1967, after having a child with him out of wedlock. Their union was a society scandal that received substantial media coverage. Meanwhile the relationship between mother and son was maintained at a great distance.

'I didn't actually see her from when I was about 12 when she came out to see me after a custody case, till when I was 18 and went to England for the first time,' Shmith recalls. During that time, she was a

> superb correspondent … I think much of my writing skill comes from her side of things. And it was like being at a correspondence school or an open university. Rather than actually going there, you acquired the knowledge, the love, all those different things, the feeling of belonging to a family that one day you would meet and that made it rather good.

But the public focus on his mother made Shmith wary of how media covered private lives.

> I really minded seeing my mother pilloried in print as anybody would, especially since she was *the other woman*. This was all going on and it did hurt me to see some of the things that were written and what some people said to me.

Tom Hyland grew up in the era of Vietnam and Watergate, when journalists were seen as heroic figures.

> I used to watch them and admire them and secretly wish I could be like them ... I think it was the ABC reporters who you would see on TV at night. The guys in Saigon, wearing what looked like safari suits with epaulettes and pockets and lots of pens and things, standing in front of some street riot or incident and speaking to the camera and holding a microphone and looking as if they knew what was going on. They looked in control. They looked sharp. And not only did they look informed, which appealed to me, they also looked as if they were doing really exciting and adventurous stuff. So, I think that influenced my thoughts when I was younger.

For others, having direct experience of the rest of the world also stoked career ambitions. The divorce of Debra Jopson's parents when she was 12 years old became one of the pivotal moments of her life.

> I moved to Sydney, and eventually we went to Beirut at the age of 16 because my mother remarried, so that was another turning point in my life, this great adventure of going overseas and being involved in a country which ended up in conflict. That conflict taught me a lot about the world and inspired me to want to be a journalist.

For Michael West, travel in Central America in 1984 contributed to his desire to become a journalist, ironically by instilling scepticism about the media. He was in Managua at the height of the Nicaraguan Revolution and spent time talking to people about the events unfolding around him.

> I suddenly realised that what I'd been reading in the newspapers about the Sandinistas [National Liberation Front] being the bad guys – the evil Marxists – and the Contras [US-backed rebel groups] being the freedom fighters … was exactly the opposite. And the Contras were the ones coming and raping the women and burning, coming in these forays from Honduras, the neighbouring country. Not that I had a great love for collectivism, but I realised that the reason this had all happened is because of repression from this dictatorship and the people just wanting to have freedom in their own country. It wasn't so much about the ensuing political structure, whether it was right or left, but I realised that the media had misled everybody, including myself. And that was the start of a great tradition in my life of never believing what you read in the newspapers or anywhere, or what you hear or anybody's political ideology.

You might think that David Marr, who is so strongly identified as a journalist, would have wanted to become one from childhood, but he wasn't really sure what to do at the end of school and fell into studying arts/law and then secured an articled clerkship at a leading firm in Sydney. He soon realised he did not want to practise law, though, when he observed how unhappy many of the firm's young lawyers seemed to be, and when he saw some senior lawyers engaged in what he thought was unethical behavior. 'I'm sitting there thinking, would this be my life? That was kind of a jolt,' he recalls.

Jane Hammond was passionate about environmental causes from an early age, attending her first rally at the age of 14, but after leaving school she had no clear idea what to do. She fell into a job at the Australian Bureau of Statistics that she found boring, before enrolling at teachers' college where she felt engaged with education, but found the experience of actually teaching primary school a challenge, as she recalls:

> I looked down one day and there's one little seven-year-old wiping his nose on my skirt. And I just thought, 'I can't do this job.' When I had kids, I thought, 'Oh, that's nothing.'

All the while she continued to attend rallies. Her road-to-Damascus experience came at anti-nuclear protests at Roxby Downs in outback South Australia in the mid-1980s, where she watched horrified as the news media abused the protesters.

> And the media were really hostile towards us. Really, really hostile. Shoving cameras in people's faces when they were trying to have meetings. You know, it was a very tense time. And I thought, 'You know, I've got to be a journalist. Because I've got to be able to have a bit more sympathy for these people. No one's listening to us. No one's understanding. So, I think I need to be a journalist.' And so that was it. That's what made me turn.

The range of impulses and motivations that bring people to journalism is wide, from idolising heroic role models to parlaying a love of writing into a career; and from being introduced to media at home to serendipitous events. Some just knew from an early age that journalism was all they wanted to do, while others strayed into it without ever meaning to, and yet others decided to give it a go for want of any clear idea about a career. A few came to it after trying, and disliking, their first choice of career. But whatever their motivation, or lack of it, they still faced the challenge of securing a foothold in an industry that even then was not always easy to break into.

CHAPTER 3

Many roads to journalism

Andrew Dodd

Simon Mann admits he must have been 'a pathetic interviewee' when he started applying for jobs after graduating from Monash University in 1980. His mum had suggested journalism, because he liked writing. At that stage he hadn't worked out that liking writing doesn't mean 'that you're right for journalism, or that you'll like journalism; they're very different things'. He applied for positions, and even got a few interviews. 'Goodness knows what I said, I can't remember much, but I wouldn't have been at all impressive.'

One day he was travelling down the coast, south-west of Melbourne, when he saw a sign on a building in Anglesea for the *Coastal Telegraph*. He knocked on the door, walked in and asked, 'Look I'm keen to be a journalist, could I write some stories for you?'

Mann remembers the reply: 'We'll take you on for $15 a day, as long as you can perhaps help clean the office occasionally and do some of those chores.'

He agreed: 'Yeah fine, I'll clean the toilets if I have to, that's no worries.'

Mann rode his motorbike down the coastal road two days a week and covered the crime beat and the local council.

'The great thing,' he says, 'was that you could have a surf at lunchtime and go for a swim and then go back to work.' The job grew into a fulltime cadetship.

Mann's story gives the impression that journalism jobs were once so plentiful that a young hopeful only had to knock on a door. However, the reality for many was that landing their first job was challenging and required determination, chutzpah and plenty of good luck.

Cadetships for the major media outlets, for example, were hard to get, as many hundreds (sometimes thousands) would apply. The difference was that many more cadetships were available.[1]

To find work, young people – like Mann – migrated to the regions. That was certainly easier as there were many more regional newspapers from which to choose.

In this chapter, we explore both the conventional and novel ways people entered the profession, demonstrating the many roads people could take into journalism.

For some, the first foray came as work experience at secondary school. That was what Sophie Tedmanson did in Year 9 at Adelaide High School. Julie Duncan, a friend of the family who worked at *The Advertiser* in Adelaide and happened to be married to the prominent Labor politician Peter Duncan, suggested she join the team of kids putting together *Showbiz*, the temporary paper that reported on daily events at the annual Royal Adelaide Show.

'I just remember that was the most exciting thing,' says Tedmanson, partly because Duncan had seen something in her; some capacity for writing and telling stories. She joined the other students each day in a trailer at the show site in Goodwood, from where she covered sheep trials and reviewed show bags.

She faced her first journalistic dilemma when she reviewed a ride and almost fell off.

'It was a scandal, because it was a really bad ride and I was really scared and it was the first time I was, like, do I write the truth, or do I not write the truth? I can't remember what I ended up writing.'

Looking back, she says the experience was 'incredible because it introduced me to journalism and it introduced me to a world that I'd never considered, because I realised that news was in my blood, I'd grown up with it, and politics and all that kind of stuff, but I never considered to make that into a career.'

Until then, she had been contemplating life as an actor and had already enjoyed success in auditions. She realised that, like acting, journalism allowed her to tell other people's stories. But as a reporter she would be working with facts and real-life events.

'So, I don't have to come up with the creativeness of a story,' she says. 'I just come up with a creative way to write that story. That was like a bingo moment for me.'

Stephen Corby was first exposed to journalism during work experience at *The Canberra Times* in Year 10. He was assigned to the advertising department because the newsroom didn't take on school kids. But one day he was allowed to go upstairs to sit in on the daily editorial conference, where he had an insider's view of how a newspaper really gets made. He still remembers how eye-opening it was.

> A lot of blokes, sweaty armpits, open-collared shirts, and a lot of shouting. I couldn't believe how much shouting and swearing there was. I'd never seen this kind of boisterous fighting – everything was a fight. Everything was 'No, we're not putting that there!' 'That's rubbish!' 'This story's crap!' 'That's never going to happen.' 'When are we going to get this, when are the pics coming in?' The photographer is flicking actual photographs across the desk and the editor's shaking his head. And just – big characters and big booming voices. I was like, 'God, for me, this is terrifying, but exciting.'

Two years later when he finished school, his mum took him back to the newspaper and, according to Corby, talked them into giving him a job as a copy kid. This turned out to be useful in the following years when he was studying journalism at Canberra University, because often his university assignments were published in *The Canberra Times*, meaning he'd score 100 per cent for his course work.

In newsrooms, copy kids were on the lowest rung of the hierarchy.[2] Mostly young hopefuls wanting a start in journalism, they were given menial tasks like photocopying and fetching the editor's dry cleaning and rarely given the time or space to write anything of substance. To contend for a cadetship, copy kids had to prove their worth by finding and writing their own stories.

Corby knew he had to produce, but at that age, by his own admission, he was timid and baulked at asking bold questions. He did write plenty of stories, but they were about sport and reviews for the music and TV pages, the kind of articles known in newsrooms by the demeaning term 'soft'.[3] These rarely catch the editor's eye.

'I was desperately trying to write stuff, and getting published was very exciting, but I wasn't pushing my barrow enough with the editor in a personal way. I wasn't getting myself in front of his face, and saying, "Hire me, hire me, hire me!"'

When the cadetships were offered, he missed out.

Most roads into a journalism job pass through a formal interview at some stage, and some leave lasting impressions on the participants. Jane Hammond remembers visiting the Commonwealth Employment Service (a forerunner to Centrelink) in Fremantle, where she found a job advertised for a journalist in Geraldton.

She thought, 'I really would like to do this. I can write. I can take pictures.' She had done photography at TAFE, so she applied. A few days later she found herself in the headquarters of Provincial Publications in Victoria Park being interviewed by the group editor, John Brown. As they talked, Brown was laying out the front page for one of the company's newspapers by cropping photos with a scalpel. Hammond remembers he had a 'beautiful picture of a boat on a fjord in a landscape'. She watched him 'cut around the boat and leave out everything else' so 'this carefully composed photo had been reduced to just the boat, that could have been taken anywhere'.

At that moment she realised there was a big difference between the art she'd studied at TAFE and journalism.

'No, we don't send women to Geraldton,' said Brown, who explained there had been a serial rapist in the town and it wasn't safe.

'Well where do you send women?' Hammond asked.

'Oh, well, maybe the wheatbelt. But we haven't got any vacancies out there,' replied Brown.

Hammond wasn't deterred. She had seen 'a glimmer of hope' and vowed to ring him every week until he gave her a job, which he eventually did at the *Merredin Telegraph*, 250 kilometres east of Perth.

Hugh Jones had what he describes as a 'very Tasmanian' interview when he applied for a position at *The Examiner*. He'd recently graduated with 'not a particularly wonderful arts degree' and was about to embark on a Diploma of Education because he was interested in teaching. At a party in Hobart he met Tim Piper, who had been working as a cadet at *The Examiner*, but decided to leave to study law. The more they talked, the more Jones liked the sound of journalism. 'Why don't you give them a ring?' suggested Piper. 'I've just put in my resignation, they'll be looking for someone.'

He was interviewed by Michael Courtney, who had returned to his hometown to edit *The Examiner* after a stint at *The Sun* in Melbourne. Jones remembers him having 'a great sense of place' and someone who 'very much liked being editor of a small town, his town'.

'Who are you and who was your father?' asked Courtney. 'Who was your mother before she got married?' He also asked Jones about his grandfather, who had been headmaster of Launceston Church Grammar.

Courtney offered Jones a job on the spot and then took him on a tour of the office. It was late afternoon on a busy news day, so the paper was alive with activity. The West Indies cricket team was in town and sportswriter Mike McCann, who went on to have a successful career at the ABC, came 'steaming in' and put his copy paper into a typewriter. Jones watched him type his byline and 'rip' out the 'slug' in the right-hand corner of the page before churning out the lead paragraph.

> And I thought this is magic. He's writing tomorrow's news. And Mike was only a year or two older than me but I thought this was wonderful … Courtney, who was a bit of a puffed-up rooster, came over and started to talk to Mike about what he was writing and, 'What's your angle going to be, Mike?' and, 'Did you speak to so and so?' and really showing off in front of me … McCann [who had] worked at the paper for a couple of years so he knew what to expect, just fed the answers back and I thought 'What sort of a career is this? This is just magic.' And yeah, so that was it. I had no qualms at all that that's where I wanted to be.

Family connections were also useful for Charles Waterhouse when he applied for a job at *The Examiner*. He was working as a driver delivering fridges and colour TVs for a Launceston business when he decided to apply for a cadetship. He thanks his mum for helping him out: 'I think she knew the general manager at *The Examiner* who was, I think, Brian McKendrick and she might have had a word to his ear. "Could you talk to my son, he wants to do journalism", or something. I certainly remember because, let's face it, cadetships at newspapers didn't come up very often, particularly at *The Examiner* and the *Mercury* in Hobart.

Matthew Moore managed to avoid an interview altogether when he applied for a cadetship at *The Sydney Morning Herald*, which may come as a surprise to later generations of applicants who must face a battery of tests and comply with modern 'workplace behaviours'. He also had an advantage over the other candidates. He had met the cadet counsellor at *The Australian Financial Review* while doing an internship. He says he flirted with her and she showed him the applications from the key people with whom he was competing.

'That was a big plus,' he says.

He was also helped by a friend who was close to people at the Law Reform Commission. Moore asked him to leak a report the commission had just written – but had not yet released – on a topical privacy issue. This helped because the candidates all had to write a story about a current issue. The inside information and the leaked report combined to make his application irresistible.

'They didn't even interview me,' he says. 'They just gave me a job.'

At the time Moore was 29 and desperate to get into journalism after years of working on building sites. However, *The Herald* had a policy that it didn't employ cadets over the age of 25. That wasn't going to stop Moore. He simply falsified his age.

Michael West tried to find work at *The Australian*, but the vocational counsellor told him he didn't have a chance because prominent politicians like Bob Hawke wouldn't want to talk to him.

'Who would Hawkie rather be interviewed by, you or a good-looking sort?' the counsellor asked. 'Back in the day,' says West, 'they just employed attractive women.'

He then applied for a cadetship at *The Sydney Morning Herald* and reckons of the 3000 applicants for the four positions he came about fifth.[4] He remembers feeling 'doleful' until soon after he got a call from the personnel manager at Fairfax, who said, 'Well do you want to go in for an interview at *The AFR*?' When West told them he didn't know anything about business and finance the personnel manager replied, 'Don't worry you'll be right.'

This was standard practice for *The Australian Financial Review*, which would let *The Herald* shortlist the thousands of candidates and do all the interviews before offering cadetships to the ones who just missed out. As West puts it, '*The AFR* were doing it on the cheap.'

The aim of any cadet was to 'get graded', which signalled the end of their cadetship and the prospect of being paid properly.

Most school-leaver cadets were awarded with a D grading after three or four years of training across several rounds such as police, sport, business and general news.[5] University graduates often only had to do a year as a cadet.

Getting graded was a big deal, as it was for any apprentice or trainee in a trade or profession. It meant the industry recognised they were equipped with the skills they needed, such as shorthand and typing and a thorough knowledge of the various writing styles, especially the inverted pyramid, which was, and still is, the go-to method for prioritising information in hard news stories.

Ross Brundrett was able to break from his cadetship early, but it came at a cost. As part of his training, he was required to study at RMIT for one day a week, meaning that his editor at the *Footscray Mail* had to do without him every Wednesday. One Thursday about a month after he'd started, his editor, Gary Sargeant asked him where he'd been the previous day.

Brundrett told him, 'That was my day off for doing that journalism course. It's in the award.'

'Well, that's no effing good for me. Bugger it,' replied his editor.

'So, he gave me a grade … I went from a cadet to a graded journalist on the strength of Gary didn't want me to be out of the office.'

Looking back, Brundrett says he might have been short-changed because he missed out on some vital training. But the higher salary was a consolation. He remembers thinking, 'How good is this … at this stage of my career and I'm already graded.'

He was still living at home and his mum asked him how he was going. '"Mum, I already got a promotion!" She was telling the whole neighbourhood.'

Brundrett's experience was not uncommon. Many of his contemporaries were also encouraged to bail out of study before completing their qualification.

Student newspapers have been important training grounds for some of Australia's leading journalists, especially before the proliferation of journalism courses.[6] At Adelaide University, a special relationship existed between the newspaper, *On Dit*, and *The Advertiser*, although law student Samela Harris didn't know this when the then editor – and future state premier – John Bannon insisted she replace him. According to Harris, Bannon took her to the Student Representative Council and proposed her and two others as his successors and they were duly elected.

At that time, News Limited offered a scholarship for student newspaper editors to become fourth-year cadets. The logic was that if they liked editing a university paper they might make a good reporter. After completing her term, Harris rang up *The Advertiser* and said she would like to take up the scholarship. Before long she was 'received in the posh wood-lined office' by the paper's manager, Ken May – later Sir Ken May – and the editor, Ron Boland.

> And they gave me the job because it was contractual that they do. But they said to me, 'If you don't make it, there won't be any more, you understand? There won't be any more. You better make a go of this.'

It was only after starting work that Harris realised they weren't referring to other university students. They were talking about women, because at that time the women who worked at the paper were corralled off in a separate section:

> They're behind glass partitions hammering away, ringing up society ladies, asking them what they were wearing to parties. That was social pages and they were women's pages. And these women were all trapped. And they glared through the glass at me because I was out there on the general floor.

From the 1990s on, internships offered by university journalism programs became stepping-stones to careers. It's the moment when the study is applied and the concepts get tested. Students often say they learn more in the first week of an internship than the rest of their degree, although that's changing as journalism programs focus more on publishing, and providing the kind of training that used to occur in newsrooms. As the mainstream news industry contracts, students are finding they have to do several unpaid internships to increase their chances of landing a continuing, paid role.[7]

Liz Wells was a student at one of the more hands-on journalism programs, at Mitchell College (now Charles Sturt University) in Bathurst, when the internship she was assigned to in Cessnock was cancelled. She found her own internship, instead, at the rural newspaper, *The Land*.

Her timing was good. A ban on live sheep exports due to concerns about disease had triggered a bigger debate about trade barriers and tariffs on imports. Wells was asked to cover it.

'That was probably the first interesting news story I got on to and the editor said, you know, "Ring [these] live exporters and ring this person in the government," and I did and I just loved that, to be able to do that.'

She was also asked to drive out to Bankstown Airport before dawn and fly to several towns across south-western New South Wales with the then New South Wales education minister, Terry Metherell. The opportunity fell to her, she thinks, because the minister's regional tour occurred on the day before *The Land*'s weekly deadline, so no one else was available.

The trip provided a valuable lesson Wells has never forgotten. One of her jobs was to take lots of photographs of the people they met to accompany her story.

However, she recalls, 'I didn't write down any of their names. I thought, Oh, I'll remember who they are. Like, I don't know what I was thinking? But anyway, there was one redeemable photograph from the whole day and that's when the editor said, Where are the captions? And I went, "What do you mean?" I didn't realise I had to actually write everyone's [names] left to right and what school we were at.'

Her rural background and interest in the plight of graziers and sheep markets – and her enthusiasm to learn what she didn't know – made a positive impression. On her last day, her boss, Vern Graham, said, 'Come into my office when you've finished what you're doing.'

'So, I came in and he said, "We really like the way you roll your sleeves up and we'd like to offer you a job," and I went, "Oh, wow. That wasn't what I was expecting."'

When she went back to Mitchell College and told course co-ordinator Roger Patching that she had been offered a job, Wells remembers him saying:

'Well the whole idea of you being here is to get a job, so go, you know, you can have your degree, it's only one kind of little project at the end [that you need to do to graduate].' So, I started there fulltime and that was the start of it all.

Patching's pragmatism mirrored that of many lecturers who helped aspiring journalists find their way into the industry. Some lecturers, though, preferred to emulate the tough love meted out to cadets by sub-editors in newsrooms. Lynne Dwyer recalls that when she was studying journalism in the early 1980s, one of her writing teachers was Peter Temple who had worked as a journalist and would later become one of the country's best known crime writers. 'He was brilliant but he scarred everybody. He was very harsh and very cynical, and we all loved him.' Students had kept the essays he had marked, even those with comments like 'Have you thought of another career?'

Heading to the regions was sound advice for anyone trying to get into journalism. Until recently, many country towns had a small newspaper. They were mostly weeklies and some were still family-run. They covered local events and acted as a kind of glue holding the community together. While the local rags, as they were affectionately known, were not bastions of fourth estate journalism, their diet of feel-good stories and news about local events, particularly crime and sport, meant they were excellent training grounds for young journalists.

The regular turnover of staff – as reporters moved on to other jobs in the city – opened up spots for young recruits. And because they ran on tight budgets, reporters were expected to work across the paper, soon becoming proficient at many tasks, unlike their city colleagues who might be stuck doing just one form of reporting.

Di Thomas remembers writing letters to regional newspaper editors and asking for cadetships while she was still at secondary school. But she had no luck because, 'I had nothing other than an HSC result.'

It was the early 1980s, when fewer journalism schools existed and they were much harder to get into, so she settled instead for secretarial college, where she could at least learn typing and shorthand skills. There she discovered she was good at bookkeeping, a skill few journalists could claim. She found interesting secretarial jobs, including a weekend role at a flying school at Bankstown Airport, but she still hankered for journalism and started applying again. In 1985, she saw an ad in *The Sydney Morning Herald* for a cadetship at the *Central Western Daily* in Orange and posted off an application.

A few days later she got a call from the new editor, Rod Kirkpatrick, who asked whether she would make the three-and-a-half-hour drive to do an interview? Of course, she said yes.

'My mother came with me. I remember driving up there in my car. I had a 1977 Honda Civic.'

She can still recall going up and over the Blue Mountains and the 'boom boom boom' sound as they drove along the concrete slabs of the old Great Western Highway.

She remembers going into the building and being introduced to the chief of staff. When she was offered the job she remembers feeling excited, because she could finally give journalism a go. She also felt apprehensive because she had also applied for a position at *The Sydney Morning Herald*. She rang the cadet trainer at *The Herald* and explained her dilemma. She then received 'the best piece of career advice' she was ever given.

> He said to me, 'Look Di, you've had one interview with me. I haven't finished the first interviews of all the applicants for the cadetships. I can't tell you at this stage whether you'd get a second interview.' He said, 'It's a job. It's a cadetship.' He said, 'Go for it. You can always come back to Sydney.'

When Flip Prior began as a cadet on the newspaper in Broome in the Kimberley region, she found it advantageous to be removed from her familiar life. She soon made friends, but says it helped to have no companions when she arrived because she was 'just devoted to work'. She was able to focus on the region's 'endlessly interesting' stories and experience a 'process of discovery'. She suspects the high turnover of reporters had a downside for the local residents, however.

'I'm sure that every time a young new journalist goes through they write all the same stories. The town just gets them on a loop.'

Campbell Cooney found himself in unfamiliar terrain too, but at the other end of the country, when he landed a job as a rural reporter in Launceston in Tasmania. It was the culmination of four years of retraining. He was desperate to get out of western Queensland, where he had been working at a gravel-crushing company and feeling unfulfilled and isolated. First, he went to TAFE to study for a Year 12 equivalency certificate, with which he was eligible to apply for a journalism course at the University of Southern Queensland. When he was finally ready to graduate, he started applying for journalism jobs and traineeships, but found only regional companies were calling him back. One day the head of rural programming at the ABC in Tasmania rang and offered him work.

> Moving to Tassie to start work as a journalist from Queensland was probably the best thing that ever happened, because it totally disconnected you from the life that you'd had before which had nothing to do with journalism. So, the only thing that they knew about you down there was that you were a journalist.

Cooney says in the first six months he 'probably racked up enough hours to take about three months' leave'. In addition to finding his way in a new place and new career, he also had to tame his accent, which was then a 'slow western Queensland drawl', acquired over years in the outback.

One day after his first on-air session, the station manager Ray Sangston played back the recording. 'I think I'm doing something like, "Yeah g'day and welcome to the Northern Tasmania Rural Report. I'm Campbell Cooney," or something like that and he is just sitting there just shaking his head and listening. And he said, "Oh Campbell, we've got a lot of work here to do with you, don't we?"'

But the ABC followed through and provided Cooney with the support he needed. 'They'd give you exercises, and they'd give you training, and they'd give you assistance.'

Even in a newspaper market as concentrated as Australia's, small independent publications have been able to rise and serve targeted audiences. Sometimes they attempted mass circulation in large city markets.

That was the intent of West Australian businessmen Lang Hancock and Peter Wright. In 1969, flush with money from their Pilbara mining operations, they established *The Independent*, later known as *The Sunday Independent*.[8] They were competing with *The West Australian* and the then separately owned *Sunday Times*, which collectively controlled the lucrative classifieds market. In her last year at Curtin University, journalism student Maureen Shelley was employed by *The Sunday Independent* as a copy kid which meant she was 'filling cars with petrol and getting the chief of staff's lunch'. Some Saturdays she worked 16-hour days for a total of $10. But she felt privileged for two reasons; because she had work when 'there were so few jobs in journalism in Western Australia' and because the job provided a ringside seat on the struggle for control of Perth's newspapers.

> *The West Australian* hated the fact that there was a competitor trying to come into its market, and so the newsagents would do things like vandalise our cars, literally. They would scratch them and dent them. It was real terror tactics trying to stop the paper being successful.

Eventually, *The Independent* folded, but not before Shelley had gained a foothold in the industry.

Christian Kerr had some exposure to journalism by earning 'execrable' pay as a sub-editor on the independent *Adelaide Review*, edited by local identity Christopher Pearson. Kerr wanted to write, but Pearson wouldn't let him. So, Kerr left and pursued alternative careers, as a press secretary to high-profile Coalition members of parliament and doing public relations for a large construction company.

That might have been the way things stayed, if it weren't for the arrival on the scene of the maverick journalist Stephen Mayne, who had held several senior reporting positions at both Fairfax and News Limited.

After a stint working for the Victorian Treasurer, Mayne made an ill-fated attempt to stand for parliament and launched a website called Jeffed, chronicling the shortcomings of the state Coalition government led by premier Jeff Kennett. It was widely read, and Mayne was only half joking when he later claimed credit for the fall of the Kennett government soon after.[9]

Mayne wanted to create a more permanent publication and asked Kerr to meet him for dinner when he was next in Sydney. They chose a restaurant near former prime minister Paul Keating's house, because they thought it would be fun if he just happened to walk by. Mayne asked Kerr to write for his new publication, called *Crikey*, but Kerr said he couldn't because he had a job. So, Mayne suggested Kerr write under a pseudonym. The dinner turned into a brainstorming session over what name Kerr would use.

'Suddenly a stroke of genius hit me,' says Kerr. 'I know who it's going to be. I'm going to be called Hilary Bray.' Mayne replied, 'What the fuck?' The name came from a character in the 1963 James Bond novel *On Her Majesty's Secret Service*. 'We thought that was inspired,' says Kerr, who continued to write under the moniker until he eventually left *Crikey* to join *The Australian*.

This chapter started with Simon Mann's easy entry into his first job. It should end with the way he later moved from regional papers to a metropolitan daily. His friend Geoff Easdown told him there was a job going at *The Sun*, so Mann went down to Melbourne to meet the editor, Leigh Stevens, who agreed to see him at 11 pm. He sat anxiously in Stevens' office, a smoky den with old newsreels and newspapers and books and dark panels. Stevens walked in:

> He was very pleasant, and he sat opposite me and he started to ask things, then he said, 'Look, I've got to be honest with you: I don't know what Easdown's told you, but all we've got going here is a job in the finance section – shares, money, that sort of shit.' I didn't really take this in, but I was keen for a job, and I said, 'Look, that's fine Mr Stevens … I'm really keen to come and have a crack at the metro papers so I don't mind,

but I have to be honest with you, I failed fourth-form maths and I dropped out of economics at university.' And there was a pause, and he tapped his cigarette before lighting it, and he took a long draw and he said, 'Terrific, when can you start?'

Despite Mann's charmed experiences, finding a job in journalism a generation ago wasn't always easy. Aspiring reporters generally had to demonstrate they were hungry and were prepared to work hard to become proficient at the craft. They needed luck by being in the right place at the right time or by having an edge over their competitors. It is also true there were many more media outlets employing journalists and that most of them invested in new recruits by providing relevant, useful training, even if it was informal mentoring in the newsroom from older hands. Fewer people were in the marketplace competing for work then but in some ways it might not matter whether the road to journalism was easy or hard, and whether the search for work was quick or slow, because those who entered journalism a generation ago had no inkling how much it would change. Those who simply knocked on the door and walked into a career, or who knew someone who was friends with an editor, may have felt the job was theirs, almost by birthright. And those who worked hard, retrained, took bold risks or slaved away to create a portfolio of self-published pieces might have felt equally entitled to their job, by virtue of the ordeal they endured to secure it. When you've won a job and built a career doing something you love, and when that work is secure and has a structure that is meant to last for a career, it must make losing that work through redundancy all the more painful.

CHAPTER 4
The first byline: Early careers

Lawrie Zion

'I lived in constant terror', recalls Wendy Hargreaves of her early days reporting for the *Geelong Advertiser*. Growing up in the nearby country town of Colac in Victoria, she thought news had always boiled down to reporting what people were talking about, but once she joined the *Advertiser* she realised it was a craft that relied on accuracy and attention to detail.

On entering the newsroom, first-year cadets were sent straight to the weather or shipping round and taught that 'even the most inane' bits of the newspaper 'can be life or death'. 'You've got to treat every word you write as if … it could really fundamentally affect someone's life – even if it's just the wedding captions', says Hargreaves.

To instil the notion of accuracy, cadets were cautioned with stories of 'fishermen who died because the tides were wrong' or the story of a young journalist who 'messed up' the shipping round which left 'hundreds of Italians' waiting for a boat that never turned up. 'That cadet got the sack', recalls Hargreaves.

Mistakes were vigorously called out. Hargreaves laughs as she recalls a 'big old sub-editor in the back corner' who would shame anyone who misspelled a name or made a grammatical error by bellowing their surname across the room. But the terror felt real, and there was another fear: missing the story.

'I think newspapers are really built on that, and it's all about competition,' she says. 'It's not just about competition with another newspaper, it's competition against the person next to you. It's healthy and friendly, but there's definitely a climate of fear underneath.'

'It was everything I saw in those B grade movies,' recalls Russell Robinson on his first days as a cadet at *The Herald* in Melbourne in 1970, straight after matriculating from high school.

'There were hard-boiled men and women in that room,' he says, including divorcees and alcoholics. 'It was a community, an absolute community, and it was just fantastic … I enjoyed it because I'd set out to win that job and it happened, and I was going to hang onto it.'

Robinson estimates he was one of more than 10 cadets in his year at the paper. He, and others who entered newsrooms in the late 20th century, felt they had been handed passports to another world. Once inside, they took the formative steps of careers that would go on to span several decades, some working for the same company until their roles became redundant in the 2010s.

Long-term relationships with readers and colleagues were forged in what were often imposing edifices that doubled as office and factory.

'You felt the presses thundering in the building,' says Michael Shmith of the old Herald and Weekly Times building in Flinders Street in Melbourne.

> It was that feeling that you were really part of it, you could do a cross-section diagram of where you fitted into it with the presses underneath and the composing room on the top floor and the journalists all scurrying around on the middle, that's what *The Herald* was like. It was like one of those doll's houses where you can take the front off and see the activity.

Just how the careers of new recruits evolved in those early years depended on the publication itself, recruits' ages, previous education, the size of the newsroom and, of course, the other journalists, who would be both their trainers and colleagues. Most were fresh out of high school.

Typically, in the second half of the 20th century, they would join as editorial assistants or copy kids, the keenest and sharpest of whom may be offered cadetships.

The cadetship system existed in the big media companies, primarily on metropolitan daily newspapers. In broadcast media, the ABC for many years had a training program for its annual intake of cadets. Across the rest of the media, whether in commercial broadcast outlets or in local, regional and rural newspapers, training was ad hoc or non-existent. There, cadets were expected to learn the basics of journalism by themselves, perhaps with the informal aid of a friendly older journalist, or at the mercy of the kind of loud sub-editor Hargreaves recalls.

On daily newspapers, cadets were supervised by a cadet counsellor, usually a veteran journalist, who drilled them in the key skills of reporting (interviewing, plain English prose) and the core tenets of journalism (such as accuracy and defamation law). Cadets took typing and shorthand classes, needing to reach a set number of words per minute before they could become a graded or fully-fledged journalist.

Cadets were rotated through various rounds, from general news to sport to business to courts to state parliament to industrial relations and so on, being introduced to the reporting of each of the main areas or institutions.

The rounds system was devised earlier in the 20th century as a way of organising the many simultaneous events and activities happening across society into a system amenable to daily news production. Such a feat of organisation against tight deadlines is why newspapers were called 'the daily miracle'.[1]

As education levels rose across the country, more cadets with a bachelor's degree were hired. In the early 1990s, less than 40 per cent of Australian journalists had completed a tertiary degree, and only four in 10 of those had majored in journalism.[2] By the time of the big redundancy rounds of 2012, graduate cadets were the norm and Year 12 entrants a rarity.[3]

University qualifications, however, did not replace mentoring, both formal and informal, which was a critical element of learning on the job in many journalists' early years.

Sophie Tedmanson was a teenager when she started as an editorial assistant in the six-person office of *The Australian* in Adelaide. She says joining a newsroom was like being inducted into a family. 'I was like their little baby. They took me under their wing,' she recalls.

In her role as editorial assistant, she answered the phone, occasionally went out to get lunches, and performed a range of administrative tasks. And while she was not expected to write stories in those first months, her bureau chief Patrick Lawnham made her read every edition of the paper from the previous six months, and cut out every single published story from the Adelaide bureau team to place in a folder 'because he wanted to send it to Sydney and prove that Adelaide wasn't getting enough of a run [compared to] the rest of the country'.

The exercise helped Tedmanson understand how many, or how few, South Australian stories were published in the national daily and also what kinds of stories made the cut.

> It was a fascinating insight for me into what I was getting into, and it helped me form my feelings about what kind of area I wanted to write about, and also the way *The Australian* represented the country and the significant people that were talking to that newspaper.

After graduating from Melbourne University in 1984 with an economics degree, George Megalogenis failed to get a cadetship in 1985, but finally succeeded the following year at Melbourne's *Sun*.

The induction was led by chief of staff, David Guthrie-Jones, who Megalogenis remembers as 'a very thoughtful person'. He says he found 'a way to look after people like me who were not very socially adept but keen, almost over-keen at one level, and talked too much or didn't really pick up social cues in a workplace like that'.

Like Tedmanson's, his training included stints in production roles. These included caption writing, which placed him in close proximity to the heart of daily decision making.

> You sat in a picture conference with the editor-in-chief, the editor, the chief sub-editor, and they worked through the pictures from pages one to seven, and you were assigned to the caption for each of those pictures. So, you got to see news judgments made every night. I spent a lot of time eavesdropping and I think that was the whole idea of where they put the cadet, at the top of the table. So, I was one chair away from the editor-in-chief.

Not all cadets scored the box seat. When Louise Graham began her career as a photojournalist she was literally kept in the dark.

> I really didn't know what I was going to be doing but they said, 'You're going to be in the darkroom. And you stay in the darkroom and we let you out for a day now and then to go out on the road.'

Her tasks were to mix the chemicals, develop films and produce the photo sales prints, as well as helping photographers if they needed anything.

'My father used to call me the pit pony.'

One common feature of training was the rotation of cadets across a range of rounds and roles. For Stephen Corby, this provided a substantial grounding for a diverse career in journalism.

> I would say it's the best training ever. You had to do sport, whether you wanted to or not. You'd see these girls doing sport, hating every minute of it. You had to do sub-editing, whether you wanted to or not. You had to do night shifts. And sit there, and learn to be a sub. And being a sub obviously makes you a better writer.

Within these rounds, emphasis was placed on developing skills in the routine aspects of journalism practice, especially information gathering. In the pre-online era, it's hard to overestimate the extent to which fixed phones in offices were central for story development.

Accordingly, learning how to extract stories from routine calls was baked into newsroom training. At *The Examiner* in Launceston, a young Hugh Jones was told he had to 'prod and probe' after his chief of staff heard him gently asking police if anything was happening that they should know about at the paper.

> I got to the stage where I'd say: 'Hi. It's Hugh Jones from *The Examiner*. You must have had lots of stuff going on there keeping you busy this afternoon. How's your day gone?' and striking a way of not letting them say, 'Nothing's happened,' or even if they did say, 'Nothing's happened,' you'd say, 'Well, surely, you've had a couple of drunks walk in the place or a car accident? Have you picked anybody out of a ditch?'

At *The Sunday Australian*, Debra Jopson also received feedback from colleagues about her approach to phone interviews.

> If I said to an interviewee, Do you mind if a quote you on that, as in the movies, they'd say: 'Don't ask that question. They are speaking to you as a representative of the media. If they're speaking to you, and they know who you are, you can quote them.

Scoring your first byline is seen as a rite of passage for budding journalists. But many wrote short news stories or contributed for some time before seeing their name in print. As Hugh Jones recalls, at *The Examiner*, usually only the lead story would get a byline, while many of the police 'fillers' didn't.

For George Megalogenis, an interview with footballer Gary Ablett senior scored him his first byline in Melbourne's *The Sun News-Pictorial*. The then Geelong player had a minor knee strain and was going to miss the start of the season. Megalogenis was assigned the job because it wasn't going to be much of a yarn.

'He wasn't the best footballer of his generation at that point. He was about to become it. Went out. Little press conference with the coach.'

But while the result was 'a very standard rudimentary story', he was excited when he saw not only his own byline, but a reference to the story in a rival publication.

'The big buzz I got that day was I read the equivalent article in *The Age* and the question I asked at the press conference was noted in *The Age*'s article.'

Two decades later, Tom Arup's first byline in *The Age* was also the result of an out-of-town football story, in this case a summary of a Friday practice match between AFL teams Collingwood and Hawthorn played in the regional city of Shepparton.

'I knew who the players were,' he recalls. But it was a night game and I had to turn around a match report for the first edition in like 20 minutes after the end of the game.'

With the story filed, Arup ordered a takeaway meal.

> I remember getting my pizza and then just freaking out about what I'd written and opening my laptop in the car and looking at what I'd written and going, 'Oh my God this is terrible.' I just remember there were spelling mistakes everywhere and calling the sub-editor and going, 'I'm so sorry, I'm sorry', and

The first byline: Early careers

they're going 'Whatever' … I said, 'Do I have time to redo it?' and he said, 'No it's fine. I've basically rewritten it' – as subs did.

Landing a front-page story on your first day in the job was rare, but in Jo Chandler's case it did happen. She had just arrived at *The Age* from a regional paper and had been assigned to write a story about a young Australian missionary who had been abducted in the Philippines.

After making some calls, she filed the story, which ran as a single column on the front page the next day. But by the time she got to work Chandler was horrified because it turned out that the woman's head had been chopped off, even though Chandler had reported in her story that her family believed her to be in good spirits. But her colleagues reassured her, pointing out that what she had written was right at the time.

> I remember Hugo Kelly going, 'You're a legend, page one, your first day.' And I'm going, 'But, she had her head cut off.' 'Doesn't matter, it doesn't matter … you're off with a running start, off you go.'

Other front-page debuts eventuated from more mundane circumstances. For Wendy Hargreaves, her first was published in the *Geelong Advertiser* after a bartender at the Geelong Hotel charged her 80 cents for a glass of water.

'This was back in '86 and it was just outrageous – tap water, 80 cents for tap water! I had a go at him and he said, "Look, this is just how it is." So, the next day I wrote the story and it got on the front page and they had to stop charging.'

For Anne Davies, encouragement from a more senior journalist led to her first front-page story, soon after joining *The Australian Financial Review*. She had received a heads up from her lawyer friends that a leading Sydney law firm, Freehills, was set to merge with another legal practice.

'I said to chief of staff Glenn Dyer ... "I think I've got quite a good story". And he looked at me and he went, "Come on, sit next to me". And we wrote the story.'

This was her first experience of the adrenaline rush that comes from breaking a story. And Dyer continued to play a role in developing her early career skills.

> Glenn Dyer really looked after the cadets ... He had, and probably still does have, a photographic memory. So he'd walk in and he'd go, 'Davies, I want you to follow up. It's on page four of *The Australian*, down the bottom, left hand side' ... And he'd just reel it off word for word. So he got us really charged up about the thrill of the chase.

The Australian Financial Review also proved to be a launching pad for the career of Steve Lewis, a recent journalism graduate of the University of Technology in Sydney. After working in a number of other roles, he started a cadetship placement at the paper without ever having read it.

> From the minute I stepped into the newsroom I enjoyed it. I think my first assignment when I was at the *Financial Review* was interviewing Richard Woolcott who'd just retired and written a book and I thought, This is pretty extraordinary for a cub journo to be given access to a very distinguished diplomat, one of Australia's finest diplomats. So I loved the fact that at the *Fin Review* you weren't ... doing ambulance-chasing stories, you were actually doing high-level stories.

Smaller newsrooms in suburban, regional and specialist publications also played critical roles in training young Australian journalists. For

Liz Wells, the collective wisdom of the two dozen-strong newsroom at her first job at the agricultural and regional news weekly *The Land* proved invaluable.

'There was a lot of experience in that room, you could just listen to what they did and look at what they wrote, and you'd look at a story and go, "Oh, right ... I should probably mention that in the lead".'

This extended to selecting prospective interviewees.

'If you get a comment from the minister, you might put that first and then the industry representative next, and then somebody from the opposition after that. So, there was a real system that I could, without pestering people too much ... fit into.'

But feedback could be bracing. After filing one story she was called into the office of editor Peter Austin, 'and stupid me, just coming out of university and thinking I was Ernest Hemingway or something, thought he was going to tell me how fabulous I was'. But instead, Austin had highlighted a section of the article and asked: 'How do you expect someone on a farm in Nyngan to read this and know what on earth you're talking about?' She stood there, almost in tears.

In 1979, Tom Hyland landed his first job as a general reporter in the mining town of Mount Isa on *The North West Star*, which serviced a wide area of north-west Queensland. At the time, the paper was an afternoon daily with fewer than a dozen editorial staff. He recalls finding many aspects of the town confronting, including the physical environment, and the treatment of local Indigenous people.

> It was a shock to me to see, this is my country and this is what goes on here. The racism was pervasive. It was vicious. People's attitudes were vicious. The conditions in which a lot of the Aboriginal people lived were just devastating to see.

Hyland did not undertake a cadetship, which left significant gaps in his training.

'What I never received, and what I always regretted not receiving, was any sort of instruction in how to conduct an interview, in how to craft a feature article, how to watch for key points … I was simply given a typewriter and a notebook.'

But beginning a journalism career at a small outback paper also had an upside.

> I got to see a small media operation, a newspaper that did everything that a big newspaper does, but just on a smaller scale. I got to see the interaction between authorities and a newspaper proprietor. I got to see how the political system works in a small town and I think … international politics is small-town politics writ large. I think if you can work out how things work, say at a city council meeting, you can basically work out how similar principles and practices apply in federal politics or even at the UN. So it's a good grounding in that regard.

Others also found that working at small publications could provide career lift-off. Simon Mann sensed this on his first day at the weekly *Coastal Telegraph* in the Surf Coast town of Anglesea in Victoria in 1980. In his case, municipal politics proved to be the bread and butter of what started out as a part-time job.

> I think the reason I went from two or three days early on to very quickly five is because I threw myself into it, and I was happy to be there at eight in the morning, and I didn't leave until eight at night, and you'd go to an all-day council meeting of, say, the Shire of Winchelsea (as it was then) and you'd come away the next two days – because we were just a little weekly free publication – and you would just pick the eyes

out of the agenda meeting and look at your notes and pull the stories together and you'd get a dozen stories out of the meeting.

Jane Hammond, though, experienced the challenge of struggling to find stories after moving to the wheatbelt to work on the *Merredin Telegraph*.

'We had a drought at that time, so I was always worried that I would never find a new front-page story. Because nothing happened.'

On one occasion, with her weekly deadline approaching, she looked down the main street and all she saw was tumbleweed.

'There wasn't even a car in town.'

Gillian Lord, who grew up and began her career in Cape Town, South Africa, before moving to Australia, was working for what she describes as a 'suburban knock and drop' in the late 1980s. There she discovered that one of the world's first gender confirmation (previously gender reassignment) people, 'Loretta of Long Street', was living nearby. After winning her trust by spending a lot of time with her subject, the still relatively inexperienced Lord wrote a profile piece that turned out to be anything but a routine news story.

'People didn't know much about gender reassignment surgery then,' Lord points out. And when the article was published the paper received so many calls from readers, they had to disconnect their phones.

'I was very lucky because she'd been photographed by this very famous photographer ... But it did teach me the power of the printed word and the effect it had on readers.'

A particularly fertile beat for breaking news stories in the 1980s was business and finance. Anne Davies was one of those young journalists writing stories at a time when Alan Bond, Christopher Skase and Robert Holmes à Court were all prominent business figures.

'They were all these larger-than-life characters. So, finance was quite an exciting thing to write about. And interestingly, these moguls worked on the principle that you had to duchess the press.'

Davies recalls receiving a phone call from Holmes à Court one Sunday when she was rostered on. 'He'd just have a chat to whoever was on the share market round.'

Such easy access could also be problematic. John Spooner, who began at *The Age* as an illustrator in the 1970s after working as a lawyer, reflects that a lot of those finance stories relied on a single source.

> If you were able to quote [Robert] Holmes à Court, you'd get a scoop that would go straight onto the front page. And you wouldn't have to be a political journalist, chopping around through a whole range of possible alternatives to that story, and double-check. You would just run with it. Because there'd often be early breaks on a big announcement.

Fuelling this was a growing excitement around money and power.

'A lot of journalists who started at *The Age* and other places with arts degrees, got bored with writing in the general newsroom, and a lot of the most talented ones wanted to work in Business', says Spooner.

Simon Mann became one of those business journalists in 1984. Soon after, he helped set up *The Age*'s personal finance section called Money Extra. In this era before the stock market crash, newspapers were beginning to understand the value of dedicated finance sections.

> These things were bobbing up, personal investment magazines started on the strength of *Business Review Weekly*, and most of the daily papers were looking at having some sort of personal finance presence. There was this kind of awakening of Australians to investment and looking after yourself, and of course it was the [Paul] Keating Treasury years that manifested

in superannuation and all those things, so it was a great time [for] informing people about what to do.

The diversity of opportunities journalism offered also added to its attractions as a career choice. If the job you were in didn't work out, or if you simply wanted a change of scene, options abounded. Tom Hyland discovered this after a stint at the *Cairns Post*, following his time in Mount Isa. He flew to Sydney with no work lined up. While he recalls feeling like a fraud because he hadn't done a cadetship, his account of what happened next as he searched for work illustrates how opportunities could open up for someone whose previous role had been working for a country newspaper.

> On my second day in Sydney, I went and bought *The Sydney Morning Herald* and looked in the jobs column. And I saw a job with a company called Media Monitors and I rang them and they gave me an interview and I think they might've offered me a job, but I wasn't sure about it. It was night work and it would've taken me out of reporting, bearing in mind that I'd only had 20 months as a journalist, and I felt I hadn't got a very sound foundation for a journalistic career at this stage.

But soon afterwards he secured casual shift work at both *The Daily Telegraph* and the wire service, Australian Associated Press (AAP), which he had contacted before leaving Cairns.

'They were in a period of expansion. And I did, I think, two or three casual shifts at *The Daily Telegraph* and two or three at AAP, and after a couple of days at AAP they offered me a permanent position.'

With journalism jobs also in plentiful supply in other countries, journalists were able to combine work and travel with relative ease. As Russell Robinson explains, The Herald and Weekly Times had a lot of overseas bureaus, but it was rare for a person of his age and experience to be given an overseas posting.

> But the attitude of the organisation then was if someone goes overseas and works in journalism, we'll take them back, and we'll encourage them. It's a cheap way of saying 'Well, we've given you overseas experience', which they didn't.

For Michael Shmith, a nine-year stint at Britain's *Daily Express*, which switched from broadsheet to tabloid format during his time there, proved invaluable for his subsequent career at *The Age*.

> If *The Herald* had been my BA, let's say the *Daily Express* was my MA and PhD thesis in one. I learnt more I guess at the *Daily Express* in over nine years about not only newspaper production … but about the value of each and every word that went into that paper.

There was also a degree of mobility between different media forms for up-and-coming journalists. Tony Walker began his career as a cadet broadcaster with the ABC's Radio Australia, eventually becoming its correspondent in the Canberra press gallery in the mid-1970s, as well as the diplomatic correspondent for the ABC's domestic and international services.

'If you look at the photographs of November 11 [1975] with Whitlam on the front steps of Parliament, I'm the reporter immediately to his left, recording his words,' he points out.

At the ABC he received the training commensurate with what was offered in large print organisations. And while he says he never felt entirely comfortable as a broadcaster, 'I really did learn to interview people and to draw people out, which of course is one of the things that you learn for radio.'

When he left the ABC in 1976, he thought he might drift away from journalism, but was offered a job at *The Age*, and soon the role of foreign correspondent in Beijing.

When Rocco Fazzari took extended leave without pay from his public service job in Canberra to work at *The Canberra Times*, he was concerned that he might be taking a risk. But a conversation with fellow *Canberra Times* cartoonist Geoff Pryor resolved his dilemma.

> I said, 'Look Geoff, I'm really concerned for my parents, I might be without a job' ... He said, 'Don't be silly Rocco, newspapers will be around forever. Don't worry about it. You'll have a job for life, just like me.'

But for Tom Arup, as became evident soon after he commenced his cadetship at *The Age* in 2008, no such long-term certainties were on offer. Early in his training, he and fellow cadet Lucy Battersby were working on stories in Mildura when they were informed of a strike following the announcement of a round of redundancies, and that they needed to return to Melbourne immediately. The strike went on for three days. Eight years later, while working as *The Age*'s environment editor, Arup would put up his own hand to take a voluntary redundancy. By then the head count in the newsroom had contracted substantially.

With newsrooms now much depleted, and cadetships relatively thin on the ground, the hands-on and extensive training and mentorship programs provided by large media organisations in the last decades of the 20th century appear to have gone forever. Their legacy was several generations of skilled and versatile journalists whose early careers developed in environments that were nurturing as well as challenging. They were given exciting opportunities and enjoyed relative stability compared to today's entrants, and consequently many thought of journalism as a lifelong pursuit.

CHAPTER 5
Copy copy copy! Newsroom culture

Andrew Dodd
Matthew Ricketson
Penny O'Donnell

Not so long ago, big city newsrooms operated like industrial factories – printing presses down below, a floor or two for editorial, another for advertising and sales, and management at the top, on what was usually called 'mahogany row'. Most newsrooms had large open-plan sections with rows of mostly messy desks. Each section had its own territory, marked by the artwork on the walls (glass-encased front pages of company collapses in Business), material piled on the desks (sticky yellow-labelled books on European art in Graphics) or strewn on the floor (dog-eared season guides in Sport). Newsrooms could be quiet places, but the nearer to deadline, the louder they became, as journalists' chatter gave way to sub-editors' shouted queries, pitched battles over story placement and eventually the growing roar of the presses below. Newsrooms smelt: of stale sweat from the adrenaline and anxiety that drive daily journalism; of beer-soaked, never-quite-cleaned carpets and, until the 1990s, cigarette smoke.

Newsrooms have always been unusual workplaces. David Marr loved them, calling them 'crazy universities'. They were:

> Full of experts on the strangest things and the most important things, people with weird arcane knowledge,

people with real understanding and experience of things that mattered, places where you could ask anybody anything, though you might get your head bitten off if you interrupted somebody on deadline.

He discovered, happily, that he thrived in such a 'noisy energetic atmosphere', punctuated with 'shouting, yahooing and jokes'. Creativity and discipline co-existed. On the news desk it was all clean copy; in Features, the prose was vivid. But all of it was about facts and all produced to unyielding deadlines. The journalists acted as free agents, asking anyone hard questions, chasing down leads and bending the odd rule. But they were also bound by their own company's need to remain profitable, by appealing to the widest possible audience, through entertainment as well as serious journalism.

That newspapers and news bulletins are always easily available disguises the skill, organisation and effort involved. News production requires dedication. Reporters think nothing of working long hours day after day and dropping everything to help out when a big story breaks, even if they're on holiday.

Newsroom cultures vary across media companies, and evolve over time to meet new economic and technological demands. They also show how the people in newsrooms have changed from blue to white collar, from male-dominated to mixed, and from Anglo to multicultural, even if relatively few of the many women reach the highest levels, and progress on diversity remains slow.

For many years, newsrooms had a strict hierarchy and were highly demarcated. Everyone knew where they fitted in the grand order, from the compositors preparing 'hot metal' pages on 'the stone' to the lowliest ones of all, the copy kids, who ferried messages around and through exposure quickly absorbed their newsroom's particular culture.

Sophie Tedmanson was employed by *The Australian* in the pool of copy kids, meaning she moved around the News mastheads and sections.

'One day,' she recalls, 'I might be on the Saturday afternoon shift from 12 till four on the sports desk of *The Sunday Telegraph* and that would involve literally getting everyone's lunches … or sometimes paying the sports editor's phone bill.'

Her job also entailed collecting printouts and 'running copy' from a journalist to the editor and back again. She remembers each paper had its own character. As a weekly, *The Sunday Telegraph* was relatively relaxed. But there was more pressure at the daily paper, which was then edited by the legendary Col Allan.

Tedmanson says she was scared of him. 'Even going anywhere near that office scared me. I remember one day having to take some orange juice in there and I was literally shaking so much that I was spilling it. That was back in those really intimidating days.'

The copy kids also kept the copy flowing between the reporters and the sub-editors. At *The News* in Adelaide, Samela Harris says the reporters relied on the copy boys, as they then were.

> We would have to hammer things out on these archaic typewriters, which we'd have to do in layers and layers of carbon copies with one paper going here and another paper going there … The copy boys being ready, you put your hand up and scream 'Copy' and a copy boy would run and grab it and take it in to the subs.

The sub-editors were often maligned as old fogeys and pedants, but they did important work, as cartoonist Rocco Fazzari came to appreciate.

'I learnt to really respect how clever they were. I thought they were the cleverest people in the newsroom and they were treated so badly by journalists.'

The reporters tended to disparage them as 'failed reporters', according to Russell Robinson, who from his first day as a copy boy at the Melbourne *Herald* saw how skilled they were. Running copy on deadline was also part of Robinson's role:

> A sub would finish the subbing and would yell out 'Copy' and you'd jump up and … you'd get the copy and put it in the tube, and clip it down and you would send it one floor up to the comp room where it would be typeset.

The copy was sent paragraph by paragraph, each on a separate page known as a 'slip'. The sub's job was to correct or change the reporter's story, while keeping track of what had been sent and what else needed to be written. Robinson remembers witnessing one experienced sub at work on a breaking news event:

> I've seen a big story where I've had to stand behind that crack sub while he changes copy, and slip by slip, I'll take one slip and run it upstairs, shoot it upstairs, and he could retain that intro, an image of that intro, and let the story flow. I was just absolutely gobsmacked at the skills.

As a copy boy Robinson also worked with the sports sub-editing table and with the telephonists who all sat nearby. He remembers the women on the phones were aged between 30 and 70 and that one of them used to smoke a cigar. They would have headsets on and pound away on their typewriters, frequently yelling out, 'Copy, copy, copy'. Robinson would quickly get the copy and run it over to the chief sub. If reporters were stuck for words or couldn't get their intros, or were drunk, as Robinson witnessed on more than one occasion, the copy-takers would do the story for them. 'They were absolutely fantastic.'

Subs seem to enjoy the same reputation everywhere. They are revered, feared and despised in almost equal measure. In Cape

Town, South Africa, where Gillian Lord was a young reporter on the *Cape Argus*, she remembers the subs' 'absolute insistence on factual accuracy' which ensured 'there would be no sloppy copy coming out of that desk, ever'. Making a mistake led to repercussions: 'If you let a literal [spelling or punctuation error] through, I mean for the rest of the day, people would be talking about you behind their hands.'

Newspapers were once so well-resourced that they employed several categories of sub-editors. 'You remember the revise subs?' asks Lord. 'And then the final check subs?' And on every subs' table there was at least one larger-than-life character. Lord remembers Tony Miller, who in his younger days used to be a 'hellraiser' and who was still 'physically getting into brawling matches, well into his 60s'. Miller had a habit of calling reporters with his booming voice across the newsroom when they had done something wrong. 'He'd gesture with his finger,' says Lord, 'and the whole newsroom would watch you do the walk of shame to Tony Miller.'

But even this gruff sub had a soft side. After a while he took Lord under his wing to show her how to improve her writing. It meant sitting next to him for hours watching him working with reporters' copy, but she valued being shown 'how to really cut something if it had to be cut and how to still maintain the integrity of the story while you're cutting'.

Back then everyone smoked at their desks and Lord remembers Miller 'was a very heavy smoker and his chest used to burble, and his face was like paper'. She and the 'copy taster' used to whisper to one another, 'Is he dead? No, he's not, he's just sleeping.'

The copy taster played an important role in many newsrooms. Lord remembers her colleague got to work early in the morning to go through all the overnight news from the wire services. She would then assign those stories to the various sections of the newspaper and inform the chief sub about any rolling or breaking stories before the morning news conference. By the time the editors and section editors came to work 'there would already be a mud map for the day's paper'.

At least one of the old sub-editors at *The Mail* in Footscray made a big impression on Ross Brundrett. Like many newcomers to journalism, Brundrett didn't know subs played a time-honoured role as mentors when he was given a cadetship at the suburban newspaper in 1975. He didn't have access to either of the two standard industry guides used at Fairfax and The Herald and Weekly Times, *The Journalist's Craft* and *Reporting for Work* respectively. What instruction he received was more like torment than tuition. He was shocked when one of the subs started rolling his rejected copy into balls and throwing them at the back of his head.

'Some days, it'd be 30 or 40 rolled-up bits of copy paper all around my desk,' he recalls.

Suburban newspapers in Melbourne were 'still making money' in those days. Brundrett remembers *The Mail* as a 'bustling newspaper publishing 60 to 80 pages a week' with a boss who 'basically kept the place full of smoke'. As well as the two old subs, the paper employed four journalists and a photographer from *The Age* who worked there two days a week. 'I was the youngest by eight or nine years at least,' says Brundrett, 'everyone else seemed ancient.' The copy ball-throwing sub was Stuart Brown, a former editor of *The Herald*, who became Brundrett's 'early guiding force' and trusted friend.

> He used to always make a point of reading my copy. If he didn't like it, you'd know, because he's thrown it back, and he'd say, 'Try again'. But he also used to type out little notes. 'She's not a lady, she's a woman'. 'You're making editorial comments. How do you know she's a lady?'

That went on for a year or two until another cadet arrived and 'a few missiles floated out towards him'. Brundrett had a light-bulb moment once he was not the only target and took on board Brown's 'commandments of journalism'. He worked side by side with the sub for seven years, mined the local crime, courts and football rounds, and wrote '30 different little pieces a week'.

At some newspapers, the sub-editors were so dominant that the paper became known as a subs' paper. Before joining *The Sun-Herald* in Sydney, Debra Jopson had worked on broadsheets and had written extensively for *The National Times*, so she had become 'used to working for what's called writers' papers. And so, having my copy changed constantly, also without consultation – which was quite common in those days – was very frustrating for me.'

The subs' table was generally made up of career-long staff. They were dedicated to their craft and over the years saw every imaginable error, routinely saving journalists from ignominy and embarrassment. They all made their fair share of mistakes too, by inserting errors rather than amendments into copy, incorrectly captioning photos or removing vital clarifying comments in legally sensitive stories. Subbing was also a job that suited people returning to work, because the hours were regular and some shifts could be contained to a nine-to-five day. For others, especially from the 1980s on, the subs' desks became populated with women returning from maternity leave, making them less blokey.

Another kind of sub existed too; the one who considered themself a writer, not someone who simply processed others' copy. That was Stephen Corby's lot at *The Daily Telegraph*, where he worked as the chief sub on Features. He was good at it, but he had been promised a writing gig. He'd been allowed to write TV guides and occasional columns when the regulars were away, but those didn't satisfy him. He lobbied the editor, Campbell Reid, without success. He even trained up people to take over from him.

But Corby remembers Reid saying: 'Mate, why do you want to be a writer? Writers are a dime a dozen. Anyone can be a writer. We've got a career path for you. We've looked after you. You're going to the backbench. It's going to be great.'

But Corby was adamant, eventually threatening to quit unless given a writing job. *The Daily Telegraph* didn't budge.

'They wouldn't let that career path happen,' he says. 'So, I resigned.'

At this point things got nasty and another facet of newsroom culture became apparent when a senior colleague said to him:

> 'Mate, you will never work in this town again. We will make sure of it. You think we're just News Limited. We have friends at Fairfax. You will never work anywhere in journalism again if you do this. How can you leave? How can you do this to us? After everything we've done for you?' I said, 'Mate, I'm not leaving because you won't give me a promotion. I just want to write. All I want to do is write. I'm not doing it – just let me write. I just want to freelance. That's all I want to do.' And he was saying, 'No, screw you'. And it was on for young and old. It was just horrible. It was like leaving the Mafia.

Newsrooms could be cruel places, as well as blinkered. The combination of deadlines and competition, as well as power dynamics within a tight hierarchy, could lead to strange behaviour. Flip Prior remembers a time earlier in her career in Western Australia when a woman was appointed chief of staff, which rarely happened. Unfortunately, it did not go well as the woman 'monstered people, in particular women, to the point where eventually she didn't have that job anymore'. Prior had trouble understanding why a woman would do this to other women. She remembers wondering if it was about self-preservation. Perhaps the new chief of staff was thinking 'It's so hard to get this position that I'm going to protect it at all costs and so if a young woman shows any promise, I'm going to give her a harder time, or be more disparaging or something'.

Sophie Tedmanson experienced an equally baffling event as a copy kid at *The Daily Telegraph* when a senior editor called her over and 'picked up a piece of paper off her desk, threw it on the ground at my feet and said, "Take that to someone"'. Tedmanson thought, 'Are you kidding me, why didn't you just hand that to me?' Tedmanson was tempted 'to tell this woman to f-off and not be so rude'. She recalls realising 'it was a bit of a game to her and that that was the way she thought you were supposed to treat copy kids'. So, instead she remembers taking a deep breath, picking up the piece of paper and doing what she was told. She also remembers thinking, 'I don't ever want to become like that. If I ever make it, I don't want to be a woman who treats people like that, that's just not the way to behave, even in life, let alone a newsroom. So, in some weird way she taught me an interesting lesson.'

The editors were ultimately responsible for the tone of the newsroom, as well as the content it produced. They had the power of feudal lords, although they themselves were answerable to the proprietor, who might be benign if patrician like the Fairfaxes[1] or unapologetically directive as Frank and Kerry Packer[2] were and Rupert Murdoch continued to be after nearly seven decades in the media business.[3] Editors generally rose through the reporting ranks, meaning they knew the industry inside out and from many different perspectives. They were rarely trained in management, though, and the relentless pace of the daily news cycle did not leave much time to hone their human resources skills, assuming that's what they even wanted.

Fazzari says editors were 'like mother and father figures that would try to keep the ship steady and make sure that by 10 o'clock every night the newspaper went to bed'. Some created the conditions where new staff could seek out mentoring and simply pick up lessons by quietly observing others around them. At *The Land*, Liz Wells learnt a valuable lesson by watching the livestock editor, Bob Arnold. On Thursday mornings Arnold fielded calls from disgruntled cattle or sheep farmers after writing about one of their competitors. Arnold was dealing with people who were both advertisers with the paper and the subject of stories, but he did not let the former influence the latter. For him it didn't matter whether someone had 'spent twice as much on advertising in the past month as somebody else'.

Steve Lewis admired Gerard Noonan's editorship of *The Australian Financial Review*, which for him made the newspaper 'just a wonderful place to work'. But, as often happens in newsrooms, senior roles change quickly. 'Gerry unfortunately was sacked as editor and replaced by John Alexander, an editor who inspired both fear and awe.' Fazzari describes Alexander as 'a real hard man', because he was relentlessly focused on bringing out the best in people.

He also remembers Alexander as mischievous. One day when Fazzari was walking across the newsroom, Alexander – huddled with a group of senior editors 20 metres away – pointed at his illustrator and called him over. As Fazzari walked over, all the other editors stood up and looked at him. With each step closer, Fazzari's anxiety grew. Alexander pointed at him again and said, 'Rocco don't you ever, ever wear brown shoes with a black belt again.' Fazzari knew Alexander, an Italophile, was 'just being funny', but he also knew 'I was really worried and frightened by being called over to this huddle of really important men.'

Not all editors appreciated high culture, and some could be fearsome. Stephen Corby's editor at *The Sunday Telegraph*, Jeni O'Dowd, was so successful in the role that she grew the gap between the Fairfax-owned *Sun-Herald* and *The Sunday Telegraph*.

Famously, O'Dowd and Lachlan Murdoch, Rupert's eldest son, then in charge of the company's Australian operations, had an agreement that if she could increase *The Sunday Telegraph*'s sales lead over *The Sun-Herald* by 200 000 copies he would buy her a Porsche. Sure enough, the following year he handed her the keys.

'She had some kind of ability to sell that paper, that had nothing to do with journalism,' says Corby. 'And she was a terrifying manager. Made people cry. You would go to news conference in the morning, you had to pitch your stories and, halfway through … someone's in tears because she's tearing them apart.'

Corby remembers a news conference when she threw the paper across the room and said, 'All your ideas are shit!' She told them, 'You all come back in, you all pitch me new ideas in an hour, and we'll keep coming back every fucking hour until one of your ideas is any good. Because these are all shit.' Apparently, O'Dowd then stormed out.

Corby and some of the older reporters were called into her office, where she said, 'What the fuck is going on? You guys better have some ideas. You're the senior journalists. We're paying you all this money. You tell me your ideas now.' Corby said, 'I just told you my ideas in there.' O'Dowd responded, 'Well, they were shit!' 'She was terrifying, absolutely terrifying,' says Corby.

Despite this, he says he had a good time at the paper; well, kind of: 'I had a good time in between being driven slightly bonkers by the culture and the madness. We were all in this world together – we were described as being "in the trenches" … you were bound together by the experience.'

In response, O'Dowd says, 'I can't recall leaving people in tears at a news conference held almost 20 years ago; but I can recall many great conferences where staff shared ideas for investigative journalism which later led to awards. Journalists on a high salary were expected to contribute ideas which shaped the paper; it was part of their job description. In those days of fierce newspaper battles the work was tough and invigorating; the tactic of calling senior writers back for another conference was mainly to stop the long lunch culture of those days – although I am not at all suggesting Stephen was part of that culture.'

Not all editors were ferocious, but many were aggressive, and demanded 'scoops'. That's Michael West's memory of Glenn Burge when he joined the Business section at *The Sydney Morning Herald*, where West 'walked into a good little team of journalists' who prided themselves on beating *The Australian Financial Review*. They were also 'hard lunching' and would spend hours wining and dining with contacts.

'There were some that used to go for hours till five o'clock and you'd nick back and quickly write your story, you know, one eye closed,' says West. 'I had to get one guy, the mining reporter, out of the toilet, who fell asleep. We had to climb over the top of the toilet to shake him. He wasn't even alert to being yelled at to get him up to go back to his desk to file.'

West recalls a senior columnist sometimes fell asleep at his desk at about six o'clock at night when he was meant to be filing. Somebody had the job to go and wake him up so he could finish his column. 'You'd get sacked for it these days,' says West.

Drinking was part of the newsroom culture for Gary Tippet, who admits he was 'a pretty big drinker'.

> We used to have the subs' club after work so they'd finish work in the early hours of the morning and then they'd go over and sit at the table where the conferences used to be and crack open beers and guys would be going home at six o'clock in the morning, crashing, and then getting up and coming back to work and doing it all over again.

As Tippet was working on a morning paper his shift ended at 10.30 pm, but much of the work would be done by dinner time.

'So, you'd go for dinner and you'd have a few drinks then and you'd come back and you'd be half cut for the rest of the night. If something happened, you'd have to do it with a couple of drinks in you.' He concludes, 'It should have been frowned on, but it wasn't.'

Rivalry and intense competition were common in newsrooms, even within the same company.[4] Russell Robinson will never forget the 'ridiculous' rivalry between fellow mastheads that almost left him without a job after a five-year stint reporting abroad. He had been a cadet at *The Herald* in Melbourne, so paid a visit, and asked editor Pat Hinton for work. The answer was, 'Sorry mate, we don't have a vacancy.' On his way out through the newsroom, which at that time *The Herald* shared with *The Sun News-Pictorial*, Robinson crossed paths with another old colleague, Don Baker, then *The Sun*'s chief of staff, who immediately offered him work. 'I remember it as if it was yesterday', says Robinson. Within 24 hours, Pat Hinton made a rival offer, explaining that he'd 'been through the books' and 'we can fit you in'. Robinson was offended. 'I'm now a *Sun* man,' he replied, and the two men never spoke again. Robinson's decision relaunched his career and he became an investigative reporter.

Maureen Shelley says that at News Limited a reporter was considered either a Fairfax or a News Limited person. She personally preferred the culture at News Limited.

'I found the Fairfax people terribly grumpy on the whole, but at News Limited they didn't give a toss about anything. They did what they did and they were happy to be doing it, whereas at Fairfax I think they took themselves all a bit more seriously.'

There was almost no industrial culture at News, but at Fairfax the staff fought numerous battles over independence and editorial integrity, especially when they believed it could be threatened by new owners.

When the Fairfax family's control came to an end in 1990 and the Canadian media mogul Conrad Black took effective control,[5] Matthew Moore and his colleagues on the House Committee (the local branch of the union) went to the annual general meeting and questioned the new owner about editorial independence.

He says, 'We put the view of the journalists to try and preserve our role in society, and there were some very combative times during that.'

Moore remembers Black's characteristically verbose retort after an argument over staff cost cuts. 'He said, "Mr Moore, I'm not here to sodomise the franchise."'

Newsrooms were driven by deadlines, which over time could wear down the most seasoned of reporters. Simon Mann says, 'You end up living on the adrenaline a lot, because of those deadlines, you know, every day you start again with a fresh canvas and away you go, and as you get closer to the deadline the heartbeat is literally rising and the pressure, and you've had your fifteenth coffee for the day'.

Newsrooms everywhere have changed. The strict demarcation of roles has loosened. Once reporters were prevented from taking pictures and writing headlines because they were other people's tasks. Now they're expected to, along with uploading videos, curating live blogs and responding to reader analytics. Mentoring has diminished with the exit of the old guard. The subs' table has all but disappeared too, meaning reporters have been forced to add proofreading to their list of duties, ensuring more mistakes make it into print and a further erosion of readers' trust. Newsrooms are more corporate and business-focused. They're less chaotic, and perhaps less creative. The 'crazy university' that David Marr so enjoyed was not present at the head office of *Guardian Australia* in Sydney where he went after leaving *The Sydney Morning Herald* in 2012. He tried to recreate it, but had little success.

The buzz and energy of a newsroom is a product of the ways so many people race the clock each day to create a record of the world around them. Newsrooms brought together people almost as varied as the audience they served, with experts and generalists working alongside newbies and lifers; the passionate and the jaded. There were drunks and jokers, the high-cultured and low-brow. Economists, telephonists, columnists, lawyers, artists and cartoonists all created parts of a newspaper that, right on schedule, ended up in the hands of the printers.

Simon Mann fondly remembers the excitement of standing next to the presses as 'they slowly cranked them up at *The Age* for that big Saturday edition'. As Mann says, it had a phenomenal capacity of 168 broadsheet pages. On one Saturday the entire paper

– including its pre-printed material – was 324 pages, a world record for a Saturday paper, according to then editor Mike Smith.[6]

> When you went down there and the bells were ringing and they were aligning the presses and slowly they hit the button and they start to crank it up, there is undoubtedly that adrenaline rush; it is fantastic. It is this thunderous pumping out of these copies and seeing them spin off and being able to grab one and look at it. Yeah, that is a great feeling – a fabulous feeling – one of the best feelings of print journalism.

Amanda Meade

Interviewed by Penny O'Donnell, edited by Matthew Ricketson

As the longest serving media reporter in Australia, first for *The Australian* and then *Guardian Australia*, Amanda Meade has had a bird's-eye view of the beauty and the beastliness of Australia's news media.

Growing up

I was born in 1962 in London, but grew up in South Africa and emigrated to Australia when I was 15. I had a disruptive childhood; my parents were both actors, and my mum was married five times. We lived in a very white suburb in Johannesburg during apartheid. I remember at the supermarket meat would be divided into regular and dog meat and servant meat, which was really cheap cuts. The servants would eat that, and then your scraps. I saw police trucks pulling black people off the street and throwing them up against the wall. I talked to servant women who hadn't seen their kids in a year.

That severe inequality I saw politicised me, and made me want to be a journalist. Many people ignored it, but my father was political and made me aware of what was going on. He was a stand-up comedian and actor. He spoke Zulu, 'cos he grew up in the Transvaal [a former province in north-eastern South Africa]. He was anti-apartheid; my mother wasn't racist, but she came from a wealthy

American family who didn't oppose the regime. My grandfather was president of the Coca-Cola Export Corporation. My parents were two sides of the coin. Black people were living these horrendous lives while we were being woken up every morning with a cup of tea; our beds would be made; we never did any washing. We didn't have any money, but we still had servants. It was such an unrealistic life.

My parents separated and my father met and married the actress Elaine Lee who later was in the television show *Number 96*. They moved to Australia, but they broke up and my dad came back to South Africa and then brought us all to Australia. My parents only really watched the ABC. When I went to other people's houses, they were allowed to watch *Blankety Blanks*. I loved watching Mike Willesee and Jana Wendt. They got me interested in journalism, though I was more interested then in being on television than print journalism. To me journalism was like show business, but not. I'd seen how hard and insecure it was to be in showbiz, but I also wanted the excitement of doing something creative.

Breaking into journalism

My dad would always buy *The Sydney Morning Herald* and *The Daily Telegraph*, and I would read them, but after school I went straight to Sydney Uni and did arts. I had a marvellous time, then I realised I had an Honours degree in English literature, but was completely unemployable. I had a vague idea I wanted to be a journalist, but didn't know how. I got a job as a trainee book editor at the Law Book Company in North Ryde and that's when I realised I had to be a journalist. Just sitting there all day with this dead manuscript, editing it, ringing up the author and then proofreading – I just thought I was going to die of boredom. I went back to uni and did the postgraduate diploma in journalism at the University of Technology Sydney.

My very first story was about South Africa. It was timed to coincide with an anniversary of the 1976 Soweto uprising. I'd interviewed the head of the African National Congress in Australia and talked to him about his journey to Australia, and compared it to mine. The lecturers loved it and were very encouraging. They told me to go over to *The Herald*, which was then on Broadway, next to UTS.

I don't know how I did it, but I knocked on the door and asked to see the foreign editor, Warren Osmond. The receptionist rang, and he was too busy to see me, and so I just said, 'Really, really, really, please ask him to come out. I think he'll really like it.' He came out and gruffly took this piece of paper and went away, and then he left a message on my voicemail, 'Thank you very much, Amanda. We'll publish your piece on Saturday on the world pages, and we'll pay you' – I don't know, it was $1500 or something amazing. Oh my God, I'd never been so happy in my life. It was literally the first thing I'd ever written. After that, I was, 'Okay, this is what I want to do.'

Arriving at *The Sydney Morning Herald*
At 28 I was the world's oldest cadet. I had absolutely no money and no financial support from my parents. It was wonderful to have a job. I thought it was a lot of money, even though in those days it wasn't. I started as a third-year cadet, going to shorthand, and doing colour stories. It was a great place to work; everyone loved it and there were so many resources. We had editorial drivers who used to sit outside and wait for us and drive us on jobs. If we worked late, they would drive us home. It was incredible compared to now. After a year they said I could go to Canberra for six months. It was terrifying. I remember covering things like superannuation, which Paul Keating was bringing in. I had to write a how-to guide; I was like, 'But I don't even understand it myself.' So, yeah, a steep learning curve, and I grew up so fast. It was fantastic. All the years I spent later at News Limited, I never felt as comfortable as I did at Fairfax. *Guardian Australia*, where I am now, reminds me a lot of Fairfax. There was something about those days where we really

thought *The Herald* was the best newspaper and there was a great self-belief among journalists at that time.

Moving to *The Australian*

Why did I move to *The Australian*? They offered me a job, and a lot more money. I was on a pretty low grade, and Chris Mitchell, the editor, offered me seven grades more. I was like, 'Okay.' I went from a J2 to a J9 overnight. I almost immediately regretted it, though, because the culture was so different. I went from feeling very comfortable with my besties at *The Herald* to feeling like a fish out of water in *The Australian*'s Canberra bureau.

The Herald was compartmentalised; you did this particular round or had this particular skill level, but News Corp is a lot flatter. Somebody would resign and suddenly I'd find myself writing 2000 words on a minister that day, not knowing anything about them, and it was very full on. After a year I came back to Sydney. I was working on good stories like the Wood police royal commission [into the New South Wales Police Service], but I was floating and I started agitating for a round.

The first one that came up was television. I thought that was soft after politics and royal commissions, but they said, 'You can make of it what you want, and you can also write news.' For the television page you would do a big feature, plus you'd do news. It was only by accident I ended up getting a column in the new Media section, because the guy who was doing Media Diary went on holidays, and they asked me to fill in. They liked what I did better, and so when he came back they said, 'Oh, sorry, we're giving it to Amanda.'

Reporting on the media

It was actually Lachlan Murdoch, when he was at News in Australia, who set up the Media section. Bizarrely, it was based on *The*

Guardian's Media section. Lachlan wanted it to cover everything, and early on it was a thick pre-printed lift-out with television listings, but also long features on the media industry, on international trends and developing media. There were 10 people working full time; now there's one or two. For a long time, the section had a reputation for being independent. We had editors who stood up to other parts of News Corp when we made fun of *The Sunday Telegraph* in the diary, or whatever. But journalists in general are quick to jump on you if you've written anything wrong about them. The Media Diary is a thankless task really because it's read by everyone in the media and any little mistake is noticed by everyone in the newsroom.

Reporting on the affairs of your own company is tricky. When you worked for News Corp you never mentioned Rupert. For a Media Diary item once I mentioned how the *Herald Sun* had written a story about these iconic Australian brands that were foreign-owned, like Vegemite. I wrote how ironic is that, when the *Herald Sun* was owned by that famous American, Rupert Murdoch. It was approved by the Media section editor and got through all the checks, but the editor of the *Herald Sun* freaked out.

Before I knew it, I had been called into the editor's office and stripped of my column. They didn't actually say it was because of that item – they said they were changing the section's direction, making it more about marketing – but it was bleedingly obvious it was about the item. The rest of the media actually wrote about it, so it was known what had happened. I remember sitting in the meeting with all these editors, thinking 'This is another dimension'. Nobody said it was because of this paragraph, making fun of Murdoch, but I knew and they all knew. After a year 'on the bench' I was asked to come back and I started all over again, but I was a lot more careful about what I wrote. I had been quite naïve at first. Within News Corp you can't make fun of the company.

News Corporation and its enemies

The biggest animosity was between News Corp and the ABC. Not the ABC to News Corp, but News to the ABC. Part of it was that the ABC was doing well in digital, but it was also the culture wars. It caused me the most angst over the years. Once, I was covering the Walkley Awards, and I was put at Kerry O'Brien's table, which happened to have a spare spot.

The next day an editor calls me into his office and he blew up at me so badly I sobbed for an hour afterwards. The whole attack was: how dare I be so friendly with Kerry O'Brien. I was gob smacked. 'But, it's my job. I cover the media. Of course I'm going to talk to him,' and he was like, 'I saw you laughing with him. What were you doing sitting at that table anyway?' I was so upset I ended up going home for the day, because it felt almost like a physical assault. I was supposed to do my column the next day, and I didn't, and they had a blank space saying I was unwell. They really thought the ABC was left-wing, and biased, and that people like Kerry O'Brien had too much power, and got paid too much. He was one they really didn't like; David Marr was another. He got a really hard time when he was hosting *Media Watch*; they would ask us to dig up dirt on them. It wasn't often explicit, but everybody knew that's what they thought, and that's what they wanted. I managed to survive at *The Oz* without doing things I wasn't proud of, and it's extremely hard.

I don't blame people who write agenda-type stories. You kind of get pressured by the news desk to do things, but I managed to sidestep doing things like that by finding another story which they could use instead. There were people who they felt they could manipulate more. Once they asked me to do a story on *Media Watch*, and the premise was: 'Who are these people? They're not real journalists. They just come along and criticise us.'

I actually did it, and the opposite was true. Tim Palmer was the executive producer and he had a Gold Walkley. He had been a foreign correspondent twice. Everybody had serious runs on the board. I handed the story in and it never saw the light of day.

The Finkelstein inquiry and the Press Council

By the time the [Independent Inquiry into the Media and Media Regulation] headed by Ray Finkelstein was set up, Chris Mitchell had been editor-in-chief for several years and controlled the newspaper's agenda. There was a specific view on how they wanted that inquiry covered and we did day after day of negative coverage. We never actually covered what was in the report, except a little bit on the day it was released. It was exhausting because a news editor would come down and say, 'Chris wants this', or, 'Chris wants that'. Everyone was expected to just go all out and get him whatever he wanted. If you didn't agree with what they were pursuing, it was very uncomfortable.

After the Finkelstein report was delivered, they decided, very cynically, to back a beefed-up Press Council as an alternative to whatever Finkelstein was proposing, even though they had never really cared about the Press Council, or taken it seriously. They had seen it as a major pain, but they decided to back it and put a lot more money into it, even though they have since attacked it ferociously.

Embracing a digital world

There were quite a few years of denial, at *The Australian* anyway, about whether any of these new forms of media, like Twitter, were going to survive. At that time the newspaper and the online desk were still separate. I would write a story in the morning about something that had happened on TV the night before, for example, and then at 4 pm the newspaper chief of staff would say, 'Can you do a story about that thing that was on TV last night?' and I would say, 'I have. It's been on the website for six hours, and it's got 200 comments.' They didn't even know it was on the website because they were thinking about the next day's paper.

Covering the media, I could see the landscape changing, whereas other people were still in their own bubbles. When Kim Williams came to head up News Corp in Australia, he tried to bring everything into the digital age, and the newspaper editors all revolted and they basically got rid of him, and they said, 'No, the newspaper is the thing.'

The editors, and Rupert, like having the papers as power in a city. I think they still cling to the idea of the influence that comes with the front page even though the news agenda has been taken out of their hands. They can say this is the story of the day, but if the public has other ideas and start bombarding social media or websites with a complaint about something – say there's a product at Target that mothers are complaining about – then that quickly moves from Facebook to *Mamamia* to *The Herald* to *The Australian*.

I got onto social media early, as I had spent several years working from home, so I wasn't inside the newsroom bubble, worrying about office politics. I was inspired by people like the late Mark Colvin, and Leigh Sales, who were on Twitter early, posting links to interesting stories. I followed them, saw who they were following and I learnt with Twitter that it's really good to have a bit of a dialogue with people. They didn't have to be famous, but you should always talk to people.

Leaving News Corporation

In 2012 I had a conversation one day with the managing editor about going from four days a week to five days, because a change in my family circumstances meant I needed full time work, and she said we couldn't really afford it because we're cutting back. In that moment, I thought, 'Really? Okay, I just want to leave, then.'

It had probably been building up; it wasn't a happy place to be anymore because there was so much pressure on us to attack all the other media organisations rather than just be reporters. I asked Chris Mitchell and he took 24 hours to get back to me, and said yes. Which was great because they could have said no, so I did really appreciate it, but then it was quite shocking because they said, 'Okay, you can go on "that" day in November.' I had less than two weeks left, and I didn't have a job.

I hadn't made any plans, or anything. People thought I had a job lined up, but I honestly didn't. I didn't panic because I had a nice little nest egg with the redundancy payment. I was determined I wasn't going into PR. But word got out and a *Crikey* reporter rang, asking if I was leaving and I totally lied because it wasn't official yet. I was dying inside – I couldn't believe I was lying – but I was terrified they would reverse it if word got out. I announced it on Twitter, and that created a bit of a stir.

I had a lovely send-off, at a pub in Surry Hills. And then, I did nothing, pretty much drove my daughter to school, and then had a coffee, and watched *Ellen*. Did nothing for several months, which was a first. It was awesome. It was so nice to be able to completely shut off and be a mum. As a single parent I hadn't really had much time off. I'd gone back to work full-time when my daughter was 11 weeks old.

I feel my greatest achievement in life is that I managed to keep going with my job and my career, even though I found myself happily with child, unexpected, unplanned and certainly I wasn't in any financial position to deal with it, and I didn't have family support.

My editor at the time was extremely helpful and said I could do my job from home. I started doing my column from home, and they let me come in one day a week for meetings and planning.

During that time social media exploded, and I found myself drawn to it; social media became my office. You can share things, talk about things online. I had someone looking after my daughter, so that saved me hours in commuting time. News Corp was brilliant about it; they let me do that for seven years. I was writing front-page news stories, from home. A lot of people weren't doing that then. I owe them gratitude for that. Mind you, I did work hard in the hours I had.

Joining *Guardian Australia*

I started writing a bit for Fairfax and *Mumbrella*, the trade publication. Then Andrew Denton quit working in television. *The Guardian* had just started up in Australia, and their culture editor tracked me down and asked if I would write something about him. I was busy that day. I was having some procedure at the hospital, and I was in the waiting room and I said, 'Oh, I'd love to do something for you but I can't do it today.' That was a bit scary.

I had thought about applying for a job there, because it was one of those dream places to work. But the jobs they were offering didn't suit me because they were for younger journalists who were able to be available over a seven-day roster, willing to work weekends, late nights, early starts, doing live blogging and I thought realistically that's not something I could do, so I didn't apply.

Then I started offering them things like a guide to what to watch on election night. I was keeping an eye on things they might be interested in. Because *The Guardian* has a completely different audience to *The Australian*. The Media section was right down into the detail of media, almost like a trade magazine. Whereas *The Guardian* doesn't care who's running *60 Minutes* or anything like that. A story needed to appeal to a general audience.

I had to rethink what stories would work for them. Things I thought they'd be interested in, they weren't. Anyway, I started offering them stories, and we found I wasn't only doing these features, I was doing news. It got to the point where I had to be there at my desk in the morning, looking at what was happening and filing for them.

Eventually they said, 'Well, it looks like we've got to give you a job, because you've created a job for yourself.' It was difficult because they didn't have a budget for a media writer. They're a start-up. They had no money. I'm incredibly impressed how agile and fast and prolific the young journalists there are, and how good they are at investigative work and live blogging. There are some other skills I had learnt early in my career, though, just by being in the newsroom, listening to other journalists interviewing people on the phone, or working closely with senior people who would help you with the questions to ask or tell you the holes in your story.

Within *The Australian*, I had been known as a defender of the ABC. When I left, I was free to write whatever I wanted about them. I did feel strongly about a need for a strong public broadcaster, and I still do, because commercial media, especially broadcast, don't cover what needs to be covered unless it is popular. Which commercial media, especially these days, is going to be able to spend six weeks doing one story about, say, homelessness or Indigenous culture, that won't make them money like *Four Corners* does? It's unthinkable to me to not have the ABC and SBS, but the attacks on public broadcasting by commercial media, especially News Corp, have accelerated to full-on war.

News also, for a period after I left, personally attacked me, through my old column, which at first was upsetting, 'cos I'd worked there for more than a decade, and then it just became funny.

All the redundancies in the media mean, I think, there are so many areas of life that aren't covered like they were before, where newsrooms used to have many, many people and the chief of staff could literally send one person out to each event that was happening. Whether it's state parliament or local councils or community events or conferences about education or health or science, people would go and cover those things day in, day out even if there wasn't a story. They would compete for the limited space in the newspaper; now there's unlimited space online, but not enough people to cover all the things happening each day in the city. Coverage of courts is falling by the wayside.

The Guardian is a big global media organisation, but it started here in 2013 with a much smaller newsroom than Fairfax and News Corp. The staff number has grown under the editor, Lenore Taylor, but there are still areas we simply can't cover. With the redundancies and then the newsroom closures, you have to ask: are there dirty things going on in society that we don't know about, because there aren't enough journalists to find them?

CHAPTER 6
The constant undercurrent: Sexual harassment and discrimination

Penny O'Donnell
Merryn Sherwood
Brad Buller

The first abusive email arrived soon after Rosslyn Beeby joined *The Canberra Times* as science and environment reporter in 2003. She'd spent most of her career reporting on climate change, the environment, and working for an environmental organisation in Sydney, so some older journalists saw her as a greenie and made life difficult when she arrived in the newsroom.

The editor who hired her, Michael Stephens, was also 'not liked' by 'some of the older men' who thought creating an environmental round at the paper was 'pandering to greenies' (seen by these men as a minority readership in Canberra). Stephens had also abolished several news rounds he considered unproductive.

One day, 'out of the blue', Beeby received an email addressed to her and copied to 'a group of about six other men ... the ringleaders' at the paper.

> It was a little email about 'Peggy the greenie' and how Peggy ... had climbed a tree because she wanted to see an endangered species ... and how she was so excited to see this

endangered species that she lost her grip and slid all the way down the tree, getting a vagina full of splinters. And how she went to the doctor and said, 'Oh help, help me' as she sort of walked in, hardly able to walk. 'Oh help me, doctor.' The doctor said, 'Oh Peggy, if only I could. But I can't log an old growth area.'

Beeby wrote about endangered species at *The Canberra Times*, and 'Peggy' was the men's mock name for her. Her male critics in the newsroom had escalated and sexualised their harassment. 'It wasn't [just] a case of should that man be calling me love or sweetie,' says Beeby. 'It was clearly targeted at me. It was insulting. It was denigrating the work that I did.'

Beeby wanted an apology, so she forwarded the email to Stephens who promptly censured the author and demanded a written and verbal apology. Beeby says, 'That sort of marked my card with some of those older men'.

About a year later, Beeby began reporting on the culling of kangaroos, which was an important local issue. Her coverage included comment from kangaroo ecologists and animal rights lawyers at the Australian National University, attracting international attention from animal welfare websites.

'It was interesting the viciousness that it attracted,' says Beeby.

On the day the 'roo culling season opened, she walked into the office to find something awry with her desk.

'Some papers had been rearranged [so] I picked them up and they had been put over the top of a toy kangaroo with its head cut off. That had to be from somebody in the newsroom,' she says.

Gender discrimination, bullying and sexual harassment have long been part of journalism work in Australia.[1] What happened to Beeby was disturbing, but she remembers other women in *The Canberra Times* also experienced harassment. Research on women in the industry shows ample evidence of an entrenched gender pay gap, discriminatory 'mummy track' roles for women returning from maternity leave,[2] and far too much intimidation, abuse or sexual harassment perpetrated by bosses and co-workers.[3] The industry has a poor track record on gender equality. The stories are awful but, as any self-respecting journalist would say, they must be told.

At *The News* in Adelaide, Samela Harris remembers that women dealt with the male-dominated newsroom 'quite well'. She says during the 1960s 'there wasn't a lot of oppression or female harassment in any shape or form' and that women 'were treated with a fair amount of respect in terms of being a sex object'. Harris did experience one situation while a cadet at *The News*, though, which led her to react.

> I'm hammering on my ... typewriter, the great big, huge clamouring old things we used to use, and this sub came and stood behind me and put his arms over my shoulders and put his hands over my breasts as I'm writing.

Harris could have been paralysed or ashamed, but her 'instant reaction' was to 'pull my arm forward and then let my elbow go back as hard as I could right into his beer belly'. The sub, who Harris says, 'had probably had a bit to drink', 'let out an almighty oomph and never did it again'. It was a cathartic moment for her. 'I've never forgotten the feeling of my elbow going into that beer belly ... It was really satisfying,' she says.

Veronica Ridge recalls when she joined *The Herald* as an 18-year-old in 1973, women were basically seen as 'a piece of meat'. There was 'a lot of sexual harassment', as well as bullying and 'very nasty characters who'd be very aggressive'. One particular older columnist gave her a 'rough time'.

'I told him that I liked the arts and show business', recalls Ridge, 'so he said he'd like to show me around'. The older journalist took her to a local theatre restaurant called Tikki and John's where he 'stuck his tongue down my throat'. 'I didn't really know what to do', she recalls, 'I was trying to be polite' but he also 'wanted to go to the Southern Cross [Hotel] and go into a room'. Eventually, Ridge did the only thing she knew and just ran. She says the experience 'opened my eyes' to the male-dominated ethos at the paper.

> It was a brutal culture and it was systematic. The bullying, the abuse of power, the sexual harassment, to the point that I think you had to be quite a strong person or be very determined or have a sense of humour to actually survive ... I didn't tell the other girls what he'd done or what any of them did and they didn't tell me. So, there was no #MeToo watershed moment. I didn't know that ... it was happening to everybody else, too. I thought that I must have been doing something like not dressing properly or provoking or flirting or I thought that I [was] doing something wrong to be constantly being propositioned.

The culture at *The Herald* also extended beyond the reporters' room and into the photographers' darkroom.[4] When Louise Graham joined *The Herald* in 1978, she was among the first generation of female photographers on the paper.[5] She remembers the initiation ritual: a senior photographer would 'pick you up and dunk you in a sink of water' fully clothed. 'It was a terrifying time', she says, 'because you knew it was coming, but you didn't know [when]'. 'They finally got me one day and just lifted me into the water'. She believes humiliation was the purpose of this strange ritual, and the cadets just had to 'cop it'.

There was also other harassing behaviour from someone Graham describes as 'an old guy in the darkroom', who would point to his shoulder and say, 'See where the budgie bit me'. Old-timers knew what was coming, but cadets would lean forward, while the old man's hand went 'Woof, right up between your legs'. Graham felt sure something was very wrong about the behaviour.

The constant undercurrent: Sexual harassment and discrimination

> I just jumped so far out of the way quickly as I could …
> I didn't know what he was [doing]. But all the blokes knew, and they were waiting for it to happen. And of course, it did happen. So he used to do it all the time to new people … He was just this leering old man. And look, underneath it all, he wasn't a bad fella, but when you think back on it you think a lot of these blokes had no idea what they were doing.

On another occasion, a photographer approached Graham from behind to 'put his hand up inside my skirt all the way to my waist'. She turned around and thumped him. 'I just gave him the biggest open hand across his ear,' recalls Graham. But what she found equally offensive was that 'none of the other blokes would say, "Hey you shouldn't do that". They would just be pissing themselves laughing.' All she could do was take a deep breath and think to herself, 'Yes, okay, if that's what you want to do.' On reflection though, she says the experience made her 'tough', and influenced her approach to dealing with colleagues in later years:

> I think people realised I wasn't going to cop it … In some ways you had to be one of the blokes, which I kind of was. I'd swear like a trooper, I'd be aggressive because I had to be, because that's what they were. Picture editors were aggressive. Chiefs of staff were aggressive. You'd remember what they were like … there was always this aggression around you so you kind of had to be like that. But at the same time, I thought I was always fair. I would never do anything like that to people.

Women were subjected not only to physical harassment, but also to sexist attitudes from male executives who underestimated their worth. For example, when Margaret Gee walked into *The Age* newsroom for the first time in the early 1970s and asked one of the senior executives why there weren't many women, he replied,

'Butterfly, in between their periods, their boyfriends and their nervous breakdowns we don't get much work out of women here.'⁶

In many cases the prejudices of senior staff meant women were overlooked for senior postings or advanced assignments. Michelle Grattan, regarded for decades as one of the nation's most esteemed political journalists, remembers an interview with Graham Perkin in 1970, where she expressed interest in joining *The Age*'s Trades Hall round. Perkin demurred, saying something to the effect that there was 'bad language there', which would not be suitable for female ears. 'I think he hadn't come to grips with the idea of sending a female to Trades Hall', recalls Grattan.⁷

Later, Grattan's elevation to the post of chief political correspondent for *The Age* in 1976 'provoked strong opposition' within its editorial ranks. According to another leading, now retired, political journalist, Laurie Oakes, 'Some executives and senior staff were convinced that a woman could not succeed in the dog-eat-dog environment of the Canberra Press Gallery.'⁸

Similarly, when Debra Jopson started her cadetship at *The Sunday Australian* seven years earlier, she was told that 'women are good at human interest stories'. On reflection, she remarks: 'How silly all that sounds now we've proven that all these women have gone into all sorts of positions in society.'

In contrast, Veronica Ridge recalls that although women weren't allowed to wear slacks, only skirts during her early days at *The Herald*, she was nonetheless among the first generation of women allowed to complete full cadetships. She was trained in many of the major rounds – courts, politics, news and business. Previously, women had to be content with 'covering recipes and society functions and what people wore' for the so-called 'women's pages'.

Photographers experienced similar discrimination. When Louise Graham started her cadetship in 1978, women were seen as 'kind of a novelty'. 'There were certain things … they just wouldn't send you on because you were a woman', she says. Graham did eventually get to shoot boxing matches, but only when she was dating a sports journalist who took her along to the events, so she could develop her skills. One night, to her dismay, she was asked to be the 'ring girl' holding the tally numbers. It was the worst night of her life, recalls Graham. 'To straddle the ropes' and have to parade around 'was terrible'.

In some ways, the 1970s marked a turning point for women in Australian journalism. Widespread social change and the influence of the women's liberation movement led to increasing numbers of women joining newsrooms, and changes to the style and content of journalism produced for women.[9] Journalists such as Nancy Dexter[10] at *The Age* and Suzanne Baker at *The Sydney Morning Herald* revolutionised the 'women's pages' with coverage of controversial subjects. And some women started to break the glass ceiling. One of the most well-known was *The Canberra Times'* Gay Davidson, who in 1975 became the first woman to head a bureau in the Canberra Press Gallery.[11] Despite these developments, discrimination and harassment were almost routine.

Wendy Hargreaves remembers starting work at the *Geelong Advertiser* in 1986 where editor Graeme Vincent asked why she wanted to be a journalist. 'I want to write sport', said Hargreaves. Like many other women around the world who have tried to break into the male-dominated field, Hargreaves experienced rejection.[12] Vincent 'laughed his head off ... pointed across the sports desk at these blokes all standing around – one of them was scratching his balls, and he said, "You want to work there?"' To which Hargreaves replied simply, 'Yeah'.

Not surprisingly, highly prized foreign postings were denied to women for many years.[13] Jo Chandler remembers how at *The Age*, women simply 'didn't get the big gigs' and were 'not going to get put on the same trajectory' as renowned foreign correspondents like Robert Haupt.[14] On one occasion, Chandler was sitting in the nearby Golden Age pub listening to Haupt tell stories of all the big issues he covered when she suddenly realised, 'Okay, so I can work really hard and I might get on the Insight unit, I might get a round, I might get X, Y and Z, but I'm never going to get *those* gigs.'

Chandler also recalls, however, that sometimes women outplayed those who underestimated them. 'We were marginalised, objectified to a certain degree', she says. But 'there was a flipside to that'. While working on suburban newspapers, she came across 'these filthy old councillors' and police who would tell you stuff, but then expect the information to be somehow sacrosanct.

> They would come back and say, 'I didn't – you weren't supposed to put that in the paper.' And you're thinking, 'You idiot, what did you think, we were just giggling and I talked to you because you're such an attractive man?'

As Chandler explains, 'They always underestimated you, and in some ways that was what we would exploit.'

> You would just let them kind of fall over themselves … I can't tell you how many times I would be writing down notes, when some guy just said far more than he should have, because you kept smiling at him.

Discrimination in the 1980s was also expressed in overtly sexual terms. For Rosslyn Beeby, this occurred early in her career, at *The Age*, years before the disgraceful behaviour at *The Canberra Times*. She was covering a state inquiry into corruption at the Richmond Council in Melbourne and overheard an ABC reporter call out to his cameraman: 'We've got to get some footage of Rosslyn for the Christmas party.' When Beeby asked what for, the reporter informed her that camera crew taped footage of women's breasts for entertainment. 'It's the tits-and-arse show, and they vote,' he said. Beeby was shocked. She thought, 'But it's the ABC. It's the ABC.'

The constant undercurrent: Sexual harassment and discrimination

Beeby also remembers the 'trail of broken women' she knew at *The Age*, who thought they would have successful careers in the industry, but 'had fallen foul of male politics to some degree'. She would find female journalists 'crying in the toilets'. 'It was not a pretty sight,' she says. Beeby believes the women were likely 'preyed upon by men'. She also saw other women who were 'moving up the ladder' and being 'given positions of trust'. Beeby would think, 'Hmm, I guess it doesn't always have to be like this.'

At the *Albany Advertiser*, Jane Hammond found many of the people she worked with during the 1980s 'very conservative' and 'very sexist'. She recalls that a couple of the men in the office would 'put girly calendars up just to give me the shits and they were always just harassing me, really harassing me'.

Similarly, Cate Swannell remembers the environment at the *Gold Coast Bulletin* was 'old-school'. She says it wasn't unheard of for a copy girl, 'kneeling on the ground to get something out of one of the filing cabinets', to hear 'one of the subs say, "Hey, while you're down there."' Swannell says it could be 'pretty rank'.

Louise Graham even decided it wasn't worth eating certain fruit at work. 'I couldn't eat a banana in the tearoom without the hooting.' There would be a 'whole lot of sexual innuendo and all that sort of stuff. So, I just thought, Okay bananas aside'.

Samela Harris recalls an incident at *The Advertiser* in Adelaide during Piers Akerman's editorship. After returning from lunch one day with one of the paper's senior writers, Akerman called Harris into his office.

> He said, 'Would you do me a favour?' ... And because I'm quite keen to go home, it's late ... 'What is it, Piers?' He said, 'Just do this for me, will you?' 'What is it, Piers? What do you want?' He said, 'Would you stand on that chair for me?' I said, 'What? Why do you want me to stand on the chair?' 'No, don't ask, just as a favour to me, would you stand on the

chair?' I was thinking, 'Gee, it might help me go home if I …' I stood on the chair. I said, 'Piers, I am standing on the chair. Does that make you happy? Is that what you want? Can I go now?' 'No, just a second. Just turn around. Turn around.' I turned on the chair and I said, 'Now I've stood on the chair. I've turned on the chair. That's okay?' He said, 'Yes, that's okay now. I just wanted you to have an uplifting experience.'

If the incident sounds bizarre, Harris recalls taking it lightly. 'It was just a bit of nonsense,' she says. 'There were colourful days with Piers, and they got fairly dramatic[15] … and it was a very different time.'

Akerman, for his part, does not recall the incident. Referencing the Queen's comments about allegations made in Oprah Winfrey's interview in early 2021 with Prince Harry and Meghan Markle, Akerman added, 'Recollections may vary'.

Meanwhile, what were men making of all this behaviour? Hugh Jones remembers the time a young journalist in her late 20s reported for duty at *The Examiner* in a 'summer top'. She was 'clearly not wearing a bra underneath', says Jones, and a sub-editor called Chris Copas[16] 'cracked jokes about her' all day. 'I mean, we all giggled because he was funny, but now in hindsight – I just cringe at the memory of it.'

Ian McArthur says there was also a 'blokey guy' at *The Courier-Mail*, who would 'pretend to polish the tip of his shoe with his trousers and then move the tip ostentatiously under the dress of a female journalist he'd be standing by'. He would 'make a show of looking under her dress'. Reflecting on this memory, McArthur says, 'That was the kind of culture … where you could get away with that sort of joke … those people have probably gone on to become respectable journalists.'

There were some men at least who objected to such behaviour. Philip Chubb was a MEAA branch president in the 1980s and backed action in a couple of 'very nasty' sexual harassment cases whose details remain confidential. At the funeral service in 2017 for Chubb, who had won a Gold Walkley in 1993 for his documentary series *Labor in Power*, Margaret Simons recalled Chubb saw straight away that sexual harassment was a 'simple matter of justice and human dignity'.[17]

There were also social practices in journalism which by their very nature excluded women from participation. Drinking culture in journalism is legendary[18] and *The Age* 'Bog Bar', located in a locker room smack bang next to the men's toilets, shows how women were not just excluded, but simply not considered.

Every night a sub-editor bought 'several slabs of beer' which were 'wheeled on a trolley' into the toilets at the paper's Spencer Street office. Reporters and subs would congregate there in between editions.[19] Similar practices occurred at *The Sun News-Pictorial* where 'The Subs' Club' convened 'out of sight in a cupboard in the subs' room'.[20] Like *The Age*'s Bog Bar, no one knows for sure when The Subs' Club started, but it became an 'institution with its own freemasonry of rituals and coded language'.

In contrast to these male-dominated institutions, the 'Mummy Bar' was a product of the late 1980s and 1990s, when not only substantially more women were working in newspapers but they – and their employers – needed to come to terms with maternity leave and post-maternity leave work.

Jo Chandler remembers being one of the first women to work on the production team at *The Age*, and she did so while breastfeeding her children. As such, she was instrumental in setting up a female-friendly alternative to the infamous Bog Bar outside the women's restroom, which they named the 'Bag Bar'. Chandler says there was a couch where women could 'either express milk or cry or both at the same time'. They hired a pump and a small fridge to store breast milk. 'Gin may or may not have also been kept in there', says Chandler. 'And tonic.'

As the 1980s ended, the journalism industry began to see improvements to the make-up of newsrooms. Numbers of female journalists increased even further, while it also became more common for women to hold foreign postings, senior roles in the Canberra Press Gallery, and even editorships of big publications.

In 1991, *The Bulletin* appointed Lyndall Crisp as its first female editor. Michelle Grattan became the first woman to edit a metropolitan daily newspaper at *The Canberra Times* in 1993, and Colleen Ryan edited *The Australian Financial Review* from 1998 to 2002. Other newspapers moved more slowly. *The Age* appointed Pamela Bone its first female leader writer[21] in 1990, but it took 30 more years before the first female editor of the newspaper was appointed – Gay Alcorn.

Despite these improvements, entrenched inequality continued in many newsrooms during the 1990s, with most women remaining in lower grades or in areas traditionally pigeon-holed as 'female' such as fashion, and to a lesser extent the arts, health and entertainment.[22]

With the turn of the century, more women were being promoted to editorships. *The Sunday Telegraph*'s Jeni O'Dowd became the first woman to edit a Murdoch-owned metro daily newspaper in Australia in 1999. It took until 2011 for Fairfax to appoint Amanda Wilson as editor of *The Sydney Morning Herald*, making her the first woman to hold the post in the company's 180-year history. A year later Michelle Gunn became the first woman to edit *The Weekend Australian*. However, even as more women were appointed to senior roles, new threats emerged, such as toxic online abuse that is overwhelmingly aimed at female journalists. Whatever improvements have been made, there remain significant problems. In the Sex Discrimination Commissioner Kate Jenkins' comprehensive 'Respect@Work' report released in 2020, she found the prevalence of workplace sexual harassment worst in the information, media and telecommunications industries.[23]

Reading these stories, one wonders how women coped with all

the discrimination and harassment. As Debra Jopson recalls, 'I've had many discussions with colleagues over the years, and we all had these techniques for getting away from those types of men who tried to exert power over us'. Many of these conversations occurred in a small group Jopson set up with Willa McDonald, Adele Horin and Caroline Falls called The Bondi Girls. 'It was like a counselling session', says Jopson. They would gather roughly every fortnight to talk about life at the *Times on Sunday* and 'how tough it was to work there'.

Veronica Ridge says the global #MeToo movement really opened her eyes and changed her understanding of the life she lived in journalism. She now knows that young women like her were harassed not only in newsrooms, but in most workplaces, and that the problem is longstanding, widespread, and continues in the present day. She raised the topic at a reunion of former colleagues from *The Herald* in Melbourne.

'We just looked at each other and went, "Oh my God." We had no idea that there was this constant undercurrent. We thought it was our own battle and we had to battle it ourselves.'

The stories female journalists tell about their experiences working in newsrooms in many ways are no different to those from other workplaces. What is perhaps different is that women journalists have been at the forefront of documenting and denouncing inequality, sexism and harassment in Australian society as far back at least as the pioneering work of Adele Horin for *The National Times* and *The Sydney Morning Herald* during the 1970s and 1980s. Initially, and for many years, though, Horin and other women journalists such as Wendy Bacon focused on women in society rather than in the media.

More recently groups such as Women in Media, supported by the Media, Entertainment and Arts Alliance, have begun documenting gender issues in the media industry, in part recognising the silencing effect of powerful men, even among a group in society whose job is to speak truth to power.

CHAPTER 7
The thrill of the chase: Memorable stories

Andrew Dodd

On 4 November 2010, a Qantas A380 was forced to land in Singapore after part of an engine fell off following take-off. It was a big story, but for Sophie Tedmanson it had extra significance.

She was helping out in the Australian bureau of the English newspaper *The Times*, which had just been established inside News Limited's Sydney offices. Her role was to use her local contacts to help the bureau through its first few weeks while her boss interviewed people for a permanent deputy. But Tedmanson was also an applicant. She really wanted the job, which was running *The Times*' 24-hour website while Britain was sleeping, and while Australia and the powerhouses of Asia were awake and making news. To have a chance, she needed to make an impression.

Her boss turned to her and said, 'You've got to find a British person on that plane.'

Stories are the currency of journalism. They are the principal products the industry creates. Reporters measure their own worth by them. Careers are defined by them. They can change lives, for both the reporter and the reported. Most of the stories produced in the daily grind of journalism are ultimately forgotten, but in every reporter's career at least a few are special. Usually because of the way they are made, or due to their impact. Here are just a few of the memorable ones, which hint at the frustrations and thrills of journalism.

So, there's Tedmanson, with so much on the line, trying to find a British airline passenger in a foreign country, and with very few clues about where to start looking. She started ringing hospitals and hotels without success. Then someone suggested she try Qantas-affiliated hotels instead. After trawling through the airline's website, she managed to find one and rang its number.

She explained to the hotel receptionist where she was from and what she was doing. 'Oh yes, we've got some of those passengers,' the woman said. 'Who do you want to speak to?'

Tedmanson replied, 'Ah, a British person.' But the receptionist explained that she didn't know who was British, so Tedmanson asked 'Do you not have their passports?'

Tedmanson knew she had to be both creative and persistent, but she was also 'trying to be really careful not to push this person too hard to then hang up on me'. She says she felt a 'wave of that journalism excitement' because she was 'almost there', meaning she was so close to getting the story. She also became aware that everyone around her in the newsroom had stopped talking; they knew that she had made a breakthrough.

The receptionist said, 'If you give me a name, I'll put you through to their room' but Tedmanson was thinking, 'Oh my God, how do I find a name? I don't know who's on that plane.' So, she said, 'Could you start reading out some names?' She decided to ask to be put through to the first British-sounding name she heard. 'I don't know why I thought that, but I was like, this is the only thing I can think of.'

To her surprise, the receptionist said, 'Okay I'll give you five names' and started reading from a list of guests, including one by the name of Manchester. Tedmanson saw it as a sign. 'Put me through to Manchester,' she said.

I got put through to someone, the British accent came on the phone and I was like, 'Oh!' And then I was like also, how do you say the right thing immediately without offending someone? And I just said, 'I'm calling from *The Times* newspaper, just wanted to check were you on that plane, are you feeling okay, would you be happy to talk?' and this person just went, 'How on earth did you find me?' and I just said, 'That's a really long story, we don't have much time. Are you okay and would you like to talk?' and they said, 'Yes.'

All journalists can relate to this moment. The point where the search for a lead or a contact or a source succeeds. It's when the anxiety of not having a story disappears, and the job of gathering the facts, quotes and other details can begin. On that occasion, Tedmanson turned to her boss, who was 'just staring' at her, and gave her the thumbs up, and she then got busy with the interview.

The passenger told her 'the whole story and the chaos that was going on'. She remembers her shorthand was terrible because she was so excited and nervous.

'That's the thing about being a journalist,' she says. 'No matter how many times, how long you've been a journalist, when you get that buzz of you've got the story, it's so exciting.' Needless to say, she was offered and accepted the job at the bureau, and worked there for several years.

As Tedmanson demonstrates, there are thrills in both chasing and catching stories even when the reporting happens remotely via a telephone or internet connection. Increasingly in under-staffed newsrooms, most stories are generated in this way, especially the breaking reports that are needed to feed the insatiable appetites of online news sites. But the thrill of chasing a story goes up a notch when it happens on the ground, and as it breaks around you.

Tom Hyland found himself in the midst of the biggest story in the country on a night in August 1987, when he heard gunshots outside his home in the inner northern suburbs of Melbourne. He rang his office and told the person on duty that something was happening in Hoddle Street, Clifton Hill, but that person knew nothing, except that some trains had been stopped.

So, Hyland decided to go outside to investigate. But when he opened his front door he was confronted by armed police officers crouched down behind cars with their guns drawn. They told him to go back inside and stay there.

But Hyland did what many journalists would do when they sense there's a huge story to be told. As soon as the police left, he went outside again, got in his car and drove around the suburb to get as close as he could to the Clifton Hill railway station. He found a group of journalists sheltering behind a building, and when he asked them, 'What's going on?', they told him to 'look out onto the road'. There he saw 'a row of bodies either on the road, or in the gutter' and says, he 'suddenly realised what had happened'.

He filled his notebook with observations before heading home again and rang the AAP's Melbourne bureau, which was then staffed by someone who had rushed back into work. Hyland told him, 'I haven't written a story; I'm just going to tell you over the phone and you send it to Sydney.' The bureau was sending it in 'takes', meaning Hyland dictated about four sentences before he transmitted it. 'I'd follow it up with another four paragraphs and that's how it went. When I exhausted my notebook I said, "I don't know how much of that is new to you or how much of that is new to AAP". And he said, "It's all new to us. We didn't have any of it."'

Only when he went into work the next day did he realise how important his reporting had been.

'I didn't think I'd done anything particularly outstanding, but I'd basically saved AAP's bacon that night because we didn't have a story and I'd gone out and got it. And I know that that had cemented my reputation within AAP.'

It says something about the power of stories that journalists tend to think of themselves as lucky when they're in the midst of something awful or chaotic. But if that is where the story is, generally that is where they will want to be. It's why it's said that reporters are the ones you'll see running towards a disaster, while others are running away.[1]

Being in the best position often requires a combination of luck and initiative, as Ross Brundrett discovered after finishing work one evening as a sports sub at *The Sunday Press*. It was the night of the 1987 election and the Australian Labor Party had set up its campaign headquarters at the Grand Hyatt hotel a block away, so he thought, 'I might just wander down there at the end of my shift.'

He strolled around the hotel and ended up on a mezzanine floor, where a door opened and someone said, 'All media now, now.' So, of course, Brundrett walked in, where he found himself in an anteroom, set up with a microphone and chairs and a few camera operators.

'Next minute, Bob Hawke comes in,' says Brundrett. The prime minister was accepting victory and the room was broadcasting live on national TV. Brundrett looked around and didn't recognise any political reporters, and it dawned on him that he was 'one of about four journalists who could ask questions'. But Brundrett had spent his career avoiding covering politics.

'I always felt that politics is the last thing I want to report about,' he says. 'You watch the football game, you know who dropped the ball, you know who took the mark, whereas politics is all smoke and mirrors.' So, what did he do?

> The questions started and the other two or three people have fired in a couple of questions. Then they're looking at me, so up my hand goes, and I asked the same crap questions I would've asked a football coach after a win. I said, 'That was a tough campaign. How're you going to celebrate?' That's when he said, 'I'll have a cup of tea', because that was during

his teetotal period, and that was of course the thing everyone said – 'Bob's sweet cup of tea', I think, and that was the line that they all used the next day. Because I had no idea about the intricacies of the campaign, having not followed it very closely. My wife was at home with some friends. They said, 'You know, that sounded like your voice during that,' and I said, 'Yeah, that was.'

Gaining access to a story isn't always so easy. Often, it's about negotiation. That can take minutes, but it can also take weeks, or even months. Sophie Morris needed plenty of journalistic persistence and tact to negotiate an interview with Ricky Muir. Soon after a surprising win – that had placed him on the cross bench, possibly holding the balance of power in the Senate – Muir had refused any media appearances after an embarrassing television interview with Mike Willesee.

Morris met with Victoria's newly elected senator and told him, 'It's not a gotcha piece' – referring to the kind of interview that confronts interviewees with details about their failings.

Instead, she said, 'I want to understand where you're coming from, and there'll be a time to press you on your position on policies, but for now I'm just trying to get a sense of who you are, and maybe try you on a couple of things, but I'm not trying to trip you up.'

In the end she only had 20 minutes with him, meaning it was difficult to get 'the full measure of the man', but her reporting did 'convey a sense of who he was and confounded people's expectations' of him and his policies.[2]

Many stories depend on trust.[3] Without it, the reporter wouldn't even get close to the people and the information they need. As a parliamentary press gallery reporter for *The Australian Financial Review* and later *The Australian*, Steve Lewis covered major stories, such as the unedifying demise of the Speaker of the House of Representatives, Peter Slipper. His principal role was to find out what was going on inside the federal Cabinet, so he was dependent on a wide circle of contacts and sources.

Lewis says, 'I had the best cabinet contacts of anyone in the gallery, and I worked them bloody hard.'

He regularly wrote about brawls between ministers and occasionally published information that had been leaked to him by high-level sources within government and the bureaucracy, much to the annoyance of the then prime minister, John Howard. Inevitably, he received 'reasonably regular' calls from the Australian Federal Police, seeking to find the sources for this information. Traditionally, many important sources were cultivated over long boozy lunches, but things had changed by the time Lewis was working in the gallery:

> The key was to build up trust. It was all about trust. So, when you rang a contact, be they a bureaucrat, a staffer or a politician or Cabinet minister, they had to trust you. They had to know that if they told you something, you would protect their confidentiality. So it was all about trust. And that to me was the most important currency, and I worked damn hard to build up that level of trust. It doesn't mean that I wasn't lied to, misled. People obfuscate, of course they would and that happened plenty of times.

Trust is hard won and easily lost, especially in fields of journalism where people are routinely misrepresented and maltreated.[4] Debra Jopson had developed a reputation for her considered reporting on Indigenous affairs, in part because she took the time to listen, so that she could get closer to understanding what people wanted to say. She says her aim was to avoid being the one who decided what Indigenous communities were saying. Instead she invested time so people could get to know her, and she resisted the journalistic urge to rush towards the big questions.

> So, I don't start like, 'You're going to have to tell me that right now. Ten points. It's over.' No. Because there is actually a lot of the rhythm that happens, particularly in remote communities. You've got to be sensitive to what people are saying.

In turn she would try to help the subjects of her stories understand her role and how she had to get the piece past her editors to reach an audience. She sometimes told her interviewees, 'I'm hoping that some of the politicians in Canberra will read it', and she invited Indigenous people to speak to them, through her stories. She would say, 'Tell me what you want to say to those people.' By doing interviews this way, Jopson was able to avoid leading the discussion.

> You're not saying, 'There's a uranium mine down the road, and I hear you're opposed to it' whatever. You're not doing that, you're getting them to tell you. So, then you get these stories, you get amazing stories from people, interviewing that way. Actually, I just remembered that I perfected the self-interviewing technique while I was pregnant, because I couldn't think of any questions. I found out that you get amazing things from people if you just shut up.

Many reporters – and the publications they work for – are driven by the need to be first with a story. Once news became a tradeable commodity, value was placed in getting information out before the competition. But it's not necessarily about being the first on the scene of an accident, or about breaking a ripping yarn about crime or corruption.

As a senior writer at *The Australian*, George Megalogenis specialised in analysis of data that revealed social, political and economic trends in Australian society. On one occasion he combined newly released Australian Bureau of Statistics census data and the re-drawn boundaries for the federal parliamentary electorates of

New South Wales to determine that Prime Minister John Howard's seat of Bennelong was undergoing significant demographic changes. Specifically, it 'was drifting from a very Anglo centric, middle to upper middle income, towards a very Eurasian profile and there was a very, very big Chinese population and, to a lesser extent, Indian population moving into that seat'. Megalogenis came to the conclusion that the seat looked more like a Labor seat than a Coalition one.

Clearly, it was a big story. He pulled together the data and showed Howard to get his reaction, and then published the material the following day. He was keen to reveal what he had because, as he says, 'the art of journalism is to get the information first and then let everybody else build on essentially your groundwork'.

The information Megalogenis revealed was crucial to Howard's political survival. The prime minister failed to win his own seat at the 2007 election, giving him the dubious honour of being only the second sitting prime minister to be defeated in his own electorate.

Being first sometimes means identifying and celebrating a person or detail that others have missed or ignored. Bruce Elder wrote a feature for *The Sydney Morning Herald* on the then little-known Indigenous singer Geoffrey Gurrumul Yunupingu.

The piece appeared on the front page of the weekly Metro section to coincide with Gurrumul's Sydney performances. Elder describes it as 'without doubt his most important' story, because the piece 'really did launch him. It was a very radical decision on the part of the editor of Metro to actually put Gurrumul, who was appearing in the small theatre at the bottom of the opera house, on the cover of Metro, when you think of all of the alternatives from movies and theatre and so on. But he put Gurrumul on the cover.' Elder says seeing that piece given that sort of treatment 'makes it worthwhile'.

Some stories defy competition conventions because colleagues across mastheads reach agreements to co-operate with one another – not just for their own benefit, but so the story itself is better served.

Michael Shmith was involved in just such a case in 1991, as the arts editor at *The Age*. He was aware that the conductor of the Sydney Symphony Orchestra, Stuart Challender, was ill with HIV AIDS, and that the rival News Limited's *Sunday Herald Sun* was planning to break the story. Shmith suspected the tabloid would focus on scandal so he and Maria Prerauer, the arts editor at *The Australian*, agreed to work together to jointly interview Challender and write separate stories that would run in their respective broadsheets before the Sunday paper could run its piece.[5] The editors of both papers also agreed to the plan, even though in the case of *The Australian* it was at the expense of its sister paper.

Shmith says the stories helped change public attitudes to HIV because Challender was 'a major artistic figure, brave enough at that time to actually come out and say he's dying'. Shmith remains 'very proud' of the story, because of the decency that underpinned it.

'I thought that was the collegial approach of journalism in exactly the right sense where rivalries could put aside any idea of a scoop in order to thwart a report that would have been far more suspect.'

Some stories are difficult to tell because they're just not fun to read. The editor might consider them too dull or 'too worthy' or just 'not sexy', meaning the reporter has to work extra hard to make them a reality.

Tom Arup faced this problem trying to get stories on climate change into *The Age*. On one occasion he was one of a handful of people worldwide given early access to a report to be published in a peer-reviewed journal in the US. The report linked the Black Saturday bushfires and the 2009 Australian summer heatwaves to climate change. He lobbied hard for the story, because he believed it 'linked one of the seminal moments in Victoria's modern history to one of the great existential threats of our lives'.

After filing his story, he kept advocating for it. He even 'hung around the [sub-editors'] desk going, "Gee this is a big deal, right".'

But it didn't help. The story was 'buried' at the back of the paper. Frustratingly, the same story made the front page of *The New York Times*.

Arup faced similar frustrations writing about the bleaching of the Great Barrier Reef. He remembers telling his editors, 'The Barrier Reef is dying guys, we've got to get going.' But he couldn't get permission to go there to report on it, and was forced to cobble together stories, using 'photos from where we could get them, along with quotes from scientists'. On reflection, he says many factors influenced why a certain type of story was favoured over another:

> Part of it is certain things clicked well so they gravitated towards that. Part of it was editorial choices made about what editors thought was important for their readers. Part of it's just always personalities in the newsroom, so strong personalities covering certain areas get to the top. And some of it's a bummer, like it's just a bummer to read about terrible things you can't control.

Some stories are relatively easy to research, but especially hard to capture and produce.

Tracee Hutchison experienced this when she worked for Seven Network's tabloid current affairs program *Today Tonight* in 1999. Seven was the broadcast host of Melbourne's annual Moomba Festival, and in that year, two of the network's biggest stars – the clowns known as Zig and Zag – were named as 'Moomba Monarchs', meaning they were asked to lead the annual Moomba Parade through the main street of Melbourne.

However, Zig had been convicted of indecently assaulting his own granddaughter back in 1994. But because he had been tried under his real name and the case had been suppressed by the courts to protect his granddaughter's identity, it had gone unreported. But all that changed when the granddaughter walked into the Channel

Seven office and wanted to talk. Hutchison says she was 'given the task of getting the interview with Zig to confront him'.

It was easy to find his phone number because he'd been doing some Moomba promotions for the network. Hutchison rang him and, in her words, 'wasn't entirely untruthful' about why she wanted to interview him.

'I said we were coming out to do an interview with him about being the Moomba Monarch, which is what we did. It's just we arrived with two cameras – two camera crews, two cars – and he knew as soon as we arrived that it wasn't going to be a puff piece.'

Looking back on the encounter Hutchison describes it as 'one of the most difficult interviews of my career'. Zig began the interview by explaining that he had just had open-heart surgery. Hutchison felt that he might be trying to warn her off, 'like he knew what was coming'. Then he 'repeatedly denied' the allegations, even as Hutchison revealed that she had the court transcripts in which he'd pleaded guilty. She detailed his behaviour of getting into bed with the little girl to read her stories while Zig maintained this 'was a perfectly normal thing to do'. She asked, 'Did that involve touching?' Finally, he conceded it did.

As they were leaving, Zig put his Moomba cape on and showed Hutchison the scars from his heart surgery.

'I remember thinking, I hope this guy's still alive tomorrow, because we're about to destroy his life.'

Uncomfortable as it was, Hutchison knew she had to do justice to the granddaughter's story, as well as to what she describes as the greater good.

'This person had destroyed someone's life and here he was being held up as the kind of monarch of the family festival. It was wrong.'

But the story behind this story doesn't end there. As the camera crews were at a nearby pub recovering from their 'excruciating' ordeal with Zig, word came through that the granddaughter had also spoken to the *Herald Sun*, which was going to break the story in the following day's paper. The *Today Tonight* piece wasn't scheduled to run until Monday. So 'we had to come back and get the story to air that night. Which still to this day, I'm not even sure how we did that.' And on top of this she and the *Today Tonight* team had to endure the anger of their own network for destroying Seven's big event. She felt as if people were saying, 'How can you do that? We're the Moomba channel, you've killed Moomba.'

Deadlines shape stories in all sorts of ways, and create stresses that can take a great toll on journalists. As a writer on *The Sunday Age*, Gary Tippet was sent to Thredbo in August 1997 to report on a landslide that had killed 18 people after two ski lodges had collapsed. Working for a weekly paper meant he had to find something new to say, that hadn't already been reported by another media outlet, including by the daily *Age* newspaper. Reporters agree that this can be highly stressful because potential story leads appear, but then disappear as others write about them. Plus that oppressive weekly deadline just keeps looming larger.

On this occasion, Tippet and colleague Paul Daley managed to find a story, when they convinced another reporter, from the rival *Bulletin* magazine, to share some of what she knew but wouldn't be able to publish until midway through the following week. She had discovered from rescue workers that the landslide survivor, Stuart Diver, had been beside his wife Sally when she died, and that she had in fact drowned because of where she was trapped under the debris. Though awful, it was a powerful story.

'That just gave us something that nobody else had,' says Tippet. 'And we ran it, it was all over the front page, and I remember we were pretty happy that we'd got this story.'

But while *The Sunday Age* had benefited from the generosity of the rival *Bulletin*, it was not obliged to assist its own sister Sunday paper in Sydney, *The Sun Herald*, which was still looking for a story late on the Saturday.

So, Tippet rang *The Age* news desk in Melbourne and said,

'Listen, it's the sister paper. Do you want to give them what we've got?'

The news desk answered emphatically: 'No, no, no, no, no. These people print and their papers are out on the street hours before ours. This means that our competition in Melbourne would see it, would run it and we'd lose our thing.'

So, Tippet remembers he was forced 'to pretend that we didn't have anything to these guys, poor buggers'. He did however tip them off so they could file something for their later editions. Tippet concludes, 'The stresses of those jobs are incredible. It's the stress of not having a story.'

Sometimes stories seem to have nothing to do with journalism, but are constructed to meet the demands of the editor, not the reader. Stephen Corby recalls many such stories at *The Telegraph*. The paper had a formula for success that entailed photographing family pets, almost regardless of the issue. For example, when Sydney's Cross City Tunnel opened, he remembers a photographer was told: '"We need a car, it needs to be a convertible, there needs to be a dog in the back, and the dog has to have a big tongue". That was the photo brief.'

Corby says he became 'the baby animal reporter' because editor Jeni O'Dowd believed animals, especially dogs, were popular with readers. On one occasion he was sent to cover a giant furniture fire on Parramatta Road. He remembers it as 'the time I really did think I couldn't do it anymore'. He was told, 'Don't come back until you get an attractive woman walking her dog in front of the fire.' So he spent all afternoon searching. He really had no option. 'If you ring the chief of staff and say, "I can't find one," they'd say, "Mate, do you want to come back in here and tell Jeni that? No. Well, just keep trying."'

> Eventually we chased this woman up her front drive. She's gone in the house. We're banging on the door going, 'Please

can you get your dog out, and come and walk in front of the fire?' And you became very good at talking people into things. You had to do it. Because dogs sold that paper. We would do the animal count on Sunday morning – count how many animals there were in the photos … As long as the story had a dog or a small animal in it, it would sell.

In response, O'Dowd says, 'I did like a mix of different photos – yes, some with animals – as before I became editor the tendency was to just run pages of photos of men in suits.' But, she says, she wishes someone had reported to her that Corby was under orders to get a dog photo at a fire, 'as I would have said it was not on. As you know, it is very common for someone who wants something done to claim the boss wants it.'

This kind of editing exemplifies what a character in Tom Stoppard's play *Night and Day* called the 'Lego-set' approach to building stories.[6] Though not the most common approach, it's more common than many journalists would like. Most journalists know how much work goes into 'getting up a story', as the industry term goes. Equally, they know the fun and excitement of discovering what's going on in the world and people's lives. They also know how much craft goes into shaping the story, and the particular craft elements needed for different mediums.

Doing all this battling the clock, against stonewalling sources, and under pressure from hard-driving (or worse) editors, makes it easy to understand why journalists find their work both energising and enervating. How many times do reporters push themselves hard to land a story by deadline, only to come in to work the next day to hear the editor say, 'That was great mate, now today …' Exhilaration and exhaustion run side by side throughout journalists' careers. Some become accustomed to this, while others slowly burn out. And that is even before we consider the sticky ethical binds inherent in journalism.

CHAPTER 8
Errors and regrets

Matthew Ricketson

There's an adage dating back to the 19th century that doctors bury their mistakes, lawyers hang theirs, but journalists print theirs on the front page of the newspaper. Mistakes are an unavoidable hazard when a product is created afresh every day, from unverified or contested information, or 'facts' confected by public relations operatives. Small wonder then that books have been filled – literally – with collections of typographical errors.

Martin Toseland, in his book *A Steroid Hit the Earth*, recalls a glorious misprint from *The Times* of London's report of Queen Victoria's opening of the Menai Bridge: 'The Queen herself graciously pissed over the magnificent edifice.'[1]

Headline errors, past or present, are obvious to all, but journalists can make mistakes in all sorts of ways, from matters of fact to defaming a person's character. Under deadline pressure it is hard to accurately paraphrase complex material, and alarmingly easy to misspell names: what if that most common of names – John Brown – is actually Jon Browne?

Journalists can make mistakes well before they even write a word, and sometimes they can err by opting not to do a story. In this chapter we hear journalists' stories of blunders they've made and why they're reluctant to dwell on them. We also hear stories of regret from inside the cauldron that is a daily newsroom; some remain seared in journalists' memories.

To begin with a self-deprecating anecdote, Cate Swannell recalls when, at her editor's instruction, she raced out to do an interview, without any background knowledge of that person. 'So Linda, how long have you been swimming?' she asked as she sat down opposite a friendly woman in that woman's home. Linda looked at her quizzically, said, 'Excuse me just a minute', walked out of the room and returned a minute later with her CV, which informed Swannell that her interviewee – surname McGill – was the first Australian, man or woman, to swim the English Channel and a Commonwealth Games swimming gold medallist.

For Veronica Ridge, the error arose from not writing a particular story. She recalls being in court paying only passing attention to the parade of driving offences when a magistrate took the rare step of banning for life a serial drink-driving offender. That's a story, Ridge thought, but as she couldn't verify the details, she felt unable to write it. Ridge spent a sleepless night worrying that someone else would, but they didn't, and the event passed into history unrecorded, leaving Ridge ambivalent.

'That was one where you've decided it's a better outcome not to publish when you don't know enough, but it was a bloody good story.'

Gary Tippet remembers misnaming a lawyer in a story, who told him in court the following day, 'It happens all the time.'

It is a remark that resonates with many members of the public. What few realise is that for most journalists making a mistake is close to a cardinal sin. Tippet was deeply apologetic when he saw the lawyer in court and Matthew Moore, formerly of *The Sydney Morning Herald*, describes the 'sickening feeling' on discovering an error. He recalls writing a 'vicious column bagging a public servant'. In his 'high and mighty attack' Moore had misnamed the hapless bureaucrat 17 times in the one piece.

Accuracy in reporting is a core skill without which the average journalist would not last long. The kind of flagrant, repeated inaccuracies and distortions associated with some shock jocks and star columnists are tolerated because of their advertiser drawing power, and their audience.

Jo Chandler recalls how as editor of the Saturday edition of *The Age* she would wait until very late at night to pick up the third-edition page proofs to read in the company-provided taxi on the way home. One night she spotted an error on page one. 'Fuck, fuck, fuck!' she cried, desperately phoning the late-stop sub-editor who copped an earful when he finally answered.

'Stop the press! You've got to put page one back on and you've got to correct this thing. And how the fuck did that happen?'

When she finally arrived home the driver, watching as she signed the chit, said, 'You look like such a nice lady.' Chandler laughs at how oblivious she had been to her behaviour.

'But I was anxious all the time about mistakes getting through. It had to be as good as it could be, and for us not to be beaten.'

Of course, anyone can make an error, but much journalism is contested and the stakes can be as high as a person's livelihood, or even their life. When journalists act as watchdogs, holding to account those in positions of power and authority, a single error can derail an entire investigation.

For instance, what do you remember about the allegation that former United States president George W. Bush shirked active duty during the Vietnam War? Probably that it was never quite proved. A 2004 report on *60 Minutes II* had relied on documents soon exposed as forged, thereby discrediting the story and, by corollary, clearing Bush.[2] But reporting by *The Boston Globe*'s Walter Robinson, later of *Spotlight* fame, beginning in 2000 before Bush became president, and in 2004, revealed that for sizeable chunks of Bush's time with the National Guard he was AWOL, and there were unconfirmed reports that official records had gone missing.[3] The allegation had been proved, in other words, though that part is not remembered.

Journalists are reluctant to admit their errors because of the high stakes for stories such as Bush's war record, but also because of competition within newsrooms and across media outlets.

Matthew Moore says misnaming a public servant was by no means the most serious error he made in his long career, but 'happily the details have gone' from his memory. The idea that being honest about errors is a sign not of weakness but of strength simply didn't wash in most newsrooms until well into the internet age, with its culture of transparency and instant corrections. Few would argue, though, that it is common practice today. Says Moore: good journalists' reputations are 'carved out of stone, and you protect it as hard as you can, because your reputation is everything and, once it's gone, it's very hard to rebuild it'.

Not surprisingly, journalists rarely dwell in public on their mistakes, their regrets or the inevitable ethical binds of a vocation that routinely pits maximising public disclosure against minimising private harm. When they do, the stories behind their stories can be illuminating, eye-popping and inspiring.

Journalists see and hear many things they are not able to report for various reasons, including difficulty verifying information and restrictive defamation laws. Sometimes, though, what journalists stumble across is just plain bizarre, as Cate Swannell found working in Far North Queensland in the 1980s. Working as a young journalist on a free weekly newspaper, Swannell was sent out with a photographer to report on a body found out the back of a fast-food store. But they could not get close enough because of a police barrier. The local police refused to tell her anything other than a man had taken his own life. After a drinking session with an anonymous source Swannell learnt it might not have been suicide.

> She told me it was a guy who'd been convicted on paedophile
> charges, been released and the parents of the kids had got him,
> killed him, strung him up, stuck fish hooks in his face and
> tried to get away with it being suicide, and did get away with

it because the cops just went, 'Yeah, fair enough, we'll call that suicide' and away it went. So, it was old-world, it was old-school.

Swannell wanted to investigate further but her editor said, 'No, that's not us. We're a free weekly. Leave it alone.' 'But it's a big story,' she said. 'Yeah it is,' he replied. 'But it's not in our interests, it's not in anybody's interests, just leave it alone.' And she said, 'Well, you're the boss.' When asked about it appearing that police may have condoned vigilante behaviour in those pre-Fitzgerald Inquiry days, she says, 'Oh, you're surprised by this? Come on. Far North Queensland? Nah, come on.'

Swannell's dilemma stemmed not just from what she was told, but in what circumstances – a night out drinking with a potential contact. Canberra political reporters used to joke they had donated their livers to the non-members' bar in the service of journalism, but legendary tales of scribbled story tips on the back of beer coasters have dissipated over the years.

Matthew Franklin, a political correspondent for *The Australian* in the mid-2000s, says that these days,

> If you are a person whose only ability to interact with a politician is over a beer, they don't take you that seriously. You become more reliant on them than you should be. I don't want people to think of me as their friend; I'm not their friend. If they've done something wrong, I'll write it, I'm not afraid of that.

The reverse is true too; politicians who spend all their time at the bar don't have much to say other than 'who's having sex with whom. But they can't actually give you a decent debate about their policy because they're not across it', says Franklin.

Ignorance about policy is by no means the only issue journalists face when dealing with sources. More commonly, politicians deploy leaks, background briefings and off-the-record comments as expertly as a third-dan black belt. 'Drops', as they are known in the industry, are media releases disguised as 'exclusives' because a favoured journalist is given information ahead of their competitors, with one caveat: you don't go to any other party involved for comment.

Matthew Moore recalls that when Nick Greiner led the NSW Liberal government between 1988 and 1992 he once gave a drop to *The Daily Telegraph* about a big wage offer to break a teachers' strike. The front-page splash was accompanied by an editorial and a comment piece inside the paper. Moore was furious and 'nearly flattened' Mark Scott, then the education minister's press secretary, later the managing director of the ABC, who held his hands up – 'Matthew, it's not me, it's Greiner'. Moore barged past the premier's secretary, saying 'Where's fucking Greiner?'

The premier asked him to calm down and said, 'Yes, we gave the story to the *Telegraph* and I would be very happy in future to give you these stories provided you give me the same deal they give me.' 'And what is that?' asked Moore. 'That the story is run without comment from the Teachers' Federation.' Moore said he could not accept that. 'Why not?' asked Greiner. 'That is what happens in Canberra.'

'He was right,' recalls Moore. 'But I couldn't do that sort of journalism. I was appalled at what I think is a corruption of the system, which continues until this day.'

Political journalists like Moore know, but usually don't say, that the minister of the Crown demanding police investigate an embarrassing leak is likely the same person who poured non-attributable vitriol into their ear about a political opponent the previous week. But leaks are the lifeblood of journalism, as David Marr once remarked on *Insiders*, and so it was not surprising that in 2009 a veteran political journalist, Steve Lewis, jumped at a leak from Godwin Grech, a senior public servant in the federal Treasury department.

Grech claimed that he had explosive material about Kevin Rudd's apparently benefiting from a Queensland car dealer, who had provided the Labor prime minister with a free car for the 2007 election campaign. 'Utegate', as it was known, ended disastrously when Grech admitted he had forged a key email. The collapse of Grech's story plunged the then Opposition leader Malcolm Turnbull into an existential funk.[4] Lewis, for his part, acknowledges the episode was 'embarrassing and humiliating', but it did not derail his career.

Old traditions of drinking with contacts have been upgraded to invitations to attend marquee events like the Rugby League State of Origin or the AFL Grand Final in corporate boxes. As a junior reporter at *The Sydney Morning Herald*, Michael West recalls 'getting on like a house on fire' with corporate executives as they were drinking and watching sport together.

What happens, though, he began to think, when a big story about this particular company erupts on the Monday, and you've been a beneficiary of their largesse on the weekend?

'I got too close to some people, and you just lose your judgment as a journalist,' West says, 'and so I just stopped taking tickets.'

He also recalls as a young single journalist chatting and drinking with a very pleasant female public relations person in the corporate box, who ensured he bought the company's line 'hook, line and sinker'.

'The point of public relations,' he says, 'is to control the media. They will have done their job if they've manipulated you into writing an overly good story about something they want talked up, or about the opposition being bad.'

Over his career West, like many, has observed the expansion of public relations: 'When I started, there was one PR guy for every 100 journalists. Now there'd be 100 PR guys for every one journalist.'

He may be exaggerating, but the shift in weight of numbers is undeniable, accelerated by the large scale redundancies across the news media since 2012. One implication is the extent to which public relations people police access to newsmakers. West remembers as a junior reporter speaking to Woolworths' chief executive Paul Simons personally for a story.

'Now they wouldn't let a junior reporter get through to the head public relations guy at Woolworths.'

It surprises him (though perhaps it shouldn't) that public relations – a multi-billion dollar industry – is not reported on or analysed as are other large industries. Not only is there a steady traffic of people back and forth between journalism and public relations, but the extent to which journalism relies on public relations handouts is not something either party likes to air.

Being manipulated or deceived is a common experience for journalists who are perennially short of time, and often on unequal terms with sources because the source knows what is going on, and the journalist is trying to find out.

For Michael West, who spent most of his career as a business journalist, avoiding risks when he needed to produce so much copy was hard.

> If you're a columnist, you don't have time to double-source everything, so you've got to trust your source. But you get that with experience. Sometimes you just get totally misled. An investment banker source, to get a corporate transaction done, will mislead you and say this takeover is happening. Stock price goes up, takeover never happens.

West would ring them back and be given an excuse but 'you've just been told a bald-faced lie in order to affect the stock price. You'll get your scoop. You will have done someone a favour and you will have disadvantaged somebody else terribly.'

Not that journalists are immune from manipulation or deception themselves in the never-ending arm wrestle between disclosure and secrecy. Matthew Moore recalls how in the lead-up to the New South Wales state election in 1988 he learnt of sizeable donations to a political party. He didn't know who had donated or when, though he had the number of the bank account into which the money had been paid. He rang the bank pretending to be an intermediary in the political party and got the information. He acknowledges there was

> a bit of an ethical question there, because we were misrepresenting ourselves as members of that account, but it was the only way to gather information about what was an illegal act, and yet was important, because it revealed who was really making donations to this party. Which should have been publicly declared.

Flip Prior felt uncomfortable when pressured by a newspaper chief of staff in Western Australia to pose as a patient in pain to see if doctors were giving out prescriptions for OxyContin too freely. She was unsuccessful in duping a doctor because 'I'm a terrible liar' and refused to continue with the story. When she came to work the next day her pigeonhole was empty. She confronted the chief of staff who told her if she wasn't interested in doing what he'd assigned there were no stories for her. She recalls crying in the toilets, thinking: 'Wow, standing up for what I thought was right and ethical meant I got in trouble. I hated that.'

Stephen Corby didn't feel uncomfortable so much as irritated when an editor at *The Sunday Telegraph*, outraged at the cost of merchandise she'd seen at a Wiggles concert, asked him to write a story 'bagging' the popular children's group. 'Are you sure, mate?' the Wiggles PR people said. 'Like, this is the Wiggles. No one writes bad stories about the Wiggles.'

Corby had to go to a Wiggles concert and interview people on the way out about whether they felt ripped off by the merchandise cost. 'No, it's fine', most said, leaving Corby to find scraps of discontent that could be fed into the story. 'It wasn't that the story was evil; it was just a dumb non-story. I could write a list of 100 000 of those. Let's write the headline, then write the story. Yes, I've written some tosh all right.'

'Tosh' is overwhelmingly what letter writers thought of the Australian version of the English motoring show *Top Gear*, says Corby, who went from *The Sunday Telegraph* to inaugural editor of the magazine *Top Gear Australia* in 2008. He published only one of the critical letters, but the company associated with the program in the United Kingdom, an offshoot of the BBC, wanted him sacked. 'It's a letters page,' he protested. At least some balance is needed.

> There were people writing in saying they hate the show. If we ran all those letters, I'd understand your problem. But I just ran one letter, mildly critical of the show, because that's the truth. But yeah, they were saying, 'What the hell is this bloke thinking?' Because you can't criticise the show. The show is the golden goose. You don't mess with the goose.

Corby survived the immediate crisis and remained happily at *Top Gear Australia* until 2012 when he was appointed editor of *Wheels*, the granddaddy of Australia's car magazines.

Tom Hyland recalls initially not filing a word of copy when he went to Cambodia in 1989. This was his first year as Southeast Asian correspondent for AAP and he was covering the withdrawal of the Vietnamese army a decade after it had displaced Pol Pot's Khmer Rouge regime.

Around 400 representatives from the world's biggest news organisations – *The New York Times*, *The Washington Post*, all the big American television networks, the BBC, to name a few – flew in for this major international news event concerning countries and past wars that had loomed large in Hyland's life growing up.

The assembled heavy-hitters of the Establishment media,

then at the height of its power and influence, exuded confidence and bravado and an 'easy cynicism' as they enjoyed long lunches, big dinners, bottles of wine and lots of laughter. Hyland meanwhile felt overwhelmed by the presence of so many journalists, and by the horror of what had happened in Pol Pot's killing fields.

'I stopped being a journalist; I felt like I was a tourist. I completely lost my perspective. I didn't have to find an original story, I just had to find a story.'

He did the required newsgathering – interviews with diplomats, visits to hospitals to talk to people with amputated limbs from stepping on landmines – but he couldn't sit down to compose a 600-word story. These issues, combined with technical problems due to poor communication technology, meant he did not file until he returned to his base in Jakarta. The technical issues were real, but were not the actual problem.

> I was intimidated by all these journalists who seemed to know what they were doing. Many had been there plenty of times before, but many hadn't. Basically, I froze professionally, and emotionally I froze too. It's the only time it's ever happened to me.

From the experience, he learnt to shed the illusion that a definitive story for an event existed, and that he had to provide it.

'Just report what you see and what you're told and what you hear. Don't make sweeping judgments, don't try to be the all-knowing expert. Just be a reporter.'

Debra Jopson experienced her own struggles with the particular difficulties of reporting on Indigenous issues, which she did in the late 1990s and early 2000s. This period took in the Bringing them Home, or 'Stolen Generations', report, federal Coalition government attacks on the Aboriginal and Torres Strait Islander Commission (ATSIC), the Walk for Reconciliation across the Sydney Harbour

Bridge and disclosures of family violence in remote Indigenous communities.

Jopson found herself caught in a series of binds that only seemed to tighten the more reporting she did. Her newspaper, *The Sydney Morning Herald*, took Indigenous issues seriously, but over time editors began reacting to perceptions fuelled by rival media outlets that the paper's coverage was becoming too bleeding-hearted.

When Andrew Bolt of the *Herald Sun* launched his notorious attack on the ATSIC chair, Lowitja O'Donoghue, over her identification as a member of the Stolen Generations, Jopson was grilled by editors: would she have written the story if she had known about it? 'It's such an incidental fact to me. Maybe, maybe not,' she said, and they jumped on her from a great height.

Bolt's quest to establish whether O'Donoghue had been given to a missionary family or taken from her parents was to Jopson a distinction without a difference. The imbalance of power was such that Indigenous parents had very few options; giving their children to missionaries was seen as the least worst of them all.[5]

As that controversy raged, and as commentators, especially on radio, fanned racist sentiment, Jopson continued to interview members of the Stolen Generations. She remembers a sub-editor asking for her copy one night as a deadline neared. 'And I just had tears pouring down my face because of what happened to these people.' This was probably the hardest thing she had to deal with, but she also knew that whatever she felt was a pinprick compared to the experiences of those about whom she was writing.

As Irene Moss, head of a 1991 national inquiry into racist violence, had said, for Indigenous Australians 'racism is like a constantly dripping tap'.[6] Simultaneously, Jopson was sometimes shunned by Indigenous people after she wrote stories about family violence in remote communities. Wearying of all this after several years, she felt she needed to move to other areas of reporting, which she did successfully, but looking back she still smarts about it. For many years the news media ignored Indigenous issues, and when attention began to be paid it was intermittent, or became mired in the culture wars, or failed to address systemic entrenched disadvantage.

Louise Graham's stint as pictorial editor at the *Herald Sun* in the 1990s ended unhappily as she felt she allowed herself to be pushed out of her role by the editor, Peter Blunden. The two had not enjoyed a good working relationship, Graham acknowledges, but matters came to a head in 1996 over a photograph of a baby published on the front page. The story was about a baby who had died while in state care. A coronial inquiry returned an open finding on the cause of death but the baby's grandmother thought she had died from neglect. The photograph was supplied by the grandmother to the journalist writing the story, Michael Pirrie.

When Graham saw the photo, she thought the baby was deceased. She felt she knew because she had once needed to bury a baby herself. She understood that the baby in the photograph looked as though she was sleeping, which was why she was concerned to tell the journalist she was sure the baby was lying in a coffin.

She recalls waiting outside the editor's door, buttonholing him when he finally came out. Graham says the editor repeated what the journalist had told him. She understood it was his call, as editor, but wanted to register her strong objection. The story and the photograph were published the next day, 29 August, headlined, 'Dying in state care' with the subhead pointing to the photograph, 'This is baby "Helen" about two weeks before she died.'

That morning the editor-in-chief of the *Herald Sun*, Steve Harris, called a meeting to discuss the issue, because he had heard that Graham had walked out of the newsroom the previous evening. Graham recalls that things got a bit heated between her and Blunden; she felt she could no longer work with the editor and left not long after. Contacted about this incident, Michael Pirrie did not reply. Steve Harris recalls a meeting being held, but not much beyond that. Peter Blunden, who is still at News Corp, as national executive editor, recalls, 'The reporter assured us the picture was provided by the baby's family, and that it was taken before the baby's death. Given that it came from the family, and the reporter was adamant the baby was alive, I supported the journalist's position.'

A coda to the incident was the source of more regret, this time for Veronica Ridge, who became supplements editor for *The Age* in 1998. In pulling together a health supplement with a story about helping babies sleep she had gone to the picture library's files and used one marked 'generic'. By coincidence the picture chosen was of a baby who had been sick at the time, but subsequently died. The baby's mother rang the newspaper and complained to someone on the pictorial desk. Ridge remembers being phoned by pictorial and that the caller was Louise Graham who by this time was at *The Age*. Graham has no memory of the call but Ridge does as she could hear the anxiety in Graham's voice. Ridge called the mother.

> It was terrible. I was in tears too. She was very good, actually. I think she could see how upset I was too. I explained to her how the picture hadn't been properly captioned. It had 'generic' on it, which meant that we could use it for any story. I was absolutely mortified and I felt so terribly sorry about it.

If the story is a sad one, first for the family whose baby died, then for Louise Graham and finally for Veronica Ridge, it underscores how accuracy weighs on a thousand journalistic decisions each day. Many of these are forgotten in the rush of daily journalism, but some of the choices journalists make stay with them, long after whatever story they worked on has been forgotten by readers. Some stories stay with journalists not because of choices made, but because of the stories' content, as the recollections in the next chapter reveal.

CHAPTER 9

Knocking on grass: Reporting trauma

Merryn Sherwood
Matthew Ricketson

As a legal reporter for the ABC, Phil Kafcaloudes was used to hearing about grisly events. Generally, he found ways to cope with the distressing matters that came before the court, until one day when he covered a case of a paedophile who abducted, raped and murdered a seven-year-old girl. He dutifully took notes as the defendant told how he pulled down the little girl's pants, tied a rock to her legs and threw her in the dam while she pleaded for him to stop, saying she wouldn't tell anyone.

What happened next in the courtroom undid him.

'I was sitting up in this gallery and I heard some whimpering and, looking at the woman next to me, I recognised her ... They had put me as a journalist taking notes next to the girl's mother,' Kafcaloudes says.

Shaken, he still filed his story, did his live crosses to the ABC studio, then went home and couldn't sleep, his face wet with tears. His partner Jackie pleaded for him to take a holiday. After a night tossing in bed, he decided to ask for it, which his manager immediately granted.

This was the last court story he filed before switching back from news to a hosting role in radio. If that had been his first day as a court reporter, he would have been okay, he thinks; the accumulation of covering traumatic events day after day had finally got to him.

> That little girl became my little girl, even though I didn't have a little girl … as it is for anyone who hears that story, they relate to it as if that's someone I know and loved and had a rock tied to them and thrown in a dam. You just go, what a horrible thing to hear. I just got to the stage I think, of so many bad stories, that I just had no emotional leeway left.

The impact on Kafcaloudes was profound, yet it describes what many journalists do every day. As Gary Tippet says, a lot of journalism has to do with violence – wars, rapes, crime, family violence, abuse, car collisions, floods, natural disasters – and journalists from early on can be sent to the scenes of trauma and tragedy. 'I'm with my first body six or seven days into my new profession,' he recalls of his first week in the job. Research has confirmed that general news reporters can be just as affected by trauma as foreign correspondents covering wars.[1]

In the news media, for many years being sent out on your first death knock – which means being sent to the house of a bereaved family to ask questions about a recently deceased family member, and maybe acquiring a photo or two – was a rite of passage. Sold to novice reporters as a key journalistic skill, most find death knocks are actually a complex lesson in the nature of grief, delivered in brutal circumstances.

The first lesson is that a journalist's job pits natural human sympathy against the need to get a story.

Tippet prefers to call death knocks 'intrusions', and still has vivid memories of one, after two young boys had drowned in a flooded quarry. One of the boys had jumped in to save the other. Heading out to their house, he had in mind advice from a 'hard-bitten bloody journalist', namely that 'when you do an intrusion, if you want to get in the door, say, "I want to do a tribute to little Jimmy who's died."'

He pulled into the driveway with Golden Earring's 'Radar Love' playing on the car radio, and then knocked on the door and uttered the phrase he immediately regretted:

> I said, 'I'm Gary Tippet from *The Sun News-Pictorial*. I want to do a tribute on little Johnny, the one who jumped in to save his brother.' And she just looked at me and she just said, 'But they're both dead,' and I felt like I'd stepped in dog shit and trod it all over their carpet.

It became a cautionary tale that informed his approach from that day on, and especially so because of what followed. Despite Tippet's inappropriate introduction, the mother invited him in and allowed him to share their story of grief.

> We sat there and we looked at photos of the kids and she and the other kids told me about them and I wrote a nice little intrusion piece. I've never tried that trick again. It was stupid and it was the wrong advice and it was totally disrespectful. She's had the most awful day of her life and then some idiot turns up on the door with some glib formulated statement to try and put his foot in the door and get in for a page five story in *The Sun News-Pictorial*. That's the biggest mistake I've ever made, I reckon, that one. But by the same token it was one of the great learning experiences of my life. It also taught me about the humanity. She thanked me as I was leaving ... and asked me if I was okay. And I think to myself, what the hell? I felt really, really low.

Aleisha Orr was working in the newsroom at *WAtoday.com.au* the day a local Western Australian family, a grandfather and his three grandchildren, were on board Malaysian Airlines Flight 17 when it was shot down over Ukraine, in 2014. There was confusion about whether the children's parents had been on the plane. When Orr found a number for what she thought was their aunt, she dialled and began by apologising for calling in those circumstances. She remembers it clearly.

> The woman who answered was actually the mother of the kids, and this was all within probably an hour of her finding out. She said something like 'You've got to be fucking kidding me', and that moment it clicked. I just remember feeling like total shit.

Looking back, she would like to make amends, but feels that would be even worse, because she would be putting her guilt ahead of the mother's grief.

Louise Graham also remembers the moment she and another reporter narrowly avoided making a painful error. Following a night-time car accident, they had arrived quickly at the family's home. 'We knocked on the door and this woman answers, and we're both looking at her and we said, "Oh we're from the *Herald Sun*," and she's said, "Yes?" And I'm … thinking, they don't know. They have no idea.' Graham quickly told the woman they must have had the wrong house, and left. The chief of staff wanted them to wait a bit and return but they refused. 'We actually drove off,' she recalls.

Russell Robinson thinks that, unpalatable as death knocks are, every journalist should do at least one, because 'it teaches you about life. It teaches you that you're no different to anybody else, that when you knock on the door you've got to appreciate people's feelings. You don't push hard. You don't lie, because I've always said to people that you could be knocking on your sister's door, you could be knocking on your parents' door.'

Flip Prior discovered early in her career at *The West Australian* she was good at death knocks. 'I've always approached journalism from a position of empathy,' she says.

> I think I was always very conscious that you're dealing with human beings. If someone started crying when they were telling me a story I'd probably sit there and start crying too, and I think that's okay sometimes. It's always trying to balance the objectivity and distance. If someone is sitting in front of you grieving, then you've got to be made of stone if you don't feel something.

Other journalists hold strong reservations about the practice. Stephen Corby remembers the first time he was asked to do a death knock, early in his career in Canberra. A young child had escaped through a hole in a back fence in Yass and been hit by a train.

> I remember sitting outside the house and I walked around the back and I looked at the hole in the fence and police tape, and I was trying to build myself up to do it. I think it must have been the first one I was asked to do, but was I really expected to do this? And I just sat there going, 'No.' And I don't know why.

He told the photographer he was going to sit in the car for 20 minutes and then call the newsroom and say the family wouldn't talk. He may not have known it, but this practice is known as 'knocking on grass'; the journalist goes to the required location, but never knocks on the door.

Corby never did do a death knock, and later wondered if he should have. 'I don't know if that makes me a bad journalist. In some ways I think it does. My colleague, who I'm very close to now, he used to do death knocks and he never had a problem with it, and I just can't,' he says.

Matthew Franklin, formerly a longstanding political journalist, is more adamant; death knocks are never acceptable. 'We tell ourselves to justify this, that this person telling the story about their kid who just got killed might be a message for others. I think that's nonsense. I think that when people are grieving you should leave them alone, they don't know what they're saying. I've grieved and I don't remember what I said to anyone at the time,' he said.

Death knocks leave deep impressions on reporters, but they are still demanded by newsrooms because they yield powerful stories. Tippet remembers being invited into the family home of a young man killed in a car accident in Sherbrooke Forest, in Melbourne's Dandenong Ranges. He sat in the man's room, with his parents, as they shared memories.

'I remember tears falling on the keyboard as I wrote the story … the [father] was a rough, salt-of-the-earth working-class man and incredibly eloquent on his grief and it was just a moving and a privileged experience for me to talk to him.'

Later, he supported the family through court proceedings and continued to tell their story. 'To have people trust you after you've written that sort of story about them is a bit of … it's verification of what you do,' he said.[2]

Most journalists will be asked to do a death knock or cover a traumatic event at some stage in their career but, equally, for most of them, reporting such events won't be a daily occurrence. Foreign correspondents cover more than their fair share of trauma and war, often at great risk.

Tony Walker remembers travelling into war zones in the early 1980s without the bulletproof vests, body armour or helmets that later became commonplace for those in war zones. He witnessed trauma in many places during a long career as a correspondent for *The Age*, *The Financial Times* and *The Australian Financial Review*. He once reported on Palestinians in a refugee camp being bulldozed in their houses by Shiite militia and in the Iraq War he saw battlefields scattered with rotting bodies. But the attitude, and practice, was simply to get on with it. It wasn't until afterwards that Walker felt the effects, a diagnosed bout of depression following a challenging Gulf War assignment that he later thought might be post-traumatic stress disorder (PTSD), a now common diagnosis for many war correspondents.[3] He believes he has avoided other ill-effects, but still wonders if the field reporting he did was all necessary.

> A lot of being a combat correspondent too is sort of *Boy's Own Annual* stuff, you know? And you ask yourself in hindsight whether it was all necessary. Was it absolutely necessary to put yourself within range of a sniper's bullet? Was it absolutely necessary to get on the plane from Cairo to Beirut when the airport was being rocketed and mortared from the Chouf Mountains above? I mean, getting off the plane, and mortars landing on the airstrip like rain. Were the readers back in Melbourne or in London, whoever was reading *The Financial Times*, was it absolutely necessary to have the correspondent on the spot describing these events? And, that's a difficult question. How do you justify putting your life in danger? What makes the risk worth taking from a professional standpoint? All correspondents in combat ask themselves this, and I think the answers are quite difficult.

BBC journalist Kate Adie – a veteran of countless coups and wars – had a deceptively simple maxim: no war is worth dying for.[4] But the answer to Walker's question is not always so simple, because foreign correspondents have to make decisions in chaotic environments with little or no idea how events will unfold; a misjudgment can mean missing a major story, or it can mean injury or imprisonment, or in the case of the famous foreign correspondent Marie Colvin, death.

Marie Brenner's reconstruction of Colvin's final days in Syria in

2012 suggest she veered towards recklessness when she went back into a besieged town after it became clear to her photographer, Paul Conroy, that the Syrian military was targeting journalists, but it is entirely possible for journalists to find themselves in trouble while exercising professional care, as Australian journalist Peter Greste found in Egypt in 2013 when he and two colleagues working for *Al Jazeera English* were picked up by authorities and imprisoned for 400 days on sham charges of espionage before being released.[5]

The abiding pressures of foreign correspondent work exist in a world that is transforming in some ways, but not in others. The news media industry is changing dramatically with companies shedding journalists even as the drum roll of wars, disasters and traumas continues around the globe. Journalists who reported on the 2004 Boxing Day tsunami that killed 150 000 in Aceh province alone were deeply affected by what they experienced. Matthew Moore, then the Indonesia correspondent for *The Sydney Morning Herald*, recalls:

> It was just terrible, terrible carnage. And you learn what the smell of a corpse is in the tropics, and you smell hundreds of them, and you just know you are coming across another body up a tree, or in a drain. And as a journalist you have all of these defences that you employ, and you're there to do the story, but you do come across so many terrible stories. The woman who had gone to the market to shop that morning and lost her whole family; those stories are just everywhere.

Moore's story also shows how foreign correspondents have to change plans at an instant to jump into a disaster zone. When the tsunami hit, Moore had been back in Australia, driving down the NSW South Coast on a summer holiday with his family. Arriving in Indonesia a few days afterwards, he found his colleagues still in a state of shock.

They were not doing things like cooking meals, they were not eating, they were just smoking. So I took a big rucksack of food up there and started to do things like, 'I'm going to make dinner for eight people and make spaghetti, and sit down, let's have a meal. Let's rent a house, let's do all these things.' You know? Life's got to go on.

It seems a prosaic thought amid a global disaster, but adrenaline sustains you for only so long, as ABC journalist Lisa Millar once found. She ran herself ragged on a diet of chips and soft drink as she endured a grim 14-day vigil, waiting for the Singaporean government to carry out a sentence to execute convicted drug trafficker Van Nguyen in 2005.[6]

For Tom Hyland, asking victims to retell stories was one of the most challenging parts of his foreign postings and reporting trips in Southeast Asia, for AAP and others. In post-independence East Timor, he remembers how difficult it was to ask torture victims to recount their experience in detail. He needed to ensure his account would be accurate, but that required him asking 'really bad questions'. For the young Timorese interviewees it was more than enough for them to say they had been tortured. But Hyland needed to ask, 'How did they do it? How often did they do it? What was it like?'

On a separate trip to East Timor for *The Age*, he wanted to find women affected by violence, to show its impact on families. He and a colleague went to a village and asked a woman to recount how her husband had been hacked to death in front of her during a massacre.

> Not only had it happened in her presence, it had happened in the presence of her children. Not only had it happened in the presence of her children, but Dad was holding the hand of his little daughter as these other lunatics hacked him to death. And the child was standing there as she told us this story. Which I duly reported on, sort of, in a po-faced fashion.

He remembers after the interview he needed to sit down and smoke a cigarette. 'I was just totally shocked by what we just heard. That incident sticks in my mind and it sticks in my mind more than the fact that I've seen just a few bodies in my life as a journalist.'

Hard though it was to report such shocking violence, Hyland had difficulty translating what he had learnt about the impact of reporting traumatic events into a later role as foreign editor for *The Age*. He remembers debriefing with a photographer who had spent six months in the field in East Timor. The photographer had received death threats and in one incident during a demonstration had been slashed by a man wielding a machete.

> What sticks in my mind more, and this is a regret, is I know when I was a foreign editor that I was handling correspondents who were seeing atrocities consistently and I never asked them 'How are you doing?' I never asked them, 'Do you want a break?' or actually said to them, 'Well, you're going to take a break.' Because I know if I'd have said, 'Do you want a break?' they would've said, 'No mate, there's stories still happening.' There was that macho culture, that I've got to keep going and I can't show weakness.

Machismo has been ingrained in newsrooms, and the coping strategy of compartmentalising or avoidance is common.[7] It takes a secure, self-confident journalist to know when he needs to take himself off an assignment, but that is what Simon Mann did when he was European correspondent for *The Age* covering the war in Kosovo in 1998–99. He won a Walkley Award for stories he wrote after being shown mass graves of Albanians who had been massacred by Serbs. After several reporting trips to Kosovo, conditions began to wear on him.

Mann and his photographer were quite different people. Mann was 40 and married with four children, who were living in Kent in a house that doubled as his office; the photographer was young and 'gung ho'. 'So I think our perspectives were a bit different,' Mann says.

Kosovo then was divided into sectors controlled by Germany, Italy, the United Kingdom and the United States. He and the photographer, Christian Jorgensen, had little co-operation from the British-controlled sector as they searched for the site of the then alleged massacres. They said, 'You go beyond this point and we have no control. We don't want anything to do with you.' Mann said they were not asking to be indemnified, just wanting a sense of how safe the area was, but the soldiers refused to answer.

Eventually they found a local commander of the Kosovo Liberation Army (KLA) who took them to a massacre site where they saw 'fingers and bits of skull poking up through the soil'. The commander had a full list of the people he believed were buried there; they took pictures of him in front of the graveyard. Mann felt they had enough evidence to write the story.

Six months later they returned, to watch a team of Belgian forensic scientists exhuming 30-40 bodies from a long trench. The scientists undressed the bodies, put them in body bags, and then washed their clothes, laying them out on long trestle tables for the local villagers to walk past and identify their loved ones.

A New Zealand police officer in charge of the operation told Mann and Jorgensen about the danger of landmines around the gravesites. Mann expressed horror, to which the police officer replied, 'Well, this is nothing, because the place up the road was so littered with mines it took us about a week just to remove them all.' The place up the road happened to be where Mann and Jorgensen had been not long before.

'It was hideous. I mean, people were returning to their homes, opening their front garden gate and then standing on a landmine.'

On their way back to Pristina (the capital) that day they needed to hide underneath a British military vehicle when a sniper opened fire. A British soldier wearing what looked to them like an alarmingly thin flak jacket asked why they were wearing heavy jackets with ceramic plates.

'It's pretty obvious, isn't it?' said Mann, to which the soldier replied: 'Yeah, but you see, if I get shot by one of those guys I'll die instantly. You'll get shot, but you'll have an agonising death because you've got those stupid ceramic plates in there.' Recalling this, Mann laughs, 'So that wasn't a great moment either.'

He also recalls learning about two journalists and a photographer from a magazine in Germany who had been stopped by Serb paramilitaries one day and shot dead in their car. He became acutely aware how easily that could have been him and Jorgensen as they drove around looking for massacre sites.

> Sometimes you'd sit there for two hours waiting to be allowed through with the nozzle of a gun very close to your head, and you'd sweat a bit on that. It was the Wild West. You did things which were unwittingly dangerous, even stupid, because you wanted to get the story, and sometimes at night you'd reflect and then perhaps not do it the next day, because you'd think 'Well, we got away with that, we don't need to do it again.'

He could feel himself fraying. Day in, day out they were driving through checkpoints past heavily armed people who 'basically don't want you there' and he remembers driving slowly back down the mountain and finally reaching Serbia where he rang his wife in London and said, 'I just want to come home.'

Once back in London, he was struck by the incongruity between the war in Kosovo and 'putting the bins out at night and kissing the kids in their beds and reading bedtime stories; it's this weird sort of two worlds'. He felt he was suffering symptoms of PTSD, but it was not diagnosed as such. He says he can bring himself to the verge of tears when he recollects some of those incidents.

'It's not debilitating, I just know it's there and it's something that I either have never dealt with, or couldn't deal with.'

He is not alone; a number of systematic reviews of research on trauma and journalism have found the prevalence of PTSD is generally higher in journalists than in the general population.[8] Awareness is gradually growing in newsrooms of the impact on journalists of covering traumatic events, prodded along by organisations such as the Dart Center for Journalism and Trauma, which have advocated for programs to support journalists when reporting traumatic events. A growing number of journalists understand the value of this kind of awareness in the newsroom.

Gary Tippet took the lesson from his early death knock and became the first Australian Ochberg Fellow for the US-based Dart Center in 2004. Phil Kafcaloudes became a journalism trainer at the ABC, ensuring he included trauma awareness in his disaster reporting course. He later did a Churchill Fellowship project focused on trauma and journalism around the world. Sally Sara, another Dart Ochberg fellow well known as a foreign correspondent for the ABC, has written a play about the issues raised in covering traumatic events, *Stop Girl*, that premiered in early 2021.

Isabella Lettini – a photographer for Fairfax – sought out support after a particularly distressing incident, when she photographed a cyclist killed by a truck and didn't realise until she enlarged the photo that the cyclist's body was spread across the road. She felt traumatised by the confronting image and was not afraid to admit it, unlike previous generations of journalists who, in her eyes, had few ways of processing trauma other than through alcohol or anger.

'I used to work with a couple of guys who went to the Vietnam War. They were angry all the time. They snapped at the drop of a hat.'

Given the nature of journalistic work, it is remarkable that it took so long for the impact of covering traumatic events to become public. In the decade to 2010, 135 mental health claims were lodged with workers' compensation authorities in Australia from journalists and related professionals, according to Kimina Lyall, a former journalist who studied the issue. Despite this, precious little discussion of it has taken place in the media.[9]

Since then a photographer and a reporter, both of whom worked for *The Age* and suffered from occupational post-traumatic stress disorder, have brought negligence claims against their employer, in 2012 and 2018–19 respectively. The photographer's case failed, but the reporter's succeeded, putting media companies on notice about their obligations to employees.

Bruce Shapiro, the executive director of the Dart Center, believes the case is important because it was the first time a news organisation had been found liable for a journalist's trauma.[10]

Whether news organisations have the capacity, let alone the wherewithal, to respond seriously to the rising tide of mental health issues is very much an open question. What is not in question is the unceasing stream of traumatic events that unfold, even as news outlets shed journalists.

CHAPTER 10
Work-life imbalance

Brad Buller

Jo Chandler had been working on general rounds for about a year before she was elevated to *The Age*'s Insight investigations team. As she recalls, she 'pushed for' the promotion because she saw it as 'a chance to dig deeper into stories and ... learn more about intriguing things'. Insight reporters had been at the forefront of investigative journalism[1] for several years, and the unit is thought to be the first dedicated outfit in Australia.[2] Since its configuration as a permanent, fulltime operation in 1973,[3] it has exposed social injustice, corruption and organised crime[4] and broken some of *The Age*'s most renowned stories, such as the plight of the Minus Children, the Victorian land scandals and '*The Age* Tapes'.[5] When Chandler joined in 1990, though, she recalls Insight was experiencing 'something of a transition'.

> They'd come out of those years [the 1980s] doing Painters and Dockers and *The Age* Tapes[6] and all of that and there was a feeling that they wanted to diversify, to be doing more social equity stuff ... I remember we spent a lot of time [investigating] aged care ... Part of the interest was to kind of diversify the unit, and that it wasn't going to be just cops and robbers and filthy backroom people.

Chandler showed initiative and wrote many front-page stories during her two-year spell. In January 1992, she exposed dubious lending practices at the ANZ Bank, which had channelled more than $100 million on 'virtually no security' to a development company called McLean Group.[7]

'It was a big [deal],' says Chandler. 'I got the story on my own' and 'showed up some of the executives with questions they didn't want asked.'

In June 1992, Chandler, together with David Wilson, revealed that a man known as Mr Fixit had been paid by members of Victoria Police to rig court cases.[8]

'That was a very legally complicated story to tell,' she says, 'but there would be ways that you could write around' it.

Like most investigative reporters, Chandler worked long hours and became deeply committed to stories that were difficult to tell. She went to a lot of lunches and dinners and heard incredible stories from a wide range of people, including both victims and perpetrators and 'bent' and 'straight' coppers.

But Chandler says many of them couldn't be printed.[9] In the end, she became disillusioned and frustrated. She thought, 'I'm out all night, my [family's] really cross at me, I'm being promised all this stuff. But, come morning, the papers would never turn up,' meaning the stories she worked so hard on would be held over or spiked. She'd ask herself, 'What was the point of doing all this?' Plus she was getting so sick. 'I was smoking and drinking like nothing.'

Many journalists struggled with juggling their personal and professional lives. Their work was exhausting and often incompatible with the rhythms of families. The profession attracted, or created, 'media junkies' who found it difficult to switch off after a 12- or 14-hour day. Even when they managed to extract themselves from their frenetic workplaces, they were still on duty, yelling at the television: 'Why did they lead with that story?' or 'What's that minister got to say?'

Discrimination was rife. Some women hid their pregnancies, for fear they'd be deprived of opportunities. For new mothers, the burden of raising children often meant an immediate shift to part-time or freelance work. Facilities for child-rearing in many newsrooms were inadequate, making them almost hostile places.[10] Meanwhile, many men and some women became immersed in an intoxicating culture, where working long hours was the norm.[11]

For Matthew Franklin, working as *The Australian's* Canberra chief political correspondent and bureau chief was 'no life'. He enjoyed the role, but remembers 'it was very hard work and very long hours'. Every morning, he'd be up early reading the newspapers and listening to radio bulletins. He wouldn't leave the office until '9.30 every night'.

Tom Hyland also recalls excessive work was an issue at Australian Associated Press. He joined the agency's Melbourne bureau in 1986, and was well regarded in the organisation. Though he enjoyed his job, he worked hard and felt he neglected his family. 'I would work late every day because that's what I had to do, or so I thought.'

Later that year, Hyland was called into a meeting with his editor-in-chief, Barry Wheeler. At first, 'I thought I'd done something wrong', he recalls. 'I had a raging hangover' because the press gallery had had its Christmas party the night before. Hyland and his buddies conducted a late-night mock parliament in the chamber of the Victorian Legislative Assembly and 'misbehaved so badly' that the Opposition leader's microphone had been damaged. But instead of getting a reprimand from his editor-in-chief, Hyland was offered a promotion. 'How would you like to go to Jakarta?' asked Wheeler. Hyland remembers he was 'lost for words', because AAP already had a correspondent in Indonesia, and he'd only been there a short time. Overseas postings at AAP or other major media outlets were rare and highly sought after.[12]

That evening, as Hyland walked home from the train, he thought 'my life has just changed, my life is about to change dramatically'. Although he knew he had to consult his wife, whose career would also be affected, the opportunity was too good to pass up.

'I was like a hound on a leash,' he says. 'I knew that if I didn't take this I would regret it.'

But it also meant more hard work and even longer hours. This became a recurring theme throughout his career:

> I saw myself as a journalist. It wasn't just my job; it was part of my identity. I think male journalists, particularly of my generation, some of us overcommitted. We became caught up in this macho culture of you don't knock off early, you don't finish after eight hours. You keep going. You don't watch the clock. I was part of that.

Today, Hyland is more reflective about the impact that men's careers can have on themselves and their families. We 'used work as a way of avoiding humdrum domestic responsibilities'. He suggests that although men *felt* it was essential for them to be at work, in fact, 'they weren't indispensable' and could well have joined the family for dinner or helped bath the kids. Hyland now recognises that working too hard has a personal toll. It can affect relationships and one's 'commitment as a parent'. He says, 'You might consider yourself a good, loving, engaged father but you're not there. Or you're not there every night. And sometimes even when you're there, your brain's somewhere else.'

The challenge of juggling work and family was especially intense for foreign correspondents who were on call 24 hours a day to report as soon as a story broke. They travelled to remote regions and found themselves in dangerous situations.

Simon Mann remembers his posting as *The Age*'s Europe correspondent as a 'fabulous experience', but his daily routine was gruelling. He'd get up between 4 and 6 each morning, depending on the time of year and the seasons, 'have a burst of activity', then work during the day, possibly with 'an hour's rest'. In the late afternoon he'd pick up the kids from school, have dinner and then 'work until about midnight or 1 am' before going to bed. But Mann would also 'try to get one day a week off where I'd try not to think about work'.

It was a demanding schedule, but Mann says his family was 'fabulously supportive'. Reflecting on the impact his career had, he says, 'the sad reality' is 'you can't do these jobs without neglecting your family a bit'. Fortunately, the nature of his posting meant he could work from home some of the time. 'Okay, I was away a lot, but when I was at home I was really home and just working.'

The balancing act had its moments. On one occasion Mann was in his office interviewing while his two boys played cricket in the corridor. 'Suddenly, the cricket would be turned into this sort of spiteful punch-up and they'd tumble through the door of the study when I'm on the phone. I'd say, "Out now! Out now!" all the time while some academic is chatting away' at the other end about a major issue. On other occasions, Mann would find himself conducting an interview with his youngest daughter sitting on his shoulders 'having a shoulder ride'. He says: 'You just had to put up with that, but that was the great joy of being at home.'

Antoinette Lattouf had never dreamt of becoming a foreign correspondent. 'I just thought, "Oh, I'll give it a crack."' Lattouf had travelled to Damascus to study Arabic and freelance after she left the ABC's *Hack* program. She filed one feature for the ABC and wrote a 'couple of pieces' before returning to Australia. 'I wasn't sure *that* life – the foreign corro life – is for me,' she says. 'I've never had my eye on a prize – and I still don't.' For Lattouf, family was more important than travelling the globe, or reporting on wars and famines.

> So many of the successful journos that I know, all the foreign corros, have such screwed-up personal lives. They're alcoholics, they're onto their eighth wife, they have four children in five – you know in five different continents. And that was something that really stuck with me ... I could easily become a 42-year-old, six-time Walkley Award-winning

single lady. Or I could marry my husband and carve out a different journalistic career.

The ethos of excessive work didn't affect only men. In fact, in some cases it was women who were responsible for setting the work pattern for male colleagues. *The Age*'s chief political correspondent Michelle Grattan, for example, had an 'astonishing' work ethic and became 'notorious' for phoning politicians or colleagues at all hours to check a fact or alter a story.[13] This became challenging for Tim Colebatch and his family when he joined the bureau in 1989.

'The bad thing about Canberra was Michelle's work rules,' recalls Colebatch. Those rules 'basically expected that everybody work … almost as long as she did'. He was expected to arrive in the press gallery by '9.00 or 10.00 in the morning and stay there until 11.00 at night'. The demanding timetable led to 'a difficult period' for Colebatch. He says if he lived life again, he would say: 'Sorry, Michelle, I've got other responsibilities in life. I'm going to have to be there for my kids and wife.' After negotiation, though, she did allow Colebatch to come in an hour or so later, and leave half an hour earlier, so that 'I worked 12-hour days rather than 13- or 14-'.

Journalism can be particularly unforgiving to women with children. Traditionally, men have dominated editorial and management roles, and their attitudes have shaped the workplace. Despite the gains made through feminism in the 1970s, Debra Jopson remembers that newsrooms 'weren't really ready for women. They definitely weren't ready for women having children and getting pregnant and … being responsible for those children.'

At *The Sydney Morning Herald*, urban affairs reporter Anne Davies realised early that a 'glass ceiling' existed for mothers at the paper. She says that in the 1990s the *Herald* was still 'grappling' with the idea that mothers could be useful to newsrooms. 'There was a lot of pressure', she says, on women to return to fulltime reporting after having children. Her superiors would say to her, 'You just can't do that job if you're not prepared to be in the office 60 hours a week.' Davies had support from female colleagues, but says the attitude that journalists would work long hours or drop everything to cover a breaking story still existed. She found this prejudice 'really hard'.

'I felt like I was always battling … that I was being judged for not putting in long enough hours, even though … I basically went back to four days pretty much straight away.'

The Age's entertainment editor Jo Roberts says, 'I don't think *The Age* as an institution ever really got on board with looking after parents at work that well.'[14]

There was a mothers' room in the old Spencer Street building, where women could breastfeed or express milk if needed, but the building lacked a crèche because 'the wisdom from on high at the time was that it would benefit too few people'. The lack of support from management and senior editors led to 'a lot of good women' leaving. 'They just weren't supported at work' which was a 'real shame', says Roberts.

> They had a chance to be a real pace-setter with that whole issue, because there was a lot of press around it at the time too, about women in the workplace and the pressure on big businesses to keep valuable staff on board. But instead, all these women were leaving the workforce in droves because they just didn't have the support they needed.

The lack of facilities led to unusual experiences for journalists who sometimes resorted to taking their children out on jobs. *The Age*'s Jo Chandler was on the health round when she took her 'screaming' baby to an interview with an eminent IVF specialist. She left her in the waiting room while she conducted the interview but 'all those people were sitting there waiting, desperately [thinking] they wanted to have babies', she recalls. 'You could hear her farting … she made such a scene.' The commotion led to the doctor telling Chandler,

'You know, you're very bad for business. They're going to be running down the hallway.'

Maureen Shelley remembers that she was treated well at *The Daily Telegraph*, while she was raising her children. She joined News Limited for the 2000 Olympics, initially on a six-month contract, but found herself still employed 12 years later.

'I was on the mummy track', she says. 'So, I wasn't looking for career advancement, I was just looking for a job that would help me pay the mortgage and allow me enough flexibility to bring up my child.'

Previously she had been a casual at *The Australian Financial Review* for about 18 months. In contrast to Fairfax, Shelley remembers News Limited was 'the best employer' she had ever had. 'Whatever people say about the evil empire and Rupert Murdoch, whatever they say, they believe in family.' Shelley says everything she asked for they gave her, 'every single thing'.

> I went to them and said, 'I only want to work two days a week because that's all I can manage' and they went, 'Okay' and then I'd say, 'I want to work three days a week' and they went, 'Okay', 'I want to work four', 'Okay', 'I want to work nights', 'All right'.

In Adelaide, Samela Harris joined the *Sunday Mail* just as a 'tough old' journalist called Jeff Jones took on the role of editor. Jones, on discovering Harris was pregnant and feeling a 'little delicate', assigned her to a new beat he'd invented called 'the pregnancy round'. This meant Harris was obliged to cover stories about spina bifida and 'spastic homes', as the paper called them.

'It was horrid,' she recalls. 'I hated it. I really hated it.' She felt she was being 'discriminated against just for being pregnant'. Not long after, she left the *Sunday Mail* to return to England. The experience left her feeling despondent about the lack of support for women in newsrooms.

You didn't mention that you had children. You didn't because that would be – 'that's female with a weakness'. You can't be vulnerable. You couldn't. There would be no understanding if you said, 'I've got to go home. My kid's sick.'

Veronica Ridge remembers similar issues at *The Age* when she had her first son in 1984 and her second two years later. Initially, Ridge worked part time and then freelance, but went back to five days a week in 1992. 'When I went fulltime with children', she recalls, 'I found that if one of the children was sick I'd have to say that I needed to go to an appointment' or 'I'd have to say that *I* was sick, which was a lie and quite difficult.' She says it wasn't acceptable 'for women to say they were supporting children'.

The fear of discrimination was so strong for Jo Chandler that she decided to not tell the editor of *The Age* she was pregnant. She believed that if she did she might miss out on a new grading. It was 1992 and Chandler was at the end of a two-year stint on the Insight team.

'I made a decision that I was wasting my time in some ways; that as much as [working on Insight] was interesting, I wasn't getting stories up … and I needed to do something different.'

Her chance came when Sally Heath left the paper's health round. 'I put my hand up for that and took that,' says Chandler. 'But what I hadn't told [the editor] was that I was pregnant and I made sure I didn't until I got the pay note.' When the memo confirming her new grading finally arrived on her desk, Chandler breathed a sigh of relief and said 'Oh, thank God.'

'I was already about four months gone and had this huge belly that I'd been trying to hide so I wouldn't miss out on a promotion. I'd been literally girdling myself up.'

In Adelaide, *The Advertiser*'s opinion editor Meredith Booth remembers so many battles fought at the paper. She was 'gunning for' a pay rise from her editor and would go into his office daily to try to get an upgrading.

'I knew what the previous opinion editor was getting paid and I was nowhere near it,' she recalls.

Because Booth hadn't told her editor that she was pregnant, when he finally did agree to the new grading, she had the freedom to say, 'Well, you know … and I'm pregnant.' Although he 'reneged on the deal' a few weeks later, 'I had it in writing so I did get the pay rise.'

The problem didn't stop there, though. 'Really, I was getting, you know, some interesting positions within the paper, but as soon as that first child came' it was 'just static career progression from then on,' she says.

It's said that people on their deathbeds never wish they had spent more time at the office. People facing redundancy can experience similar feelings, which manifest as anger or regret about all the long hours they dedicated to a workplace, especially one that ultimately failed to value them or their labour. Tom Arup felt almost melancholic when he exited *The Age* as a young reporter still in his prime. 'I wish I'd left the job at work more than I did,' he recalled. 'There were too many hours spent after hours worrying about the job.' He recognises his work was important, but believes 'it didn't need to be my identity or my life.'

These days he still gets together with old colleagues for whom their work *is* their life. 'I desperately want to say to them: "Go for a walk, go for a swim, go for a surf, talk to someone else about their life, just don't" – yeah, it shouldn't be your life.'

Former ABC journalist Tracee Hutchison says redundancy was all the more painful because she had sacrificed so much for the job. She was 52 when she was forced out, and 'at the peak' of her expertise, 'after giving my life to my profession … I was kicked out as menopause kicked in and it was just brutal and devastating. I just felt betrayed. The loss was overwhelming and the payout covered a year of complete debilitation. I'm not sure I'll ever really recover from that.' In addition to feelings of betrayal, Hutchison says:

> I think there are particular issues for women, certainly of my generation, who really struggled with decisions around having children, and when the timing might ever be right in a competitive professional environment to do that. In my case, I always put the job first. I was always thinking, No, I've got to – I can't take time out to do any of that because I've got a career to have. That's come at great residual sadness and grief, particularly when you realise that you're just thrown out the door with a redundancy.

News media has always been an industry that makes work-life balance difficult. Long, irregular hours are the norm. If a story breaks, or looks like breaking, you are expected to drop everything and start working on it. And a perception that you're not a true journalist if you don't persists even today. As Tom Hyland recalls, excessive work isn't just part of the job, it is an integral part of a journalist's identity. The very phrase 'work-life balance' would never have been invented in a newsroom. Blokes were certainly not encouraged to think about it; indeed, an unspoken code existed among many, that real life was what happened in the newsroom.

Women arriving in the industry were not initially welcomed, and life was made difficult for them in several ways. Many were not treated seriously as journalists or were given less important stories to work on. If they had children, newsrooms were ill-equipped – literally – for new mothers. This is changing, but grudgingly on the part of some, and only gradually at that.

What was changing was the technology in the newsroom, but not always in ways that benefited workers. Rather than making life easier, it often made the job more stressful and rushed and difficult to escape. It also made family time harder to protect and, ultimately, it made jobs much less secure.

David Marr

Interviewed and edited by Matthew Ricketson

Seemingly effortless success characterises David Marr's career, but he has always remembered an early mentor's words: 'David, don't try so hard to be original, mate. Being good's original enough.'

Growing up

I was born in 1947 on the North Shore of Sydney and grew up in Pymble, an intensely respectable suburb. Mum came from a professional family, basically medical, and my father was an engineer. The family company for the best part of a century had been making iron in Sydney, a good deal of it for the Water Board. I have always proudly said that if you seek my name look in the gutters, on manhole covers stamped 'Marr Sydney'. I was a bit of a sport; less a dour Marr, more one of my mother's family and its flamboyant characters. There's a way in which parents sort roles to their children, and my brother was my father's and I was my mother's. I went to Sydney Church of England Grammar School (Shore) and I realise now so many of my teachers were people who'd been mashed up in the war. They were odd broken men, angry, not particularly good teachers. I was a brilliant lazy boy; if I couldn't do something off the top of my head I didn't bother to do it. Languages took learning and so I dropped them, but in the final years at school I had two or three brilliant teachers and they saved my life.

The family took *The Sydney Morning Herald*. You certainly didn't toy with *The Daily Telegraph*. When I was a little boy I would go with my mother when she was playing tennis at this big sprawling house in Turramurra that had piles of *Punch*. They were thrilling. Not only mountains of back copies, but the latest issue. I would lose myself in them for hours.

My mother's brother returned from living in London in the very early 1960s and he subscribed to *The Observer*. Beautiful airmailed copies on rice paper arrived at his flat every week, and I thought that was just heaven. You never imagined there could be a newspaper of that kind in Australia – an intelligent, beautifully designed, marvellously written newspaper. I felt I was living in a hermetically sealed world and these papers gave me a sense of breaking out of [Robert] Menzies' Australia. I was becoming interested in politics. In my final years at school, I became a passionate devotee of Gough Whitlam who promised a transformation of Australia. It was a cause of profound dispute with my father.

I had announced I wanted to be a writer, but my parents thought I had to have a qualification to 'fall back on', so I went to the University of Sydney in 1965 to do arts/law and like my brother, I moved into St Paul's College. English was the subject I most enjoyed. We had very good history lecturers, and philosophy was as dry as mouse turds, and psychology I really couldn't bear.

Embarking on a career in law

In those days final-year law students worked as articled clerks and I got a perch in Sydney's leading law firm, Allen, Allen & Hemsley. I was actually articled to the last of the Allens, a splendid eccentric who came to work every morning on a Lambretta motor scooter. He, more than any teacher I ever had, taught me to write, by being made to write and rewrite plain legal letters. I could do the fancy stuff, the poetry, but funny old David Allen taught me how to make my meaning clear. He considered that a first-rate mind in a first-rate law firm spoke to its clients without jargon, with complete clarity and brevity.

By the time I'd finished and qualified as a lawyer I knew that I did not want to practise. I noticed that the most interesting younger members of the firm, people in their 30s and early 40s, were desperately unhappy and their unhappiness was clear. Also, I remember one day in barristers' chambers listening to these incredibly respectable lawyers contrive to steal a large bequest from Sydney University. I'm sitting there thinking, Would this be my life? That was kind of a jolt.

I remain, even now, so much a lawyer in my thinking. I'm so glad I had that basic training, and I don't know how I could've operated as a journalist in the way I've wanted to operate, if I hadn't had that training. It makes you unafraid to read legal cases and unafraid to read the law. I'm astonished the number of journalists who stumble around asking people, 'What did the High Court decide?' 'Have you read the decision?' 'No.' 'Read it, don't be afraid of legal documents.' Also, the law is a window into commerce, political power and influence. That world is permeated with the law, and if you've got a grasp of that you've got a grasp of the DNA of power. I'm very grateful for all of that, but I wanted to leave it behind.

Choosing journalism

I escaped to Europe, partly because I was trying to resolve the terrifying contradictions I had about sex, and to be somewhere where no aunt and no friend of my mother's was ever going to come around the corner. Sitting on the other side of the world, I also became intensely curious for the first time about my own country. I think I understood even then that the primary driver for me in journalism is explaining things to people. I've got an explainer's imagination.

So, having decided to get into journalism I came back and wrote four letters and I got four job offers, because I had a law degree.

In those days the notion that somebody with a law degree wanted to be a journalist was completely remarkable.

I had two offers that really excited me. Max Suich, at *The National Times* rang me and said, 'Come in and talk to me on Tuesday'; Trevor Kennedy, at *The Bulletin*, rang and said, 'You've got a job if you say yes now' so I said yes.

My career at *The Bulletin* was limited by difficulties I had with the Packer family. The Packers were principal clients of Allen, Allen & Hemsley, so when Kerry found that a former solicitor, as he thought it, was now a rookie journalist, he asked me to do some legal chores of precisely the kind that I had most despised doing, and I said no.

That limited my prospects. But it was an absolutely defining moment, I really chose journalism at that moment. Then, they'd decided to do a double-page spread of people gossip and I was to edit it. It was a big opening because it required some humour and good writing and interviewing people.

For my first edition Helen Suzman, the South African politician, was in town and I interviewed her, and I was a huge admirer of her stand against apartheid. I wrote her up in the most glowing terms; that was the end of that job for me.

Of course, it transpired years later that the Packer family were doing business deals with Mangosuthu Buthelezi, Mandela's rival. I think they just thought I was a soppy small 'l' liberal softie. Trevor Kennedy wanted to send me to cover the fall of Saigon. It would've been my first serious assignment. Word came down from Kerry's office that I was to meet with him and Trevor. Kerry came to Trevor's office and hung from the door like a kind of ape. He looked at me and looked at Trevor and said, 'We're not sending fucking him.' So I thought, 'Fuck this,' and applied to go to *The National Times*.

Editing *The National Times*

The National Times was part of this coming to grips with modern Australia, or let's say the actual Australia, and the other idea of course was that it would be an intelligent Sunday newspaper. At 33, after five years on staff and writing an angry biography of the Chief Justice Sir Garfield Barwick, I was offered and accepted, of course, the editorship.

Vic Carroll, a phenomenal journalistic talent, sat with me for the first month, and he gave me a piece of advice, which I've never forgotten though he forgets having given it to me. He said to me one day, 'David, don't try so hard to be original, mate. Being good's original enough.'

I was editor of the paper in effect for two years; it nearly killed me. I went from being an adventurous deputy to an overcautious editor. I overworked other people's copy. I didn't grow in the position; in fact, I shrank. I found myself so cautious, so worried all the time. But we did have some triumphs and one of them was the best thing I've ever done in journalism.

David Hickie was one of the young guns on the paper writing about crime and corruption. He knew the former New South Wales premier Bob Askin was dying because – now this story *has* to be told – his father was Askin's surgeon. David was working on an important story about Askin's corrupt dealings with Sydney's gambling families. We were ready. Askin died on a Wednesday, *The National Times* went to press on the Saturday, was published on the Sunday and the state funeral for Askin was due the following Wednesday.

I remember us wondering whether there is a decent interval for reporting the life of a crook, and I emphatically decided there was not. Why would we delay a week? This is a newspaper; we had a scoop. So, we went to press with a front-page headline, 'Askin: Friend to Organised Crime', above a fabulous photograph of a younger Bob Askin smoking a fat Havana cigar.

The impact was simply enormous, because it was the first time in print that anybody had really brought these accusations home. In those days the Fairfax editors used to go to the Lodge once a year and have dinner with the prime minister. Shortly after that article was published, it was dinner with Malcolm Fraser. He went me about the article and all of the editors of Fairfax joined with me in arguing with him about the levels of corruption in New South Wales. And it was a seminar for him on corruption. He seemed surprised.

Writing Patrick White's biography

I was on a panel in Perth with Craig Munro, who had written a book about a peculiar character, the publisher Inky Stephensen. It's a fascinating book and no pages are more fascinating than those dealing with the setting up of his first publishing venture in Sydney in about 1935 where it is revealed that the principal investors were Ruth and Dick White on condition that Stephensen publish the poems of their son Patrick. Now that detail contradicted everything Patrick White had ever uttered about his parents, about their indifference to his ambitions, about their hostility to him being a writer, everything. I thought how much I'd like to read a biography of White, and it came to me at once that I would write it.

When I started the Patrick project all I wanted from him was a truce. I didn't want him doing what Garfield Barwick had done: instruct his friends not to talk to me. But when I turned up to negotiate some sort of deal he said, 'Come in, turn on your tape recorder, let's start.'

I began to collect the letters Patrick believed everybody had dutifully followed his instructions and destroyed. God bless them, they hadn't. As the material flowed in, I knew I had a huge project on my hands and a project of such richness that I was not going to rush it.

So, I'd applied to the Australia Council and I'd got some generous support from them, and I also applied to the bicentennial outfit, whatever it was called, because they were giving writers grants and I was awarded a $25 000 grant by them and a few days before it was to be announced I thought, 'Oh shit, I'd better warn Patrick so he's not surprised by this.'

I rang and told him and he said, 'I'm very unhappy to hear that because I've been doing all I could to keep my name completely out of the bicentennial celebrations.' He thought those celebrations jingoistic, that they were not going to acknowledge the role of Indigenous Australians, they were to be self-congratulatory in a way that he found distasteful and he didn't want to be seen as an icon of the Australia being celebrated. I should have been aware of this but I wasn't. He said to me, 'I would hope you would reconsider accepting that grant.' That $25 000, which was going to buy me a lot of time.

A couple of days after this phone call, I went to the theatre and Patrick was there. We'd been getting on so well and he just looked up from his seat to my seat with this puzzled look, like 'What are you going to do?', and I decided that the project was more important than the grant.

So I rang the bicentennial people and said, 'I'm not going to take the grant.' I told Patrick and he thanked me, and shortly after that he discovered how much money it was and he was flabbergasted. A few weeks later, he produced a big box and said, 'Here, I think you will find these useful' and they were all his photographs. That was his way of thanking me. Boy, was that the right decision on my part.

He had no reason to believe I could pull off the biography, and so as the years went on he was taking a big gamble. By the time I delivered the manuscript I was as exhausted, as spent as I have ever been in my life. It was nearly 300 000 words long; the final writing was a period of about a year where I just ceaselessly wrote. Occasionally my phone would ring and it would be him on the other end just saying, 'When are you going to finish that fucking book?' and slamming down the receiver.

We had a deal that after I'd sent the manuscript to Jonathan Cape in London he could have a copy to read and we would discuss any errors. After I delivered the manuscript to his house, I disappeared on a four-wheel-drive expedition to the tip of Cape York. I wanted to be as far from him, as inaccessible, as I could.

After I returned, he rang and delivered a verdict I've never put on the record before: 'It is as it should be. I read much of it through tears.' But he added, 'We need to sit down and talk about some things. Can you come round tomorrow?'

Next day I found him sitting at his dining table, with his copy of the manuscript, and pointed at a seat opposite for me, with my copy, and he started to read to himself from the beginning. He was frail by this time and could only do it for about half a day at a time, and he made me sit there for nine half-days while he read it in front of me.

The complete turd was making me read my own book. When I realised what he was doing I kind of collapsed. It became clear to me that this was punishment. It was also an opportunity to talk about some issues again. I think he might also have wanted me to look at my own text, and without exactly saying so he wanted me to understand what pleasure he had from a lot of it, and pain. It was actually one of the most remarkable experiences of my professional life.

He would roar with laughter at something in the manuscript and I would always hope it was one of my paragraphs, and it never was. It was always something from one of his own letters. It became a joke between us that it wasn't me. He was thrilled, really thrilled to be reading again in the very early 1990s letters he had written in the 1930s and 1940s. They were good and he knew they were good.

I did a lot of rewriting in the process; I asked a lot of important questions and we clarified things and he made not one single request that anything be removed from the manuscript. And the book was a much better book because of that really painful process. He taught me so much.

I emerged from those years of writing much more grown up,

more adamant about my own beliefs. White's view was, you don't cave in, and that became my view much more strongly – that you stand by your beliefs and you don't trim them. The book sold very well indeed, and I was able to clear my borrowings. I worked out one day, in my Presbyterian way, what it earned me for the six and a half years I'd been engaged in the book. Everybody said, 'You've made a fortune, David'; 'Yeah, as a B grade journalist.'

Going back to daily journalism

I was never going back to journalism, but John Alexander lured me back to *The Sydney Morning Herald*. It's thrilling to be in a huge newsroom. They were these crazy universities full of experts on the strangest things and the most important things, people with weird arcane knowledge, people with real understanding and experience of things that mattered, places where you could ask anybody anything, though you might get your head bitten off if you interrupted someone on deadline. You've also got company, noise, a lot of shouting and yahooing and jokes. There's something very pleasing about discovering you can work in the most concentrated way in that noisy energetic atmosphere. I discovered I'm made for that kind of place.

At this stage, the late 1990s, *The Sydney Morning Herald* Saturday edition was making a profit of $1 million a week. Ditto *The Saturday Age*. There was the space to write 4000–5000 words, even more, for a topic that deserved it. You had time, you had resources and there was an enormous audience reading your work.

Whenever I'm researching a subject, I write a timeline. They go back to my training as an articled clerk. Timelines are something lawyers use a lot; absolutely accurate accounts, sometimes broken down to the hours in a day. Once you get the chronology completely set the truth of claims and the causation become much clearer. And so does the narrative. The gap, as well as the intimate connection, between chronology and narrative is a huge subject.

Narrative is one of our greatest inventions and all different cultures have different ways of telling narratives. The fundamental rule is that, however much you go back and forth, you give your readers the impression of being taken through time in an orderly fashion. If they trust you, they will let you lead them into the most complex and difficult subjects because they trust you to bring them out alive at the other end.

Hosting *Media Watch*

I think *Media Watch* is a uniquely useful show. There's nothing quite like it anywhere in the world that says, journalist to journalist, directly down the camera: 'This is what you've done wrong.' We would do it to the ABC and we would do it to Channel 9 and we would do it to the *Northern Territory News*, though we always loved the *Northern Territory News* because it was just so damned funny.

Up close you saw the working of News Corp as a political threshing machine. The combination of very good journalism and news reporting that came with their political vendettas – it's such an interesting operation. With good reporting comes the appalling commentary and appalling reporting that gives News its political clout. Their response to criticism on the program was visceral, usually nasty and almost always *ad hominem*. We learnt how much the public loved that program.

And we learnt how to lose friends. There were unrecovered friendships among colleagues I was very close to at Fairfax. I don't mind; I think a friendship that can't survive exposure on *Media Watch* isn't well based.

But the reality of *Media Watch* is that its subject is shit journalism; 'Here's a night of shit journalism and next week tune in again for some more shit journalism.'

I thought three years was long enough. It was time to go back and do some shit journalism of my own and bring to bear all I'd learnt. But there's an Anglican bishop side of me that doesn't mind denouncing people.

Life after Fairfax

Journalism, with the help of the union, was a trade you could go into and marry and buy a house and have kids and put them through school, and if you were any good at it you were a reasonably prosperous member of the community. The economics of the industry are now so shattered that that's just no longer the case.

Longform narrative, which is my first love, was becoming harder to do in newspapers; they were shrinking and the taste for it really wasn't there any longer. Even *Good Weekend* magazine was shrinking.

At this point along comes Morry Schwartz's Black Inc. and the *Quarterly Essays*. I found the format terrific: 25 000–35 000 words on a big subject that took me about two or three months to write, and *The Herald* gave me time to do that. *Quarterly Essays* have impact, they move public discussion, they are little books on contemporary political subjects filling a place that's disappeared from newspapers. They are frequently reviewed as books, somebody usually runs an excerpt from them, and of course they're online too. I found I could write something I love – biographical essays – and most of my *Quarterly Essays* are in the form of little biographies. That's how I've dealt with this range of malefactors: George Pell, Tony Abbott, Kevin Rudd, Bill Shorten and Pauline Hanson.

Peter Fray was a good editor of *The Sydney Morning Herald* and I like him very much, but he had tired, perhaps not unreasonably, of me disappearing for weeks at a time to write for other publications. When *The Monthly* asked me to do a big narrative piece about the Black Saturday bushfires in 2009, Fray first gave permission, but changed his mind a couple of hours later. I was terribly disappointed. I had wanted to write that story. I was finding a lot of nervousness around my work. It pissed me off to have editors hinting, 'Just be careful, David.'

The characterisation of me, driven by News Corp, as somehow ideologically extreme did catch on a bit. I have to tell you that the notion I am a serious leftie is not one shared by serious lefties. Just

David Marr

how timid *The Sydney Morning Herald* had become I only realised once I started writing for *Guardian Australia*. To be told just to go for it by its editor, Katherine Viner, was wonderful. She didn't give a damn who *The Guardian* upset. Such a different newsroom, though, small and quiet. Nobody shouts. Nobody cracks any loud jokes. They try not to disturb each other. I'm doing what I can do to reverse that situation.

CHAPTER 11
Chasing clicks: Changing technology

Merryn Sherwood
Andrew Dodd

As a long-time racing writer on *The Courier-Mail*, Bart Sinclair had seen several generations of new computers arrive in the newsroom. Each new machine came with different software and posed new frustrations for a non-technologically-savvy journo. So, on his last day, after four decades' service, he decided to make a stand.

At his farewell, several colleagues, including editor-in-chief David Fagan, gathered around his desk and gave generous speeches. At the end of his reply, Sinclair said, 'I've got one more act.' He pulled out a big piece of wood from under his chair, swung it at the computer on his desk and smashed it. There were 'bits of computer flying everywhere,' he says. 'That was my last parting gesture.'

Sinclair had spent some time setting this up. He had collected the timber from a nearby railway line a few days earlier. But what his colleagues didn't know was that the computer was already broken, and had been sourced from the IT department, where it was about to be thrown out. The shock tactic worked.

'David Fagan was going to pass out,' Sinclair recalls. 'He thought it was a brand new one sitting in the newsroom.'

Many journalists have a love-hate relationship with technology. Forgotten now, but the source of major workplace disruption in the 1980s was the replacement of typewriters in newsrooms with clunky, deskbound early personal computers, known as 'video display terminals'.¹

Fears about 'repetitive strain injury' afflicting journalists was nothing, though, compared to the impact of the internet's arrival in Australia in 1993 through the world wide web. The first newspaper to create a website was *The Age* in 1995 and within a few years most other news outlets followed suit.²

However, the established media was slow to recognise the possibilities offered by the internet, and had difficulty adapting to the elemental change it created. In the Melbourne bureau of *The Australian*, for instance, journalists weren't given access to the internet until the late 1990s, and that was confined to one computer on the newsroom floor.

Media companies, and the journalists working in them, were accustomed to being the source of information for people. They jealously guarded this power. The internet not only massively increased the amount of information available but, for the most part, made it freely, instantly and globally accessible.

That said, no generation of reporters has seen technology evolve so quickly or change with greater effect. Endless deadlines now 'roll' throughout the day and night. Journalists are now almost always reachable, and therefore on call. They now also have direct feedback with the public through social media platforms. New technology has improved storytelling and created a wealth of new sources for news and information. But the advent of this new age has also made work more intense and stressful,³ and media organisations have largely jumped at small 'random acts of innovation', rather than large-scale sustained change.⁴

One Saturday afternoon in April 2012, Cate Swannell first experienced what digital technology could do for journalism. Though the *Gold Coast Bulletin* didn't publish an edition on Sunday, she was in the office writing online coverage of a local council election alongside a cadet and a photographer. She received a call from an off-duty colleague who told her there had been a shooting and stabbing at a local shopping centre at Robina Town Centre, and the building had gone into lockdown. Swannell jumped on the phone, called police reporters and as many photographers as she could find. That afternoon, the paper's online site carried rolling and extensive coverage of the incident, including videos, picture galleries and breaking stories. For the first time – that she could remember – the newsroom used the website first, rather than waiting for the paper.

> That was the first time I felt like we'd actually gone, 'It's Saturday and we don't care because we don't have a paper issue tomorrow, but look what we can do if we put in an effort now'. We had three times the amount of clicks that we'd normally get on a Saturday. It suddenly started to feel like the journalists were excited by the idea of covering breaking news in a breaking fashion rather than just waiting till tomorrow to write the follow-up.

As technology has changed, so too have journalists' expectations of 'normal'. David Marr says when he started out at *The Bulletin* and *The National Times*, and even later on *The Sydney Morning Herald*, he might work on a piece for two to three days, file it on Thursday and be happy to see it on Saturday.

'Now if I file a piece for *The Guardian* at 10 in the morning I'm on edge to see that it's up on the site within an hour, "Oh good, it's there," because the job's not done until it appears. I'm thrilled by that, I find that really thrilling, it's so immediate,' he says.

But opportunities created by digital are not always welcome. Ross Brundrett remembers he once featured prominently in *A Current Affair* story on Luddites and he long resisted getting a mobile phone. 'I guess the old fallacies about old people being resistant to change are probably true in my case,' he says. It was 'something that never really sat well with me, because I just wanted to write stories'.

Meredith Booth was working at *The Advertiser* in Adelaide in the early days of online when she saw how social media made reporting more intense and difficult. 'It brought a lot more stress with it as well. You had to be on the ball all the time,' she says.

Jane Hammond remembers just how quickly things changed. 'I came in one Saturday and the instruction was, "Oh, you have to use Twitter now" and I'd never heard of Twitter because it was quite new at that point.'

Often the journalists had to negotiate these new platforms, without instructions or guidance from above, which added a lot to the stress. Cate Swannell says there was one time at the *Gold Coast Bulletin* when an IT staffer managed to tweet the embargoed front page 12 hours before it was due to be published. As a result, Swannell drew up some company social media guidelines for employees in lieu of a formal company policy. New metrics and measurements were also quickly put in place. Suddenly journalists needed to be on social media platforms and paying attention to things like 'bounce rates' (the time it took for readers to move from one story to another).

In many cases in this era of change, it was the journalists who were keen to try new ideas and concepts, but they were baffled by the frustratingly slow response from management to support them. Debra Jopson remembers editorial conferences at *The Sydney Morning Herald* when reporters and editors would gather and listen to a presentation on, say, the latest iteration of the internet in Australia, only to find that '10 minutes later our tech writers, or whoever, would say, "Oh my God, that's so old. They're so behind."'

At *BRW* magazine, Kate Mills tried to improve the magazine's antiquated website, but couldn't get the tech support. 'It was a very ancient platform,' she says. 'I mean loading it up, it was like taking tablets of stone up the mountain, quite frankly, to get the thing to launch every week.'

Dean Mellor was working on the motoring titles at ACP's magazine stable, and had been pushing for a new website, even before he started having potential advertisers ask in meetings if they could buy space on it. An ACP–Ninemsn deal was holding things up, and he couldn't seem to make any ground.

> It got to the point where we had advertisers asking us, 'How can we advertise on your website?' Every title review meeting I'd go, 'Now, let's talk about the website' and they'd all shut me down and say, 'Well, there's nothing we can do about it.'

Samela Harris helped lead the online revolution in Adelaide at *The Advertiser*, but initially she was only able to put up stories after they had been in the newspaper. 'It seemed counter-intuitive … the papers were very slow catching on. Frustratingly slow catching on,' she says.

At *The Age*, Tom Hyland wanted to write long features and embed links that would take people to source documents or videos, or potentially write longer pieces online than he was able to fit in the paper. But he was frustrated. 'I couldn't insert a link,' he says. Another frustration was that he couldn't create different versions of the same story for print and online.

'I might have a richer, longer story which might run to 2000 words for online where there's no space constraint, [but] there was no editing capacity to have two versions of the same story.'

This lack of digital innovation wasn't unique to Australian journalism. International reviews of research found that at least in the early 2000s journalism didn't take advantage of new digital possibilities quickly enough.[5]

Maureen Shelley, working in a senior management role at News Limited, could see how the continued focus on print was playing out at the highest level. Shelley says Rupert Murdoch had the chance to update the pagination system, to a version that Fairfax had already switched to, but instead spent the $40 million it would have cost to build a new printing press at Yagoona.

'There was a commitment to print. There was a recommitment to print with that print centre,' she says. 'My sense was that Rupert was never fully engaged in technology.'

Alysson Watson had been working on a larger innovation strategy at the *Newcastle Herald* to streamline its operation for online. The proposal was to take journalists and editors from their respective rounds and create a central news hub, where they would work together on breaking stories, in an almost 24/7 operation. Reporters could be sub-editors and vice versa, and reporters would train to take photographs and produce video. She led focus groups and discussed how they would change rostering, workflow and work practices. But then came a major round of redundancies, and it all fell by the wayside. Watson says,

> I felt really robbed of the chance to try and make it work ourselves, and I felt really upset that Fairfax didn't want to listen to its own staff. I think at a local level, had we been left to our own devices, we might have been able to make a better go of it. In hindsight, maybe not. But I did feel robbed of the chance to try and reinvent ourselves.

Rocco Fazzari was an in-house illustrator and cartoonist at *The Sydney Morning Herald*, who did manage to lead his own reinvention, but only because he invested heavily in it. Fazzari initially had to argue for his own computer, as he struggled to break from the perception he was just an illustrator.

'It's not that they didn't want to give it to me. It was just like, "What for, Rocco? You're drawing. Enjoy your life. Why do you want to ruin your eyesight with one of these damn things?"'

But once the digital department caught on to Fazzari's enthusiasm, he was able to start his own blog, in which he detailed life in the art department – making it one of Fairfax's early successful online strategies. But he also took it further by downloading tutorials on video editing and special effects on his iPad to watch on the bus trip to work. He also stopped watching TV, and after shifts would work for two to three hours at night refining his skills further, and then collaborated with others to produce public works. A music parody he animated was nominated for an award at the Australian YouTube Awards in 2005. Everything he learnt was self-taught, illustrating the lack of investment in training staff for new skills. Fazzari found it fulfilling, but he also recognised that he had to embrace it.

> By 2005 or 2006 I could see that it was the future and I could see that the only way I could survive in the industry was by doing that. But it was also the fact that I actually enjoyed it. I loved it. I loved the challenge, it was different. All the things that I had learnt were coming together, you know, being creative, being conceptual, telling the story and, doing it really quick and entertaining people was Wow, it could go out there and be everywhere at the same time.

Photography also changed dramatically. When Louise Graham started her cadetship at *The Herald* in Melbourne, she worked in a darkroom, using chemicals now deemed dangerous, like ferricyanide, to bleach prints.

And the process to send photographs from interstate or overseas was laborious. Hugh Jones recalls watching photographer Andrew De La Rue of *The Australian* transmit a photograph from the blockade at the site of Tasmania's proposed Franklin Dam in 1982. It involved unscrewing the telephone in the hotel room, clipping in wires from a picturegram machine, and then putting the print onto a drum.

'The drum started revolving and there was a little needle and effectively, like an old gramophone record, the needle just went along and picked up the image millimetre by millimetre as it went through,' he says.

Jones estimates it would take about 30 minutes to send one picture. 'If you look at newspapers from the time, there are all these sort of really grainy, lined photographs and that's pretty much how photographs were transmitted from remote places,' he says.

The inevitable switch from film to digital didn't mean the end of innovation, as Isabella Lettini discovered when she started at News Limited as a staff photographer in 2000. She was on digital right away, which was still in its infancy.

'It was very antiquated back then. And very low megapixels. The quality wasn't so good, so we had to do the best we could with what we had.'

Soon, though, photographers weren't just taking pictures. At the *Gold Coast Bulletin*, Cate Swannell needed content for the website and encouraged the paper's staff photographers to capture video while they were out on location shooting stills for stories. It involved 'a lot of re-education all the time'. She knew it wasn't always easy for the photographers to do two jobs at once, but she remembers asking them 'Can you just take a minute's worth of footage with your iPhone?' Soon, though, photography became a less valued skill, as journalists were also asked to take photos, often on their mobile phones.[6]

Innovations were happening in every part of every media business, and inevitably they had implications for jobs. Almost no role was safe. As well as reporters and photographers, sub-editors and even editors were squeezed out, meaning the oversight and quality control of news production immediately suffered.

Simon Mann estimates that when he started at *The Age*, four or five sets of eyes would be looking over a story before it was published. 'You'd be back and forward to the chief of staff', he says. 'Then the news editor, then the sub-editor who was subbing a story would come over with queries and you'd go back and check things, then go back again, another sub would pick it up, then a check sub would look over it and then the proofreaders would look at it and finally it'd be in the paper.'

In 2011, Fairfax made the cost-cutting decision to outsource all of its sub-editing to Pagemasters, the external company already handling some of its feature pages and special editions. The decision was met with criticism,[7] as it took away many of the key checks that Mann describes. At that time sub-editors could simply stand up at their desk, walk over to a journalist, and directly ask any questions they had about a story. Outsourcing the work to Pagemasters meant the stories were sent off site, in some cases out of the country, to be subbed.

Concurrently, News Limited was undergoing its own revolution in sub-editing, but with a centralised subbing workforce inside its own operation. In the new model led by Hugh Jones, the Melbourne 'subs hub' saw sub-editors from the *Herald Sun*, *Sunday Herald Sun*, *The Weekly Times*, *mX* and the suburban *Leader* newspapers all come together on one floor in the Herald and Weekly Times' Southbank office.

Some of the initial feedback was promising. Subs who worked exclusively on the sports desk were suddenly encouraged to write entertaining headlines for the suburban newspapers. Jones worked hard to build and maintain morale and gave generous recognition for the work. But he also began to see problems, because the new arrangement challenged several traditional sub-editing practices.

One of those was the way subs worked closely with journalists and editors on rewrites. For example, if an 80-centimetre story needed to be cut to 40 centimetres, staff in the subs hub couldn't do the work. 'No big things. No rewrites,' says Jones, 'which meant taking away some of the appeal of subbing, and indeed that's what happened. A lot of people lost interest.'

Sports editors who had been at the paper for 30 years and prided themselves on knowing facts like 'the height and weight and the reach of Muhammad Ali and who won the 1934 Cox Plate' told Jones,

Chasing clicks: Changing technology

'Every word that passes my desk, I really care for. You're devaluing it because you're just making me a copy shifter and all you're really asking me to do is check the spelling and the punctuation and send it on its way.'

As Queensland racing writer Bart Sinclair says, his stories were no longer adapted for betting markets in his own state, because they were being subbed elsewhere.

> It became a source of frustration for me. And there were a lot of mistakes made. I was coming to the races and copping some personal abuse because I was seen to be the figurehead for racing in *The Courier-Mail*. It was very hard to have to accept that when it was out of my control.

Cate Swannell saw the effects of centralisation too. She says her own paper's subs 'had been slowly massacred basically, culled', and those who remained 'all ended up working for *The Courier-Mail* but sitting in our office', meaning that the *Gold Coast Bulletin*'s material 'went through *The Courier-Mail* and came back and was read by a group of subs that we weren't allowed to talk to because they now didn't work for us'.

> These were people I'd worked with for 23 years, and we weren't allowed to talk to them during the workday, they were down the end of the newsroom. We had to walk past them to get our coffee and we weren't allowed to talk to them in case we gave *The Courier-Mail* information about what we were doing. Go figure. So it became really odd.

Technological changes also affected the way newspaper pages were laid out. Jo Chandler loved the creativity that came with an almost blank page. She would plan in her mind how the different elements could be arranged.

'You'd use a light font or a bold, you'd use panels, you'd use illustrations, you'd get a cartoon, and nothing was formulaic,' she says. 'You'd look at the shape and think about your pages and think about how you could present that in a really appealing way. I loved that jigsaw puzzle element of it.'

But slowly this freedom disappeared. There were fewer pages overall, and the pages that were left had to accommodate the advertising, leaving less space for stories. Then a new editorial news system was introduced, with a set of fixed templates from which editors needed to choose.

> I remember going to the chief sub on behalf of all the other subs, saying, 'What are we, trained monkeys? This is appalling. Where's the skill in this? What, you just hit a button and you're told how the page is supposed to look?'

Many sub-editors felt they had been pushed aside and were no longer a key and valued part of the newspaper production process. This hit Hugh Jones during a conversation with a veteran sub, who told him,

> You know what I really don't like about this, I can see all the argument for it. I understand. But I come in, I can't sit in the same chair every day. Some bloke's been fiddling around with the height of it and I wanted to have a picture of my wife and my family on my desk. I feel like I just lost my home.

This sentiment was also being felt over at Fairfax as the real impact of digital disruption started to hit. Senior journalists faced the reality that management was more concerned with the bottom line than with quality journalism; an opinion that had already been voiced in Australian media industry reports and research.[8]

Tom Hyland vividly remembers a staff meeting in 2012, at which everyone was told about an impending wave of mass redundancies. He put up his hand to ask then chief executive Greg Hywood a question.

> I asked the question in good faith. 'When we go to this new integrated model, where print and digital are integrated and it's one newsroom structure and we file for digital first, rather than for print and then think about digital, when we do that in this new world how does that change the way we do our journalism and the ethos and the culture that we bring to the journalism?' And it was a sincere question and his answer was, 'Well, one thing you won't do is write boring-as-bat-shit old *Age* stories.' And that was his answer. And there were some gasps among the older generation in the room. To me, it was a slap in the face and it was also the moment when I realised that my time here is rapidly coming to an end. That what I do is not valued here.

Similarly, Jo Chandler remembers a meeting she attended in Sydney, where it became apparent that senior management was focused on the bottom line rather than quality journalism.

> One after another they stood on the stage. And one stood up and talked about how they had screwed the printers … as their whole profession was being sold down the river. And at that stage there were still picket lines outside the building. And we were supposed to be trying to support them while they got their redundancy packages sorted out. And the manager responsible for them delivered a report that basically talked with great pride about how many ways they were screwing these guys over. And everyone applauded. And then he talked about how they were going to come in under budget and everyone applauded again. There was no talk about journalism.

> There was nothing about the quality of what we did. There was absolutely nothing. And the real sense of it was that they were a media company trying to figure out how to transition and that the journalism just really was – it was kind of an impediment to whatever they were going to become. And I was really dismayed by this and I felt like the scales had fallen off my eyes.

These cuts followed the decline in newspaper revenue, due in turn to the sharp increase in digital advertising. In her senior national editorial development role for News Limited, Maureen Shelley had been privy to the increasingly dire news about Australia's print media. In leadership conferences, in closed circles of managers and editors, the finances were laid bare and indicated that 'basically the income just fell off a cliff', Shelley says.

'Around that 2010–12 period, what they used to call the rivers of gold, the classified advertising – recruitment, real estate, and motor vehicles – those three major sources of income for newspapers, disappeared. It was just like catastrophic failure of revenue.'

But Shelley remembers also hearing from a friend, a senior recruiter for a major government organisation, who hammered home where those dollars had disappeared.

> She went in there, she analysed how much was being spent at one newspaper title [for recruitment ads], which was $4 million a year. And she went and actually looked at where they got their successful candidates from. And none of them came from that advertising. So she proposed that they stop, there was a bit of an outcry over it. And she said, 'Well, look, what I've done is I've tracked where our successful applicants have come from, and they've all come from our own website, and we can advertise on our own website at no cost or we can continue funding a newspaper to the tune of $4 million

a year.' And they said, 'Well, we'll try it for six months, see how it goes.' And of course it had absolutely no impact whatsoever on their successful continual recruitment of good candidates. And so she was just one example. And of course that was replicated across [other] organisations and businesses.

Shelley saw how this played out in sheer numbers. She estimates that in 2000, when she started at *The Daily Telegraph*, 380 people worked in the newsroom, when she left in 2012 there were only 80. News organisations had ended up here because they had done too little, too late to address the threats of disruption. This was a common lament.

As a property editor at *The Age*, Alysson Watson worked on the real estate supplement *Domain* before it went online. Each week she had pages and pages of full-page ads from real estate agents.

'It was just a must-have,' she recalls. 'If you were buying or selling that's where you were. You were in that section ... the rivers of gold were a very real thing.'

But she slowly started to see the rise of online alternatives, like <realestate.com.au>, and the move of car sales from classified sections to the internet, and realised what had happened.

> There were still those who were saying ... we've always been here, and we can ride this out, this is a bit of a fad, this interwebs thing. Of course, clearly it wasn't. But I don't think I could have seen the extent of the devastation. The extent to which, once advertising became really cheap online, and once news became free online, we would never recover from that. For a long time we just kept our heads down and hoped that we were special enough that we would survive.

Cate Swannell was at the *Gold Coast Bulletin* when its website became one of the fastest-growing in Australia, and had seen the possibilities of digital on that afternoon spent breaking news. She considers the failure to transform the business model as a missed opportunity.

'How do you monetise these clicks?' she asks. 'How do you convince advertisers to spend money on a website? The advertising on the website was always sold at 10 per cent of the cost of the print ads, so even when you did get revenue it was minor compared to the print revenue. That's always been the problem,' she says.

Debra Jopson watched *The Sydney Morning Herald* miss those same opportunities as the paper waved goodbye to the very people who could help it adapt to new technology. She sums up the frustration of many:

> Believe it or not, a whole lot of the people who were more digitally savvy left in the redundancy rounds and some of the so-called print dinosaurs stayed behind because they were too frightened of the world out there. So let's say when Amanda Wilson was editor, I used to talk to her all the time about how absolutely and utterly frustrated I was at the lack of the digital media training that we were getting and how we really had to do it and, you know, get more of the newsroom up to speed, not just some corner of it but everyone, and she said, 'I agree with you, but I can't get the management to do it. They've got to pay for it and they're not going to do that.'

This chapter began with Bart Sinclair smashing an old terminal on his desk, suggesting it was the journalists, particularly the old print reporters, who were most hostile towards the technology that was sweeping across the industry. But the picture that emerges from the stories of reporters, sub-editors and photographers is more complex.

Most could see how the digital and online revolutions were challenging nearly every aspect of what they did, and many tried to adapt. Some even agitated for the changes they hoped would give them at least a fighting chance of remaining viable. The same can't always be said for the proprietors and managers of news businesses who were either slow to react or reflexively cut costs in ways that sometimes revealed how little they valued journalism. Editors often found themselves in the middle, trying to downsize in ways that saved at least some of the business.

As digital and online technology led to the loss of advertising, the true costs of producing journalism became apparent, and the inevitable cuts to positions and mastheads began. The rivers of gold were evaporating. News deserts were beginning to form.

CHAPTER 12

Should I stay or should I go now?

Matthew Ricketson
Timothy Marjoribanks

Dean Mellor was enjoying a family holiday in Thailand when a chance meeting with an American businessman gave him an inkling that James Packer's sale of his magazine empire might not end swimmingly for journalists like him. Mellor's career had been progressing nicely; after several years writing for magazines like *Overlander 4WD*, he moved to Packer's publishing arm, Australian Consolidated Press, as deputy editor and then editor of *4X4 Australia*.

Packer had been savvy enough to sell out of the television and magazine empire built by his father, Kerry, and grandfather, Sir Frank, at the height of the market, in 2006, scooping up $5.6 billion.[1] The purchaser was CVC Asia-Pacific, a company with zero public profile in Australia, which didn't bother them; there was a reason for that, as Mellor learned over a drink in Karon Beach.

The American said he worked in private equity and Mellor said, 'That's interesting. My company's just been bought by a private equity firm.' The man's face had 'you poor bastard' written all over it. 'What's wrong, mate?' Mellor asked. The man explained: private equity firms buy companies, then, to pay off the debt incurred in buying, strip the companies bare and offload them a few years later.

'It never turns out well for the employees,' he told Mellor. He was right.

The once handsomely profitable magazine arm of Packer's business was squeezed hard over the next few years, before being sold to the German-owned Bauer Media in 2012 for less than one-third of what it had been worth a few years earlier. Mellor began contemplating his own exit.

Mellor's predicament is a common one among thousands of journalists working in the nation's largest media companies in the 2000s. Some, like Mellor, were unaware just how much and how quickly the business of media was changing, while others, especially those in management or those who reported on media could see what was coming.

The period leading up to the big redundancy round of 2012 was marked by the differing fortunes of the major media companies. Fairfax Media became – by some measures – the largest media company in Australia in 2007 after the merger of Fairfax with Rural Press. However, it gradually became clear the price of the merger was too high, and the share price plummeted.

The disclosure requirements on companies flowed through to differing public perceptions of their performance. As a share-listed company Fairfax Media needed to disclose details of its finances to the local market that News Corporation Australia, with corporate headquarters in the United States, could avoid. Fairfax looked as though it was wobbling while News continued asserting a commitment to newspapers. But both were struggling, and failing, to find a new business model.[2]

The print media had always been a hybrid business. Stripped to its essence, for well over a century it had been about connecting advertisers with prospective customers, using journalism to attract their attention. That sounds like a brutal reductionist's view of journalism's role, but that was the commercial reality, even if the Fairfax family, the company's original proprietors, did not dwell on it publicly, preferring instead to foreground their commitment to the press's vital role in society. Not that it is false advertising; more a matter of putting the most attractive wares in the shop window. After all, as media historian Mitchell Stephens notes, all societies throughout the ages have had a hunger for news.[3]

Media companies like Fairfax earned part of their revenue from the cover price, but the bulk they received from advertising. The elegantly compiled bundle of news, entertainment, service information and advertisements that underpinned newspapers' business model was unstitched by the internet, which enabled the creation of stand-alone websites meeting customers' individual needs.

By the mid-2000s, if you wanted to hunt for a house or a car or a job you could do that for free. Instead of wading through pages of newsprint, you could narrow your search and quickly turn up precise information. The new online classified advertising sites could undercut rates, because they had none of the other costs associated with gathering and distributing news. In the early years of the 21st century print media companies aimed to massively increase their audience by publishing online as well as in print to offset dwindling classified advertising revenue. They could no longer charge advertisers anywhere near as much as when they had a monopoly on classified advertising. But most print media companies, overseas as well as in Australia, made what – in hindsight – was a catastrophic mistake of giving away their journalism online for free.

Soon they were haemorrhaging dollars and, not surprisingly, their journalists began to notice. Michael West, who became Business editor of *The Sydney Morning Herald* during this period, recalls being asked to find creative ways to cut costs, such as reducing detail in stock market tables, to save one or two pages of newsprint. He began calling contacts in funds management companies, asking them, 'Do you think we'd lose anything if we lost the options?' A media business reporter left, but West was not allowed to fill the vacancy for what had become an especially important round. Or perhaps that wasn't accidental; throughout this critical period for media companies in Australia, few chief executives wanted to publicly discuss the seriousness of the threat to their businesses. West tried asking Fairfax stablemate, *The Australian Financial Review* for access to their media and marketing stories, but they wanted to charge *The Herald* for them. 'We were constantly filling these gaps with a mad sort of patching in,' he says.

When Fairfax Media was not trying to rein in costs on its finance news, it was still producing lavish publications such as *The Sydney Magazine* that was inserted into *The Herald* (its Melbourne counterpart was inserted into *The Age*) replete with all manner of celebrity lifestyle stories on glossy stock. Kate Mills worked at another Fairfax magazine, *Business Review Weekly*, which was expected to shed positions in the move to digital-only publication. Mills was offered work on *The Sydney Magazine*.

'You remember the big glossy *Sydney Magazine*? I hated *The Sydney Magazine*. I mean it was all the things I don't like about Sydney – in a magazine. I was like, kill me now.' She had enjoyed the 'integrity and the business values of *BRW*' so was left thinking, 'Oh well, where am I going to end up in all of this?'

Matthew Franklin was having similar thoughts, but for slightly different reasons. He was an experienced journalist with News publications. He began in Queensland where he and Chris Mitchell forged a close working relationship, and he moved on to become chief political correspondent for *The Australian* in the 2000s under Mitchell's editorship. Franklin considered himself a successful news-breaking reporter, but it became increasingly clear to him that for 'my career to prosper further, I needed to become partisan'. He had discussions with senior people at his newspaper who he recalls told him,

'The paper's stance is this and to go further you need to think more about the sort of stories we're interested in.' That wasn't put to me in any sort of, 'You've got to start being unfair,' or anything like that. It is, 'You have to think, from your own perspective, what you're comfortable with, and what you want to be in life, what you want to do.'

The message being sent both explicitly and implicitly in such discussions was that career advancement in this organisation would require Franklin to be comfortable in adopting the organisation's specific perspective and focus. But Franklin was becoming less comfortable. For example, he had 'ideological difficulty' with the Finkelstein Inquiry's recommendations in 2012 to increase regulation of the news media, and he also had difficulty with the newspaper's partisan response to them. In particular, he didn't like what he calls personal-agenda-driven journalism.

'You can read certain newspapers where you don't have to read the opinion pages because they're all written by someone with the same opinion or it's the same column being written again and again and again.'

He recalls his then wife, Caroline Fisher, saying in this period he seemed increasingly tired and not himself. Franklin was also thinking about his family, as Fisher was navigating the move from journalism to academia, which required a PhD qualification. After 28 years at News, a redundancy package would be a circuit breaker from high-pressure work that was wearing on him; it would give time for his passions – gardening and guitar playing – and it would clear their mortgage. The struggle was over his sense of identity. He remembers thinking, 'Who am I? … Well, I'm a journalist. That's what I am. I get stories. I write stories', and in discussions with his wife saying, 'I've just realised I'm actually a father, I'm also a husband, I'm also this, a guitar player.'

The majority who took redundancy packages in 2012 were

journalists with around 20 years' experience.[4] They had worked hard to establish their reputations, but were still up to two decades from retirement. Franklin was 48 when he took redundancy and Jo Chandler was a similar age but an unwillingness to do things a certain way for advancement was not the predicament she faced.

The kind of journalism to which Chandler was committed was falling out of fashion. Trips to Rwanda or Papua New Guinea to report on complex humanitarian and social issues were expensive and funds for them were drying up, as was interest among senior editorial executives, even though Chandler had won a Walkley Award for such work in 2009.[5] She found herself fighting not only for the time to do the stories she deemed important, but avoiding those she thought trivial.

'I would have to enlist some pretty fancy footwork to dodge the daily stuff.' She recalls an idea emanating out of an editorial conference, 'Why don't we send Jo to do colour on the Cup?' 'I can't do this again,' she thought. She hated the Melbourne Cup, she hated writing about drunk socialites and she had done this story many years before. Why should she still be doing it? Chandler hid in the toilets for two hours. 'I took my phone; I worked, but I didn't come out because I was so determined I didn't want to get this brief.'

She didn't think she was being precious although she knew she was alienating some colleagues in the newsroom. She knew the stories she pursued were by no means easy to get or write; she would be up late at night doing background reading and she would be writing about the crippling impact of poverty in developing countries. She was, however, a senior journalist earning good money, and 'my byline isn't pumping out. I am not visible and in a place that is under siege, to not be visible is death'.

Compounding this, she was a member of *The Age* Editorial Independence Committee, a group of staff members formed in 1988 when it looked as if English media tycoon Robert Maxwell was about to buy *The Age*.[6] Where Maxwell epitomised the interfering proprietor, by the 2000s the threat was the dislocation between the newspaper's traditional editorial identity and clickbait, as it became known, pushed out on the online website. Chandler recalls:

> I was a serial pest putting my hand up at those things, saying, 'No, that's not part of *The Age* culture and it's not in the Charter of Editorial Independence.' And I was constantly fighting battles with Online and you get characterised as kind of a dinosaur that you are against Online. 'No, I am not against Online but I am against a culture that is sensationalising.' I thought we were devaluing our masthead. We were just going down the same road that all the others were and how were we any different to Ninemsn? There were a few instances where we ran blatantly sexist, appalling tits-and-arse pictures on the website and local parochial stuff and things that would never get in the paper editions, but they were running online. I was constantly calling them out. And that puts you on the nose ultimately with people.

Chandler's growing apart from her beloved *Age* manifested in plans to write books enabling her to explore issues like climate change in depth.[7] Across the city, in the Melbourne bureau of *The Australian*, George Megalogenis was also juggling daily reporting with book-length journalism. He analysed his own situation as incisively as he had the nation's economy over the past two decades. As a well-paid staff journalist on the national broadsheet, any travel he did was paid for by the company and he had bypass-the-PR-officer access to people in positions of power and influence. Megalogenis further reflected that authors, by contrast, are not only looking for an idea to sustain 80 000–100 000 words, but are always 'fighting for cashflow'.

'Mega', as he is known in media circles, was already toggling between daily and book-length journalism, emulating the model of the newspaper's editor-at-large, Paul Kelly, who has been combining the two since publication of *The Unmaking of Gough* in 1976. This model can work well for both journalist and employer. As Megalogenis commented, editors say, 'Take time off, mate, and when you come back of course we get first dibs on your new stories.' Megalogenis was also enjoying success; his 2012 book, *The Australian Moment*, was reprinted three times and sold around 20 000 copies.[8]

So far, so good for Megalogenis, but the news cycle in the digital economy was speeding up, with newspapers needing to move to 24/7 coverage, and *The Australian*, long shielded within News from cuts, calling for 20 redundancies among its 300-plus editorial staff. Megalogenis did the calculation – four weeks' salary for each of his 27 years' service equals two years' precious research time for his next book – and decided 'that minute' to put his hand up for a package. He knew, too, that if he stayed he would need to be 'taking on somebody else's responsibility'. And he sensed that his next book, about how migration had shaped Australia's history, might be harder to square with his day job.

'I couldn't imagine *The Australian* would be running on the front page some epiphany I've had about the Gold Rush or the Irish orphan girl migration scheme in the 1840s and 1850s.'

Megalogenis sensed the redundancy round of 2012 was a 'tipping point' for the media industry, and he was right. It began with Fairfax, which shed 380 – or 20 per cent – of its editorial staff in June. But News soon followed, and redundancy rounds continued over the next few years before both companies seemed to realise that no more staff could be cut without drastically damaging their product. Both began modest reinvestment in editorial resources, but then in 2020 Covid-19 smacked into the media, and many other industries, setting off more job cuts, and even closures, especially in regional media where the scale of loss was huge, with significant long-term repercussions, including the growing prevalence of news deserts.

There had been redundancy rounds before 2012, though they were smaller and sometimes done for different purposes, as Matthew Moore, a longtime member of the House Committee (the local union branch) at *The Sydney Morning Herald* explains. These rounds, especially at Fairfax, were tied up with the rapid expansion of its newspapers in the 1980s and 1990s as editors created more and more sections, for food, personal finance, education, entertainment, whatever seemed likely to attract more advertising. All required staffing; as long as the industry remained buoyant, editors could go on hiring sprees, poaching journalists from rival organisations, often for inflated prices.

John Alexander was famous for this during his tenure as editor of *The Sydney Morning Herald* in the 1990s, paying people up to $400 000, according to a senior journalist on the paper, Debra Jopson.

'Every now and then there would be a bit of a downturn, and so they would have a redundancy round,' she says.

Moore recalls it got to the point where journalists might take a redundancy, go somewhere elsewhere for a period, come back and then perhaps take another one a few years later.

This happy, if haphazard, state of affairs had changed by 2008 when the impact of the internet on Fairfax's profitability forced its then chief executive, David Kirk, to announce the first major redundancy round. As many as 550 staff, including 100 journalists at *The Sydney Morning Herald* and *The Age*, were let go.[9]

Between then and 2012, more journalists left, but in small numbers and without publicity. In 2011 most of the sub-editing roles at Fairfax's newspapers were cut, or outsourced to the custom publishing house Pagemasters, which soon needed to employ some of the laid-off subs to staunch the increasing numbers of typographical and grammatical errors wounding the newspapers' credibility.[10]

If these staffing cuts began eroding the newspapers, the redundancy round of 2012 punched a hole in them. In the 1990s and early 2000s *The Sydney Morning Herald* was regarded, even by competitors such as Chris Mitchell, editor of *The Australian*, as one of the best newspapers in the country. One of *The Herald*'s senior journalists, Anne Davies, began noticing that even though she and colleagues wanted to keep doing what they'd always done, they couldn't. If a major story broke or if it had been a tumultuous week in politics (alarmingly common during the prime ministerial chaos of the Rudd-Gillard-Rudd-Abbott-Turnbull-Morrison decade), too many experienced people were no longer around.

'We would have had a choice of half a dozen senior writers who could swing into action to provide analysis, and a fly-on-the-wall account of what happened when there was a leadership coup, but suddenly we couldn't do that. It was like having your arm cut off,' she says.

Incisive analysis and inside accounts may have been thinning at *The Sydney Morning Herald*, and at *The Age* for that matter, but at one of Fairfax's recently established standalone news websites basic reporting standards seemed to be slipping.

Aleisha Orr joined the Fairfax-owned news website *WAtoday* in 2012. Three years later, while on maternity leave, she began noticing a trend for *WAtoday* stories to attribute quotes to other media outlets. That could have been a good thing – crediting a rival media outlet instead of passing off a quote as your own work – but Orr grew suspicious that journalists at the website were not doing their own interviews. When she returned from leave, she asked to talk to an editorial executive.

She recalls, 'I just wanted to check, I've come back and things have changed a bit. I keep seeing these stories where they're pretty much ABC stories or someone else's stories and we're just rewriting them, we're not doing the journalism.'

But she remembers being told that when they needed to do things quickly this was the publication's preferred method.

At *The West Australian*, Jane Hammond became increasingly irritated by some of the values that seemed to underpin editorial decisions. By her own admission, Hammond was too much of a 'bleeding heart' for the newspaper, but she arced up one day when an editor said a story she proposed about a study of disadvantaged children needed some 'attractive children' for the picture. 'I'm not asking people if they've got attractive children,' she said. 'Yes, you are,' said the editor. 'No, I'm not.' 'You will do what you're told or I'll give it to someone else,' said the editor, to which Hammond replied, 'Give it to someone else then,' which Hammond says flummoxed him. Because she has children, Hammond says she knows what a bluff looks like. Then the head photographer went over to her desk and said, 'Oh, Hammond, come on you know the score. I know what you mean but it's *The West Australian*. We can't give them fat children. We can't give them ugly children.' I said, 'There's no ugly children. They're all gorgeous.' 'Come on,' said the photographer. 'They'll choke on their Weeties if they see a picture of a fat kid.' Hammond smacked the palm of her hand into her forehead, saying, 'Look, you'll have to get what you get. I'm not going to ask that question ever.'

Rosslyn Beeby says she faced hostility, some of it apparently gender-based, when she objected to the new requirement to file stories for *The Canberra Times*' website within an hour or so of a news event. On one occasion, when the ACT government issued a report on its environmental options, Beeby only had time to read the press release and the executive summary. But, to her dismay, she realised that was all the online news desk wanted. Beeby knew there could well be more news buried deep in the report and, sure enough, there was, but by then the news desk's view was, 'We've done that. We've covered that. Move on.'

Initially she would get angry and resist, saying 'I want this story in the paper because it's important', but after doing this for a while she felt she was turning into a parody of herself. She would go home exhausted. She could see the news media was changing and not in ways she liked. She remembered working on *The Age* in the 1980s where editors and journalists thrived on taking risks. That no longer seemed to hold true, even though the craft of journalism, not to mention the business of media, needed to embrace boldness and innovation if it was to survive.

Beeby recalls, 'I thought there is no future here. Yes, I could probably put my head down and stay here for another five years. But I think I'd be quite mad at the end of it. Because the pressure will be intense.'

It is hard to overstate the demoralising effect on staff of round after round of cuts. Debra Jopson could see editorial budget cuts caused by declining classified advertising revenue constricting her ability to get out of the 'glass box' Fairfax office in Pyrmont and on the road to talk to people for stories. Employment prospects elsewhere in the media were drying up because of the same commercial pressures. 'You could see it all happening, and it's like watching a collision coming at you,' she recalls.

Peter Hanlon, a longtime sports journalist and editor at *The Age*, also 'could sort of see it crumbling and falling apart. So many good people and good co-workers weren't there anymore.' He was still writing stories, sports features mainly, that he felt worked well and which received good feedback from readers. Being in the newsroom would leave him shaking his head, however. 'Things that seemed to be important were so frivolous, and the really big picture stuff, important stuff, wasn't being done.'

The role of editor of *The Age* or *The Sydney Morning Herald* (or any metropolitan daily newspaper editor, for that matter) had once been the pinnacle for many an ambitious journalist, representing significant influence in a city and requiring high-level journalistic skill and tough-minded editorial heft.

In the big redundancy round of 2012, a restructure of senior management roles in Fairfax stripped power from the editor's role, which was soon visible when the incumbents, Paul Ramadge and Amanda Wilson respectively, decided to take redundancies rather than remain in their positions.[11] Hanlon is not alone in observing that the people who then took on these roles were trying hard, but their hands were tied.

> They just didn't have any power. They couldn't change things. They couldn't really maintain the sort of line or culture or what *The Age* stood for. They didn't have the energy, perhaps; they didn't have the resources, certainly. Crazy things were happening. Competitions to decorate each desk at Christmas time became a really big deal, and money would be spent on those things.

Hanlon remembers those in charge of the company would fly down every now and then and 'address the floor, and leave everyone wanting to throw themselves off the top of the building. They'd tell us they really were invested in quality journalism, and things are fantastic, and we're getting rid of another 120 of you ... That wore me down.'[12]

It wore down Tom Arup too; he was a reporter at *The Age* but, where his former colleague, Peter Hanlon, is laconic, Arup thinks in arresting metaphors. He had begun a cadetship at the newspaper only four years before the big redundancy round of 2012, but served on the House Committee and was frustrated by the company's unwillingness to recruit the creativity and commitment of its journalists to help solve the problems besetting Fairfax.

He watched successive redundancy rounds roll out in 2013, 2014 and 2015. As colleague after colleague left the newsroom he'd reset himself to the new reality. Brief periods of normality would be punctured by the next set of gloomy financial results, after which a new round of redundancies would be announced. He likened it to those times 'when you're feeling sick and you vomit: the second you vomit you feel really great. Your body releases all these endorphins, the toxins are out of your body, and you get half an hour of feeling

"I'm back", "I'm all right". And then you start feeling sick again. Those years were like that.' Arup's metaphor is apt even if it might fall foul of *The West Australian* photographer's desire to avoid making readers choke on their Weeties.

The sheer difficulty of making the decision to leave a newsroom is underscored by the experience of Tim Colebatch, who had worked for *The Age* his entire adult life – when Fairfax offered redundancies in 2012 he stood to leave with more than three years' salary. He equivocated, though, persuaded by colleagues that his departure would be a real loss for *The Age*. It would have been; as economics editor, Colebatch was long identified with the newspaper's coverage of the economy, but three years' salary and post-*Age* plans only to work on his garden? Colebatch decided to withdraw his application, which had been accepted. His colleague, economics correspondent Peter Martin, was 'really peeved' as he had been promised the economics editorship once Colebatch left, which made the next 15 months 'difficult' in the newspaper's Canberra bureau.

As Colebatch neared the then statutory retirement age of 65 and as yet another round of redundancies was offered, he decided he had to apply, but this time he was rejected. He told them, 'I don't really think you've got an option, because I don't know of anybody who has been rejected for redundancy at the age of 64.' He was right, and he left at the end of 2013 grateful for the generosity of Fairfax's redundancy provisions, but feeling comfortable with the amount as he hadn't applied for a pay rise since the early 1990s.

What the stories in this chapter reveal is that the question of whether a journalist opted to take a redundancy or stay with their employer depended on what was happening with their media company, with their individual outlet and, equally importantly, in their own life, both in the newsroom and at home.

Some remained committed to journalism and would have stayed for the rest of their career. Others were beginning to despair at where journalism seemed to be heading, while others still had been frustrated for some time, and the worsening financial state of the media magnified that. A handful who were in a strong position within their organisation could afford to weigh their options pragmatically. But really, many were confused or uncertain or flat out unknowing about what exactly was happening to an industry that had been so strong for so long. They began casting about for directions, if not life boats.

CHAPTER 13

Pickets and payouts: Unions in the newsroom

Penny O'Donnell
Brad Buller
Matthew Ricketson

Alysson Watson recalls she 'was at the barricades at every opportunity'. After starting her journalism career in the mid-1980s as a cadet for the *Newcastle Herald* she joined the Australian Journalists' Association (AJA). At first, she found the daily routine of the newsroom staid, with 'quite earnest people' bashing away on keyboards. She soon learnt it was different late at night, when the printing press started up. 'You could certainly feel it once it started', she remembers, feeling the building moving, hearing it, smelling it. Intrigued, Watson became acquainted with the 'fantastic, militant bastards' of the Printing and Kindred Industries Union who worked downstairs.

She remembers them as 'old school' unionists, workers who 'stood together' on pickets and knew how to 'to bung one on', a reference to bringing about strike action. For Watson, the printers offered 'a good example' of unionism. She subsequently became a member of the *Newcastle Herald*'s House Committee, and a workplace activist. In those days, before the merger that in 1992 formed the Media, Entertainment and Arts Alliance (MEAA) as a super-union for creative professionals, the AJA covered news reporters, subs, photographers and artists.[1] The House Committee's role was to defend their working conditions and interests on site. Watson saw it as serious work, and became involved in industrial action for some years.

Many journalists were less involved or less interested in their union than Watson, whether out of apathy or due to their employers' hostility to unions, but the prospect of large-scale redundancies focused their attention. They learnt, and perhaps began to appreciate, the generosity of the redundancy provisions the union had negotiated for the two biggest media companies, News Corporation Australia and Fairfax Media, back in the late 1980s.

The union's then federal secretary, Chris Warren, recalls before then the industry had far less need for redundancy rounds, and the standard payout was 12 to 16 weeks' pay.[2] The Hawke Labor government's 1987 media ownership laws substantially concentrated media ownership, and forced the closure of two metropolitan dailies and one weekly newspaper.[3] During this the union negotiated for the printing industry's redundancy provisions to apply to journalists. These were two weeks' severance pay plus four weeks' pay for every year of service, uncapped. This meant if you had worked for one media company for your entire career, you stood to walk away with more than three years' salary.

In the early 1990s, News Corporation capped the payouts at two years of salary, but as Warren's successor, Paul Murphy, acknowledges, compared to other industries the redundancy provisions at News and especially Fairfax Media were at 'the higher end of the spectrum'.[4] Warren put it more plainly; at his farewell speech in 2015 he said the redundancy conditions were one of his proudest achievements after 28 years serving the union.

In 2012, when mass redundancies were announced by Fairfax Media, Watson says the House Committee moved quickly to try and save jobs.

'We were very vocal, very anti, very gung ho, in that we need to stop this. We need to try at the eleventh hour to stop this, and we will do that.'

By 2015, when the next mass redundancy round started, her thinking had changed. She says everybody's thinking had changed. The *Newcastle Herald* House Committee's sole aim was to 'make sure that people who lost their jobs were well treated, and people who stayed were well treated'. Yet, as Watson recalls, people getting tapped on the shoulder 'were told not to talk', a directive that only fuelled uncertainty and speculation, with people taking bets on who was going. Management–staff relations quickly soured to the point where 'our general manager bravely stood up a couple of times, in front of everybody, but he soon saw that that was an arse-kicking to nowhere'.

Meanwhile, the union kept negotiating until it convinced management to be flexible in deciding who would be forced out. As Watson sees it, flexibility meant 'horse trading' around people's futures: 'Here we've got someone who's not a sub-editor who wants to go. But we want to let them go. Can we save a sub-editor? Can we …?' It sounds awkward, even callous, but Watson says she would 'never criticise the union for what it did'. Winning 'a bit of wiggle room' around redundancies saved some people's jobs. Under the circumstances, that was better than nothing.

For many Australian journalists, joining the Alliance (MEAA) has been a matter of principle. They have loyally paid membership dues because they believe the union supports and protects journalists and journalism. And, over the years, their allegiance has been rewarded, not simply because of the generous redundancy provisions, but because unionism has delivered them other tangible gains: from establishing equities around pay, conditions, leave and entitlements, to collective pushback against proprietorial interference in content and other attempts to devalue journalistic skills.

What is more, even the 'free-riders' who never joined up benefited from the redundancy arrangements. From mid-2012, media employers were bent on large-scale job shedding, but enterprise agreements meant they had to at least offer voluntary redundancies before involuntary dismissals.

Some journalists became frustrated, even disillusioned, that the union had no power to save jobs or improve working conditions for those left behind in digital newsrooms; many others have remained grateful to the MEAA for easing the trauma and uncertainty associated with redundancy.[5]

Gillian Lord anticipated major job cuts at *The Canberra Times* after Fairfax Media news executives from Sydney paid a visit in mid-2012. The 'men in suits' talked up journalism's 'glorious future', using jargon and platitudes that left staff 'very, very worried' about their prospects.

'*Canberra Times* journalists were not paid a lot of money,' Lord says. 'There were a lot of people with young kids, or kids that were still at school, and many of them on a single income.'

For Lord, the messaging about voluntary redundancies had the feel of company 'propaganda', and assurances that 'it's all voluntary, nobody's going to be pushed' rang hollow. She believes management's handling of the process was 'quite unforgiveable' for its lack of communication with staff. She also recalls, with gratitude, that the union stepped into the breach to ensure newsroom staff got their redundancy entitlements.

'The union was fantastic,' she says. 'You could say, "I'm thinking of leaving", and they would calculate your pay-out.'

For TV reporter Antoinette Lattouf, the 2012 voluntary redundancy process at Network Ten was far more casual. She does not recall management consulting staff on workplace change, but says 'everybody kind of knew' about the job cuts before they were announced.

'We're a room of communicators and big mouths. It's bound to get out,' she says. Lattouf had a new job lined up at SBS and volunteered to leave without seeking union assistance.

We were quite a contingent of young journos, and I don't believe the union has much penetration amongst Gen Y,

> even Gen X ... I recall the union came one day and, even if you weren't a member, you could go in and have a quick chat. But the union wasn't a huge part of the conversation.

Rocco Fazzari had worked at *The Sydney Morning Herald* for 28 years as an illustrator, when his employment was suddenly terminated in May 2016. A total of 30 editorial staff were dismissed on the same day. Fazzari felt shocked and humiliated.

True to his craft, he drew an illustration of a tree being felled, and posted it on Facebook, along with the message, 'Feel very much like that tree. I'm not in a good space. Any support grateful.'[6]

By then, MEAA members at Fairfax Media were already holding stopwork meetings to express no confidence in the company's management. Fazzari appreciated union support.

'My father told me two things when I first started working: "Get super and join the union." So, I've always followed those rules and they've been very good things to stick to.' Yet, that didn't stop him from disagreeing with the union's efforts to save his job.

> I didn't want to go back ... I just couldn't do it. I didn't want my job 'saved'. I wanted my career. And that's a totally different thing. All my dedication, all my loyalty, that mattered for nothing, a big nothing. I got my full entitlements, but it's only money. I know money is important, but I never got a watch. They used to give out watches to people, or even a certificate ... it was just nothing, just bad.

Fazzari wanted practical advice on what to do next. He attended an MEAA workshop for people seeking re-employment. There he heard former journos tell their stories about making the transition from fulltime employment to freelancing. 'That was really good,' he says. 'I talked to people there and I felt pretty confident.' Fazzari saw a way to re-start his working life, and to put the past behind him.

> I no longer respected management, their strategies were confusing … It was a relief not to be managed by people you had no respect for. I guess it must be like being a soldier and thinking 'If my captain says charge over the trenches and go for it, I wouldn't do it. I just wouldn't do it'. It was a relief.

Like Fazzari, Ross Brundrett was an active union member and had 'a strong belief in unionism'. When he was young his father had been 'shafted in his job because the union was weak', which led to him joining the *Herald Sun* House Committee in the 1990s. His enthusiasm waned over the years, though, and he no longer maintains his union links.

Brundrett became 'disillusioned with the union a while ago', feeling 'like they were powerless to change the things that were bad … their usefulness has been dissipated'. In Brundrett's view, unionism today has lost its effectiveness:

> Once they had less people in the workforce … taking an active role, then they ceased to become able to influence things in any real way. It became more of a tokenism rather than a real influence. It's great to be waving a flag and be heroic, but if they cease to have a real effect on the result then it – you're really just – it's tokenism, that's all it is. It doesn't have a real role to play.

The *Herald Sun*'s Wendy Hargreaves was also 'a big believer in the union' for many years. Like Brundrett, though, she says they have become 'disabled' and lacked 'firepower' to fight News Limited's plan to put staff on individual contracts rather than the award. 'It was sad to see', Hargreaves recalls, but there was 'a culture of fear' at the company that 'made you feel very lucky to have that job'. She says the staff were forced to play by the company's rules.

'You'd walk out and stomp around and try and get the company's attention with a walkout ... that just didn't work because the papers still came out ... Strikes were completely pointless,' she says.

Similarly, Stephen Corby, who was chief sub-editor of Features at *The Daily Telegraph* in the late 1990s, remembers the industrial culture at News Limited was 'so broken'. 'Being at News Limited, it kind of broke me from the union thing', he recalls. In contrast, during his cadetship at *The Canberra Times*, Corby was on the paper's House Committee and right from the start was deeply involved in negotiating for cadets. 'I saw at Fairfax there was a strong house and it worked there,' he says.

Some of the managers at News Corp at that stage had been schooled in union busting while working at one of Rupert Murdoch's UK newspapers in the mid-1980s. Hugh Jones was among several Australians who broke picket lines at the Murdoch-owned Wapping plant during the newspaper printing union's historic 54-week strike.[7] The plant was surrounded by a 'big fence with barbed wire on the top and spikes'. Each day he was ferried in and out of the site in 'a bus with grilles over all of the windows'. He remembers the 'masses of people' trying to block the trucks loaded with newspapers each evening and how 'the police would set up with their horses and, as the trucks would come out of the print site, the horses would charge at the pickets with a dirty great semi-trailer behind them, so they would be knocking people over to clear a path for these trucks to come steaming through'.

The hostility to unions became so pervasive at News Corp that Matthew Moore could not bring himself to accept the job he had been offered at *The Australian* in the 1980s.

'I remember going in there to be interviewed and just having this acute sense of how different the culture was,' Moore recalls. 'At Fairfax, we've fought these battles, stood out on the streets handing out leaflets, not actually that much fun to do, sacrificing a day's wages for what we thought were good principles about the editorial integrity of the papers.' 'Those things,' says Moore, 'News Limited journalists would never be involved in.'

Many rank-and-file MEAA members have stepped into activist roles in the workplace or the union, as Alysson Watson did, and they have seen the tougher side of employer–worker relations. Samela Harris worked at *The Advertiser* in Adelaide for 27 years and is on the MEAA's national media section executive, and convenor of Women in Media in South Australia.

> I have always been in the union … and that's never been something that furthers you in that corporate world. In fact, it's the opposite. Because of the nature of the beast, a union is quite important to protect and advance people who work for these large, fairly ruthless corporations. I think it's very good for the small people to stand together, to have some power. It's just something that's natural to me.

Harris was always passionate about new technologies, and so had good reason to believe she would survive *The Advertiser*'s switch to multiplatform news production in 2010. She knew the union was monitoring changes in the workplace. 'Whatever the situation is', she says, the union 'stands up'. In this case, where staff were expected to rapidly diversify into digital journalism, the union was 'trying to ensure that the pay was commensurate'.

Harris took most of the employer-paid training courses on offer, worked hard, and mastered 'everything', from the latest content management system to blogging, even becoming the paper's inaugural online editor. But it didn't save her job, which was made redundant in 2012, leaving her without 'a place' in journalism.

'If you're not a journalist working for somebody, then you're just somebody writing a diary, or a blog, or entertaining yourself with your skills,' she says. 'It's a craft. It's a discipline. We're workers.'

Harris believes the union has been 'significantly de-powered' in recent years, but remains resilient.

'It's not going to give up,' she says. 'Because it's people of solidarity who want to ensure that everything does not die.'

At the ABC, Tracee Hutchison was disappointed by the MEAA, although she says the Melbourne branch's Louise Connor was 'fantastic'. She's also critical of the Community & Public Sector Union (CPSU), which represented the bulk of the ABC's staff. She says one official thought the union could 'take the government on' and stop them from shutting down the Australia Network. Hutchison remembers asking him, 'What planet are you on? ... How about you just go and knock on [the ABC's then managing director] Mark Scott's door. Forget about Julie Bishop's door, and DFAT [Department of Foreign Affairs and Trade], because we know what they think.'

She says the CPSU 'got the campaign wrong' and had a 'flawed strategy' because it had taken on the wrong people. 'They needed to take on the ABC and they didn't.'

Tom Hyland's career in journalism began at *The North West Star* in Mount Isa in 1979. The newsroom got a computer editing system around that time. Hyland remembers the introduction of this new technology, because journalists working on metropolitan dailies around the country went out on strike in protest.

In 1980, 2000 members of the AJA formed pickets and stopped work for five weeks, demanding compensation for the added work of using visual display terminals, and, eventually, they won a modest allowance.[8] Hyland became a union activist too after landing his second job, at AAP in Sydney.

'My view is that you should be able to campaign for better working conditions,' he says, 'and that is not incompatible with your obligations as an employee or your obligations as a journalist.'

He soon found management saw things very differently. 'I naïvely thought that my employer would simply judge me on the quality of my work, rather than my industrial activity,' he says. 'In fact, I was being judged on my attitude towards the hierarchy. So I left.'

Decades later, at *The Age* in Melbourne, Hyland was equally disgusted by management handling of staff job cuts in 2012.

'I should've seen that coming,' he says. 'I concede there was a commercial imperative to take drastic action. That's why I say there should have been a negotiation with some of the older journalists. Maybe you would work part-time, who knows? But there was no consideration of any sort.'

Tom Arup was a member of *The Age* House Committee during the 2012 redundancy round, and knows exactly how the union tried to partner with management in handling 'the tidal wave of job cuts'. He says, 'We tried to get management to accept a model of engagement with journalists on the floor'. It was a European model in which a small panel of journalists met regularly with senior Fairfax Media management to work through issues that arose from declining revenue and to try and avoid job cuts. According to Arup, the panel sometimes argued, 'We don't need to cut these people if we save money here'. However, the attempt failed, due to what Arup calls 'arrogant' management in the company's Sydney headquarters.

> My issue with them … is they had no editorial brand direction for these great mastheads. They just shut their eyes, cut, and hoped for the best. They had these great mastheads, with these great identities that they needed to protect, and they let the editorial part of that disappear by incentivising the wrong things. That has proven to be a disastrous management decision, because it's eroded the best thing they had, which was their brands. You look at *BuzzFeed*, you look at *The Guardian*, they know what they are. And same with the conservative leading media too. The guys I worked for didn't work that out.

Alysson Watson has mulled over the questions of why workplace change and large-scale job cuts were often poorly managed, and what could have been done better. While she admits managers may have 'had their hands tied', the clear-eyed conclusion she has reached is this: 'We all could have been cared for much better than we were'. Watson's role as Features editor of the *Newcastle Herald* was eliminated in the 2015 redundancy round, leaving her with two options: to redeploy or take voluntary redundancy. After 30 years in the one newsroom, she took the redundancy package and left the *Herald*. Militant to the end, she has no trouble calling out the bad guys when it comes to job loss in journalism.

'We love to hate our CEOs in Fairfax,' she says. 'It's just a thing, and that's fair enough, because they're generally cutting things.'

Journalists who moved into management positions have very different stories to tell. Cate Swannell landed an unexpected pay hike when she was appointed as deputy features editor, and later, in 2009, online editor for the digital edition of the *Gold Coast Bulletin*. In those days, promotion to management positions at the *Bulletin* entailed signing an individual contract, and losing union coverage.

'The bottom line was you got more money, immediately,' Swannell says. 'I got a 15-grand boost to my annual income just by moving onto contract.'

All the same, it was a big decision for a longtime union member, and someone who calls herself 'a leftist-pinko-commo-lezzo-weirdo'. The most inexplicable part of the story is editor Bob Gordon's willingness to offer 'inflated' wage increases to his veteran staff.

'There were a lot of people in the newsroom at that time around my age,' Swannell says, 'and I think Bob made a concerted effort to hang onto us, to keep all that experience in one spot.'

Yet, by mid-2012, Swannell had lost her well-paid contract job in a wave of mass redundancies across News Corporation's mastheads. She found it hard 'to be out on the market again', but says she has no regrets: 'It was good at the time!' In 2014, she renewed her MEAA membership.

Dean Mellor was editor of Bauer's *Australasian Dirt Bike* magazine in 2013 when the company announced it was moving all the motoring titles from Sydney to Melbourne. He did not want to go. Yet, as an editor, he had no right to the award redundancy entitlements. The fact that he still paid union dues meant nothing. He felt 'screwed', until some senior editors at Bauer managed to persuade the company to offer payouts equivalent to the MEAA award. Mellor says he would have got 'a hell of a lot less money' without the editors' intervention. Although Mellor ended up benefiting from the union's negotiations for redundancy entitlements, he still feels the union was 'pretty much useless' and didn't offer him any advice. 'There was nothing they could do,' Mellor recalls.

Stephen Corby had similar experiences at the Bauer Media-owned *Top Gear Australia*. 'The union was particularly hopeless,' he says. On the day after the company announced a round of redundancies, it met with staff and the union. As Corby recalls, 'Basically they stood at the front of the room and said, "We don't have any answers. We didn't see this coming; we don't know what to do, we'll get back to you." And everyone left that meeting just feeling more flat, I think, and more let down than they were before.'

Di Thomas has been a union member for over 30 years. Before her promotion to editor of *The Border Mail* in October 2012, she had been a union activist on the newspaper's House Committee, in various roles. Most journalists resign from the union when appointed as editor. It is a management position that puts them on the other side of the fence in workplace negotiations. Yet, Thomas kept her membership going because she saw value in the MEAA as a professional organisation, and for its continuing work with regional media outlets. Her decision proved awkward in 2015, when 39 of the 64 staff in *The Mail's* editorial department faced job cuts. Thomas was critical of the union's reaction. 'Their response is to try and intervene when redundancies are mooted,' she says, 'rather than "How do we help people move on?"' She found the twin roles of editor and union member difficult to balance. What perhaps hurt more was the loss of camaraderie with union staff. For years she had been 'the go-to person' when they needed entry to the building, but now no one 'asked how I was!'

When Louise Graham agreed to take on a corporate services role at *The Age*, she was relocated from the editorial department on the third floor to the fifth floor of the newspaper's old headquarters in Spencer Street. Up there, she saw 'a totally new side of the business'. She describes it as being 'all about infrastructure' and other things that journalists 'frankly don't want to know about'.

To the delight of her new manager, Graham soon realised that she was able to find new ways of saving money so that 'the journalism side' was left alone. 'So I'd look at stationery, for instance,' she says, 'and then I did a new deal with new stationery people that saved us 200 grand. That was a couple of jobs downstairs. He was really into that.'

Graham spent two years in this 'cost-focused' role before returning to editorial operations. In that time, she had a lot of conversations with people about upcoming redundancies. 'I hated that,' she said. 'It takes a toll. They're your friends.'

Journalism is high-pressure work, but for some the inevitable stress that comes with being a journalist is compounded by the harmful, manipulative or malicious actions of colleagues or employers. There is bullying, mistreatment, and even senseless humiliation. Union intervention is often crucial in stopping the sexual harassment of female staff, but less effective in changing everyday sexist behaviour in blokey workplaces.

Liz Wells's first job at the weekly rural newspaper *The Land*, combined news reporting with press photography. She recalls getting a rate of $3 or $5 for each of her photos published in *The Land* and, given the small amounts, she would tally up and submit a claim for payment every three months or so. The claims were usually in the amount of $300–400.

However, at one stage, the general manager refused to pay the claim, telling Wells it should have been lodged within eight weeks. Puzzled, Wells rang the AJA and was told that she had 'a long amount of time, like 12 months, or 18 months' and therefore, according to the award, had to be paid. She shared the union's advice with her manager, and recalls him saying, 'Oh, alright then, I'll pay it.' Wells says, 'That was worth all the fees I paid to the union!' Looking back, Wells remembers other 'bad stories' of unpaid work experience and vague promises of work made to interns who spent their time getting the coffees. She says, 'exploitation of people happened a bit in journalism' and it was 'pretty rotten'.

When veteran Adelaide journalist Samela Harris reflects on her career, she concludes 'I was always paid the pittance.' She believes being a single mother affected her pay rate.

> Doesn't matter how nice they are. If you come in as a single mum and the jobs are finite, they've got you. They've absolutely got you. And up to the end of my days, I was paid extremely inadequately. Young journalists would get paid far more than I was in my last senior years because they're more flexible.

As leader of the Women in Media (WiM) network in South Australia, Harris now fights for gender equality in newsrooms. WiM started as a union wage parity initiative, but is now an independent national body dedicated to improving the working lives and career opportunities of all women in media. Harris describes the network as 'the most shining offshoot of the old media', saying 'out of the negative comes the positive'.

A recurring theme in these journalists' reflections is the weakened state of both journalism and unionism. They worry that job cuts and declining union membership have diminished collective bargaining power, giving employers unbridled control over workplace change to the detriment of journalists' editorial independence and journalism standards.

David Marr has been a union member since the start of his career when, to him, it was an effective organisation with good awards that ensured reasonable prosperity. The industry's business model has been 'shattered' by the internet, which in turn has diminished the union's power. 'I don't think it can be as remotely effective as it once was. The world has just changed.'

Some see this loss of union effectiveness as a recent development, directly linked to the introduction of digital-first publishing from 2012. For example, House Committee members who tried to give voice to journalists' collective interests in the move online saw their managers had less and less interest in the union's views. They also saw concerns for the quality of journalism dissipate as digital business models faltered. In the words of one journalist, 'There was no hand on those wheels'.

Others take a longer, often more jaundiced, view. They look back to 1992, when the AJA merged with other unions to form the MEAA to represent all creative professionals. And, even now, decades on, they lament the union's expanded coverage across the media industries, blaming it for diluting unionism in journalism.

What emerges from journalists' stories of the union's role in their working lives is, first, straight-up gratitude for the union's muscle in negotiating generous redundancy packages. There's also some appreciation that the union was one of the few, and certainly one of the earliest, public voices warning about the looming threats to journalism.[9] The union worked out quicker than most that as media outlets were struggling to create new business models, the journalism they published and the journalists who produced it were of vanishing importance to the companies. Less well understood was that the union itself had to cope with competing demands. At the time that it was most needed by reporters facing retrenchment, it also faced the existential threat of the loss of those members, meaning it had to focus on retaining and even recruiting people as the industry downsized rapidly.

CHAPTER 14

Mate, this gives me absolutely no pleasure, but ...

Andrew Dodd
Timothy Marjoribanks

Sydney Morning Herald illustrator Rocco Fazzari remembers getting to work early on the day he was retrenched, because it was the newspaper's staff flu shot day. He put his bag down at his desk and bumped into a young graphic designer who, like him, came from Adelaide. The young man was stressed because he thought he was going to lose his job, so Fazzari reassured him, 'I think you're alright. I think you're stressing over nothing. Don't worry about it, you'll be fine.' In truth, Fazzari didn't know, but he felt he had to cheer him up. When Fazzari got back to his desk after his flu shot, his phone was ringing.

> I picked it up and it was the editor-in-chief and he said, 'We need to speak to you. Can you come to the office and can you bring your union rep with you?' And I thought, 'This is unusual' and I said, 'Well have you got bad news for me?' He said, 'Yes, I'm afraid so.'

The careers of a great many journalists have ended with phone calls like this one, followed by difficult meetings in which they're told their position no longer exists. This chapter is about the process of retrenching journalists. It captures the sharp end of the redundancy process, when media companies make decisions about who goes and who stays, and how they then break the news, before pointing people towards the exit. It's also about those who leave; how they react, and the effect the process has on them personally. Many agree it's a confronting and emotional time, even when it is entered into voluntarily. The process can be calm and considered, even compassionate. But sometimes it's cold and clinical, and occasionally cruel. Either way, it's life-defining, deeply personal, and many of its moments become seared into the memories of those who go through it.[1]

Fazzari was asked to go down to the third floor of the *Herald*, which by May 2016 had been emptied out by previous rounds of redundancies. In the corner, in a big room, behind a partition, the editor-in-chief and his direct manager were waiting for him. 'I walked in with my union rep,' says Fazzari, 'and one of them started saying, "Look you know we really appreciate what you're doing, but you are no longer part of our future plan. You don't do what we consider to be part of our thrust into the digital future. So, you know, I'm afraid to tell you that you're going to have to go."' Fazzari recalls being speechless. 'I didn't say anything. I didn't trust myself.' The editor continued, 'It doesn't mean we didn't appreciate what you've done, we just, you're no longer required.' Fazzari looked at the union rep sitting next to him and noticed 'her jaw just dropped'. He remembers feeling sorry for her, before correcting himself, 'What am I doing?, I'm supposed to be feeling sorry for myself.' He looked back at the editor, who was explaining that he was giving him two weeks' notice, but added, 'You're quite welcome to go now.' Fazzari says, 'I took this as a hint, "Please go."'

Fazzari went back to his desk, where he had wanted to work that day on an unfinished drawing for the paper. 'I don't think it would have been good to stick around. I couldn't have coped with it,' he says. He noticed that other staff members in his area 'just got up and walked away'. He wondered how they knew so quickly and concluded they just didn't know how to respond. 'I didn't say anything to them,' he says. 'I finished my drawing and walked out. And yeah, it was a very strange feeling after 28 years.'

Fazzari had been working in an environment where retrenchments had become an ever-present threat. Staff at Fairfax, and many other media companies, had come to expect downsizing,[2] although that didn't always mean people were expecting it to affect them personally. Many, including Fazzari, felt they were doing what the company wanted and reskilling in ways that would be of benefit in the digital environment. Against this, there were warnings that, no matter what journalists thought and how they performed, the crisis facing the media was beyond anyone's control.[3] Sometimes these warnings came in mass meetings, like the one organised at the magazine publishing business Bauer Media.

Dean Mellor was editing *Australasian Dirt Bike* when the staff were called to a meeting in the basement of the Civic Tower in downtown Sydney to be told all Bauer Media's motoring titles were moving to Melbourne.[4] The publisher explained the Melbourne move 'wasn't a done deal yet', but Mellor says the staff didn't buy it. 'You could tell it was [already decided], otherwise they wouldn't have told us.' Mellor remembers everyone was 'floored' by the announcement. 'We're talking 50 or more people sitting in this room just going, "You're joking? Where's that leave us, what do we do?" There'd been no decisions or no mention of redundancies or payouts or anything like that, and everyone just pretty much freaked out.'

On other occasions, a quick conversation had a similarly unsettling effect, as Tom Hyland discovered during a reorganisation at Fairfax. The company was designing a new newsroom to integrate the print and digital operations in Melbourne, Sydney and Canberra. Staff had been assigned to committees and working groups, but Hyland was convinced it was 'a rubber stamping process' because a model for change had already been created. One day his boss turned up at Hyland's desk and said, 'You know that under the new newsroom model the job that you do for *The Sunday Age* as international editor, you will no longer do that. This job will no longer exist and you will go into a pool of senior writers to be assigned as to be decided.' Hyland replied, 'Yeah, I understand that.' The boss then said, 'Good, because it was my duty to tell you that.' Hyland estimates the conversation took about 35 seconds. 'That was how I was officially informed that what I'd been doing for the past six years didn't exist anymore. And I realised that she also was under instructions – as part of the consultation process – to tell each member of her staff what this new model meant for them.'

Inevitably the warnings turned to reality as job cuts were announced. Mostly they came in the form of voluntary redundancies, but if managers wanted someone gone or if they failed to reach their targets, the cuts would be forced. That's what happened to the highly decorated *Age* cartoonist John Spooner when Fairfax needed to axe over 80 jobs across the country. The union had negotiated for a few to be saved, meaning *The Age* had to lose 20 positions. As Spooner recalls, the newsroom was already pretty thin by that stage. 'Someone gets a cold and there's a big problem, and so, taking 20 out was huge.'

He was summoned to a meeting and was also encouraged to 'bring a friend'. Spooner asked the House Committee representative, Gina McColl, to accompany him. The editor-in-chief and an HR staff person were waiting, and the head of cartooning and design joined them by phone from Sydney.

Spooner says 'every section was being asked to make a cut, probably with a target of dollars'. He believes his managers made an assessment of the other celebrated cartoonists in Melbourne before targeting him. 'They would have looked at [Michael] Leunig and said, "No, keep him." [Ron] Tandberg, "No, can't get rid of him.

Spooner's next.'" He assumes it was also because he was on a good salary and getting rid of him would 'clear up a lot of problems'.

But Spooner wanted to hear the reasons for his sacking. 'Well, why am I being made redundant?' he asked. He remembers the voice on the phone saying, 'Not enough skills in the digital area, social media, animation, things like that, where we're going forward.' Spooner needed clarification. 'You're not saying I'm not skilled in what I do?' Then the editor said, 'Look John, it's just about the money.' Spooner turned to the union rep and said 'Gina, take that down. I want this on record that I'm not being sacked because of my skill, it's because they needed the money more than they needed my work.' Having established that point, Spooner says he walked out.

Over at *The Herald* and *Weekly Times* building in Melbourne's Southbank, Hugh Jones was asked to come to the office of the editorial manager, Alan Armsden, who was sitting behind the desk and, in Jones's words, 'looking a bit green'. Next to him was a junior person from the human resources department, who Jones says was 'looking yellow'. He sat down and remembers Armsden saying to him: 'Mate, this gives me absolutely no pleasure, but your position's been declared redundant.' This didn't surprise Jones because his job of reorganising the news operations and creating a central subs hub was mostly finished. Then Armsden said something that Jones thinks might have been rehearsed: 'We've had a look around the building. There are no vacancies that meet your skills. Therefore, you're being paid out.' Jones says while the news didn't 'come as a bombshell', it was nevertheless 'still a shock'. This happened on a Thursday and Armsden explained that the company wanted to 'finish him up' the following night, but he had 'argued with them' that, because Jones had been there for 20-plus years and was 'a real company man' and had held 'senior management roles', it would be wrong to send him out the door so quickly. 'So, if it's okay, you finish up next Friday,' he said.

Jones needed to process what he was hearing. He remembers part of his brain was saying, 'Well, here's an opportunity to walk out with a cheque in your pocket and do all those things that you wish you wanted to do and couldn't because you were working', while another part of his brain was contemplating 'leaving a company that I knew had great problems, but nevertheless had a great loyalty to and felt that I had contributed to and felt I was part of the place'.

And while this was going on, the conversation turned to money, demonstrating that sometimes people facing redundancy need to defend their rights. According to Jones, Armsden told him, 'You get all your entitlements and a year's salary.' Jones replied, 'I think I'm entitled to more than that, Alan. I'm pretty certain I've got an agreement that was four weeks' pay for every year of service, and I've been here for 23 years. Therefore, I'm entitled to a hell of a lot more than a year's salary.' They agreed to check. Although the HR person initially said she couldn't find any evidence to support his case, Jones had a copy of his agreement, which had been organised by former editor-in-chief Steve Harris and included a number of clauses that were on the union award, including the more generous redundancy terms.

It was resolved when the head of HR, Ugo Gulia, returned to work the following Monday and rang Jones. According to Jones, he said, 'Mate, mate, I don't know what's going on, this has come totally out of the blue. I knew nothing about it. You're absolutely right. Leave it with me. I'll make certain it's right and I'll get you the right figure.' Jones says 'it took about three or four days to sort out. The HR manager later told him 'he'd gone into meetings with HWT management, who had been unaware that I had been on this particular agreement.'

Isabella Lettini knew that photographers were not immune from the cuts sweeping across News Limited. But she didn't think she would be targeted. Everyone told her she'd be safe. Even her fellow photographers said, 'Oh, no, you won't lose your job, you're good.' So she was feeling secure when she was called to a meeting with her boss. As Lettini says, 'All the oldies were going because they thought they're going to retire anyhow. And I thought, well, it seems to be a pattern, all the oldies are going, I'll be staying.' She continues, 'And then, this big brick fell on my head ... and the boss goes, "Um, I'm sorry, but you're being made redundant."'

Like Spooner, Lettini needed to know why, but never felt she got a satisfactory answer. She remembers her boss saying, 'Well, we can't tell you, you know, you're just, unfortunately, one of the ones.' He referred to a questionnaire that she and her colleagues had been asked to fill in. He told her 'You scored under other photographers'. Lettini asked, 'Can you show me where I went wrong?' But he refused. 'And that's what I felt cheated about,' she says. 'I fought to have a look at where I went wrong, and they wouldn't tell me.' Her mind was racing. What could the real reason be? 'And that's when I thought, well, the year before, I had breast cancer ... that's the only thing that I could think of.' She reflects:

> I was enthusiastic about my work. I loved my job; they knew I loved my job. And, as I said, even my fellow photographers were shocked. They were like, 'You? Why are they getting rid of you?' Like, they just couldn't believe it. It was just a massive shock ... It was a stab to my heart.

At the ABC, the process of deciding who should go became especially competitive, because it pitted colleagues against each other for jobs that had not been axed. Uncertainty had descended on the corporation following the 2014 federal Budget, when the Abbott Coalition government slashed its triennial funding, and in an instant created the same sort of crisis for the national broadcaster that was crushing commercial media companies.

While almost no department was safe, attention quickly turned to the international divisions, where substantial cuts could be made without losing a lot of domestic programming. Campbell Cooney had a sense of foreboding when the head of news, Kate Torney, called a meeting in the newsroom. The management team explained which programs would stay. The only radio program to survive would be *Pacific Beat*, along with the TV flagship program *The World*. Radio news bulletins would stay, but only on weekdays and at reduced hours. Radio programs *Connect Asia* and *Asia Pacific* would be axed.[5] All correspondent positions would go, as would the Canberra bureaus. The staff were told there would be redundancies, but they were also told how they could reapply for their own positions. 'It was a Darwinian experiment,' says Cooney, 'in which the people most aligned with the ABC's future goals would be selected. And it became known as the Hunger Games.'[6]

Under this model, if there were 40 people looking for jobs and only 20 positions, the ABC would assess whether the candidates had 'the skills that they require for the future ongoing needs of the ABC'. If someone did, they might be offered a job. If not, they were given redundancy. At that stage Cooney said, 'Yes. I'd like to be considered for redeployment' and was told to wait for two or three weeks for an answer. In the meantime, he says he was 'just sitting around'.

> We'd just basically given up, really. I mean you know the program you were working on. We were filling stuff. I was almost prepared to put stuff in [from] the *Western Australian Country Hour* at one time just to fill a hole. You really didn't care.

Cooney was given more information about the position for which he was being considered. When he discovered it entailed more production than reporting, he said, 'I don't think I'd really seriously want to be considered for it.' He told his manager, 'If that is what redeployment is, then I don't know if I want redeployment.'

Financial columnist Michael West says a form of Hunger Games was also playing out at *The Sydney Morning Herald*,[7] but it wasn't one based on skills. He had been called by a manager who sacked him over the phone. Two days later the editor-in-chief rang him and, according to West, 'gave me some sort of prepared thing out of the human resources handbook about no longer, you know sort of core activities going forward or whatever'. West says it's 'a morbid culture when you've got people that are paid to sack their own staff. Who are they going to sack? Well, they're not going to sack their mates first. It doesn't come down to a competency thing.' When he was dismissed over the phone, he was told 'It's a voluntary redundancy program so you can pretend it's not compulsory redundancy'. West replied, 'So you want me to lie, like you want me to start lying now at this late stage in my career?'

For many others, redundancy really was voluntary. And the motivations for going were many and varied. Some decided to go because they feared that if they didn't, they would miss out on the opportunity for a redundancy payout and on the chance to explore new opportunities. In most workplaces, staff were able to ask their HR department for their 'numbers', which detailed what they would get in a redundancy settlement.

Sophie Morris was on maternity leave with her second child when another redundancy round was announced at *The Australian Financial Review*. 'I wasn't disgruntled, I wasn't frustrated,' says Morris, who was proud of working at the *AFR*. But she was curious and asked for the figures. When they came back, she worked out she would have to work more than a year because of the tax advantages to earn the same amount. But it got even better when a friend suggested she get the numbers checked because the figure had been calculated at her part-time rate, rather than averaged out over the past five years. 'I don't think it was malicious,' she says. 'It was just an accounting error, but when I pointed this out to them it bumped my payout up.' Nevertheless, she says, it was a difficult decision to leave:

> Once I'd seen the numbers then I had to think about it seriously and it made me confront that decision about where is this industry going, where will I be in five years, if I stay here what is my future at this company, am I just going to be doing more of the same? I like what I'm doing, but I can't stay doing it forever.

The fact that Morris was on maternity leave, and away from the office every day, made her decision easier. An important factor for others was their age. Those close to retirement had to weigh up the value of a payout, which could keep them comfortable until they could access their superannuation, against the very real prospect that they might never find work again. Age became acutely important for David Marr, who needed to act urgently to get out of *The Sydney Morning Herald*. In previous redundancy rounds the thought of applying hadn't crossed his mind. But in 2012 he really had no choice.

> I'm a great prevaricator and I prevaricated and prevaricated, and there were only a few days left for you to put up your hand and it was a Friday and I popped around to my friend, somebody whose judgment I always trust, Matthew Moore, and said to Matthew, 'Look, I turn 65 tomorrow, I think it's probably time for me to go, I think I should put up.' He said, 'What? You turn 65 tomorrow? Unless you go today that's going to be taxed not as a redundancy payment but as income, David, and you're going to lose half of it.' This is just my incompetence with money and my dithering, and all of these things came to a head, and so I thought, Well fuck, I'm going to do it.

So Marr walked into the office of editor-in-chief Peter Fray and said, 'I'm putting up my hand.' When Fray begged him not to, Marr pointed out his impending birthday. 'What? We've got to get you out of here this afternoon.' Marr said, 'Yes if you can', so they did. There was a 'hiccup' during the afternoon because for some reason Wikipedia had listed his birthday a day later, so the people in HR thought they had an extra day. Marr remembers somebody came back to him saying, 'Haven't we got a day up our sleeve?' and he said, 'No, it's tomorrow.'

Environment reporter Tom Arup had already discussed voluntary redundancy with his editor-in-chief Andrew Holden in what he calls a 'semi voluntary round' at *The Age*. Arup told his boss, 'Andrew, I'm done.' He was feeling exhausted and asked if he could go to Paris to cover the impending climate conference as his last job and then 'never come back'. Holden gave him a good hearing, but the plan didn't eventuate. Instead, he decided to 'wait in the long grass' until the next round came, which sure enough happened quickly because, as Arup says, 'they just didn't have the luxury, they had to get the sheer numbers out'. He quickly showed his interest. 'I reckon I put my application in 20 minutes after the round opened,' he says. And on the day the round closed he was phoned by the new editor-in-chief, Mark Forbes, who told him, 'We're sorry to see you go, but your round has been accepted.' Arup remembers fist pumping in the air and Forbes asking him, 'Do you want to finish up tomorrow or what?' Arup replied, '"That's quick, I'd like to say goodbye to everyone and have a drink", so I finished up the next week and that was it.'

Amanda Meade had decided she wanted to leave *The Australian*, in part because her work had become less enjoyable. She says the motivation to go 'had probably been building up, because it wasn't a happy place to be anymore because there was so much pressure on us to attack the ABC and attack all the other media organisations rather than just being reporters'. The paper was becoming increasingly ideological 'and it just became really, really uncomfortable'. As she says, 'I just decided that I would leave and just take my chances, really.'

Similar motivations surfaced often in surveys of Australian journalists who opted for redundancy.[8] These people were not happy to be going, but were at least relieved to be getting out of unhappy or even toxic work environments, dominated by unpleasant cultures or the anxiety of constant restructures and redundancy rounds.

Meredith Booth says the newsroom at *The Advertiser* in Adelaide was becoming depressing. 'There was a bit of a dead-man-walking atmosphere in the newsroom, with people knowing they were going, and probably not pulling their weight as much.' She says the people left behind were feeling extra stress because 'they could see the newsroom emptying out'. They were losing colleagues and friends and every departure meant there were fewer people to complete the same amount of work.

'I have been back to that newsroom,' says Booth, 'and it pales in comparison to what it once was. It's like an echo chamber, you can see a colleague four desks over, and you're surrounded by nothing.'

Isabella Lettini experienced a lack of motivation following her sacking at Cumberland Newspapers in Parramatta. She had been hurt deeply by the redundancy, but was still expected to turn up to work for several months. Initially, she just couldn't do it. 'I actually didn't come in for a couple of weeks. And at the end, my editor, who's a lovely guy, said to me, "Listen, I'm just going to tell you for your own good, I'd like you to come in to work." And I said, "I can't. I'm too upset." And he goes, "Well, you have to because I don't want you to miss out on money when you leave."' She rallied and just before she left, she remembers she photographed a police arrest as it unfolded in her own neighbourhood and handed it to the paper. Her colleagues, who could see how she'd been treated, asked her why she was doing it. She told them, 'It's because I love my job.'

And therein lies one of the tragedies of a disrupted industry. Lettini, like so many journalists of her era, loved her work and practised it with skill and dedication. She took pride in doing it well and would generally think nothing of working long hours, or in her own time, to capture a compelling image for the newspaper. She was seemingly born for the role, and if the industry was in a healthier state would probably still be practising it within a vibrant newsroom and enjoying the thrills and challenges of such a creative and demanding job. It says a lot that even while the redundancy process was spitting her, and many of her colleagues, out the door, she found the motivation to keep on reporting.

Redundancy in any industry can be undignified and painful. What in theory is meant to be a decision based on impersonal business requirements quickly becomes deeply personal, perhaps even more so for people who are so passionate about their craft and who have spent a lifetime doing that work. Journalists' experiences of redundancy are also profoundly influenced by the approach of management, and the extent to which managers are able to see beyond the business case to the individuals involved, many of whom have been long-term colleagues.

At the same time, redundancy can provide opportunities for renewal. Some journalists found ways back into the industry, or paths into new careers, drawing on their journalism skills. And a few, like Lettini, even went through redundancy again in other media companies as the rolling rounds of retrenchments reached into every sector of the media. Unfortunately, it appears media companies are still not attuned to the feelings of acute loss experienced by those going through redundancy, even though there is a clear need for greater empathy.

The process of being retrenched was tough, but for some what was to follow would prove even harder ... the last days at work.

CHAPTER 15
The walk to the lift: Last days at work

Andrew Dodd

Hugh Jones knew that his last day at the *Herald Sun* would be 'a little awkward'. He had spent several weeks managing his subs hub staff through a period of transition, which meant shifting them to News Limited's central payroll. Part of his job was to assure everyone that these were just administrative changes, and that job losses were not inevitable. The one job that he knew had become redundant was his own.

After Jones had explained this at a staff meeting a week earlier, some people had taken the news badly and started crying, not just because he was leaving, but because they knew if such a 'rusted on' manager was vulnerable, then they all were. Jones had already explored his options within the company, but had come to the conclusion there was 'no will to find me a job.' This had been hard to take because, Jones recalls, 'I've pretty much done everything in this organisation over a period of time. I could pretty much turn my hand to anything.'

Jones wanted to say goodbye to lots of people on his last day, but he realised a 'grand tour of the building' would be impractical. So, instead, he went out to lunch with a few of his colleagues. When it came time to leave, he emptied the contents of his desk into a box, including pens and pencils and old reference books, and 'things that were mine or that I'd had so long I couldn't remember who they really did belong to'. He headed to the lift and down to the lobby where he was met by Gordon, the 'big tall' security guard who Jones had known for years. Gordon looked at Jones and said, 'I'm supposed to search everybody's boxes when they leave the building ... but in your case, walk on by.'

Such a small gesture, but a profound one. It was a demonstration of trust by an official at the very moment an ex-employee might feel most aggrieved about the company. It was a moment of decency in a process that could be anything but.

Almost every redundant journalist has vivid memories of their last day at work.[1] For many it was a day punctuated with similarly profound moments; sometimes happy and funny, but often sad or painful. It was a day when the way they were treated by others really mattered and when their relationship with the physical office they worked in, and the people they shared it with, changed completely.

Some suddenly became uncomfortable in a place where they had worked for years. In others, it manifested as a kind of revulsion that has kept them away ever since. The final day was also when many were hit with the reality that their life's calling and self-identity had shifted. Some found themselves asking, 'What am I now, if I am not a journalist?'[2] It was also a day of celebration, if that's the right word, conducted among people who were sad to see them go, or fearful for their own future, or fatigued by the sheer number of recent departures. And there were practical considerations too, such as handing back security passes and packing the accumulated mementoes and notebooks of their career into boxes, before a final parade, or furtive dash, to the exit.

Tom Hyland remembers a mixture of anger, self-pity and pathos as his young daughter helped him carry his box out of *The Age* after 15 years of service. This was not how it was meant to happen. On occasions when he'd imagined his own retirement, he'd seen a very different kind of departure.

> I thought there'd be a dinner, somebody would get up and make a really funny speech and people would have gathered embarrassing anecdotes and maybe [fellow reporter] Lindsay Murdoch might've said 'Remember that time you went to Cambodia and didn't file a fucking word.' I thought that's what happens when people retire. I, sort of, hoped, maybe. But there were 67 of us [who] walked out and none of us had that farewell.

For some of those made redundant, that type of lack of acknowledgment made their final day at work most difficult. Hugh Jones remembers none of his colleagues in senior management found time that day to check in with him and say goodbye. 'Not one of those people made any attempt to get in touch with me and I've thought about it afterwards, yep, that would have been pretty embarrassing for them – you know, pretty awkward for them but [it was] pretty weak really. They knew me – all of those guys knew me really well. I worked with them all for a long time.'

Wendy Hargreaves had recently been moved from the ninth to the tenth floor of the same building, after the *Sunday Herald Sun* was absorbed into the daily paper. She found herself sitting next to the secretary, which was a strong indication that her position had become precarious. As a feature writer she was surplus to requirements so when her redundancy was announced her departure came quickly. She says she was gone within a day or two.

> I just put everything in a box and walked out. There was no fanfare, there was no cake. It was 'See you later.' It was awful because there were so many other people going through the same pain. But there weren't enough people on the ground to do the right thing and organise the farewells.

At *The Canberra Times*, Rosslyn Beeby had attended too many 'interminable farewells for people' and chose not to have one herself. But even so, she was shocked by the almost complete lack of acknowledgment for her years of service. There was no effort to do anything, she recalls.

> I thought, Gee, it is so kind of aggressively graceless in that you could have written a card. You could have said, 'Oh, sorry … you appear to have snuck out.' You could have rung up the florist and sent a bunch of flowers. It's just a grace thing. It's a thing that you do.

While she felt let down by the company, at least one employee did stand by her. On her last day the chief sub-editor, who owned a wildflower farm, brought in a bunch of flowers and told her 'I'm buying you coffee. When you go, just come and walk past my desk and say "Elvis is leaving the building" and we'll meet up and have a coffee.' It was a simple act, but greatly appreciated, and they've remained friends ever since.

Peter Hanlon chose to sneak away from *The Age*. A few days before his departure he told the sports editor, Chloe Saltau, that he was leaving. They went and sat in a quiet room upstairs and he remembers they both had 'a bit of a cry'. About his last day, he says, 'I found it incredibly hard. I ran away, to a degree.' He eschewed the normal practice of a farewell speech. 'I did the leaving-work equivalent of – what do they call it? – ghosting at a party,' he says. 'So you just go to the toilet and disappear. I sort of did that leaving *The Age*.'

He did have a farewell but not on the premises. We 'deliberately had it away from *The Age*, offsite. A long way offsite.'

At Network Ten, TV reporter Antoinette Lattouf was in no mood for celebrating on her last day. She had found herself another job, but several others hadn't, including some who had worked at Ten for two decades. She remembers it being a 'really tough time for some people' because they were distraught at not having a job to go to. She felt it was not the time for a big bash or for beers and happy emails.

> You know it was such a strange time and so many people were taking redundancies and there were so many leaving drinks and I just went overseas and didn't say anything. I packed my desk and I left. I'm still good friends with a lot of people from Ten, so I thought those who I wish to stay in contact with I will, and I have … There wasn't any announcement. There wasn't a farewell drinks. There were no see-you-later emails. I just left.

Campbell Cooney had made the mistake of staying around past midday on his last day at the ABC's Radio Australia. He was waiting for a lift from a colleague, but was feeling increasingly uncomfortable about being in an office with which he had already cut emotional ties, and which had dispensed with him. He says if he hadn't been waiting he would have 'gone at lunchtime, just packed my bags and gone, walked out the door. No one would have cared. No one would have worried and I would have been happier about it, doing it that way.'

A week or so later he felt trepidation again, this time at the thought of going to a farewell party that had been organised for retrenched staff at an inner city bowls club.

> I just remember waking up on the Saturday, this farewell from ABC Radio Australia was going on, and thinking, 'I can't do this. I just don't want to do this. There will be lots of people there, like the managers, who I'd lost a lot of respect for. They are going to be there. I don't want to be doing fake hugs and kisses. It has gone.

The walk to the lift: Last days at work

Cooney, like many others, found solace and support in meeting up with former colleagues who had also been through redundancy. 'That was more the going away,' he says. 'It was like a shared experience.'

Tom Hyland ended up marking his departure from *The Age* with a similar lunch, along with other former colleagues. One of those who attended the small gathering was Simon Mann, who had also left without a farewell party, despite his seniority and the fact that he was saying goodbye to any prospect of fulfilling what many thought was his promise of becoming the paper's editor-in-chief. On the day of Mann's departure, the opinion editor, Sushi Das, realised that no one had even arranged a card, which she quickly rectified. Mann appreciated the gesture. As he carried his box of stuff to the door he bumped into the current editor-in-chief, Andrew Holden. 'He just gave me a wave,' remembers Mann. 'I don't think it had clicked with him that I was actually going for the last time.'

One of Jo Chandler's regrets on leaving *The Age* was that because so many people were going she missed out on receiving a specially commissioned cartoon by one of the paper's great cartoonists. 'My greatest disappointment is that, if I had left a year or two before, I might have got a Tandberg cartoon.' She would 'never have' got a Spooner because they were 'not on speaking terms' by that stage due to Spooner's controversial views on climate change. And what about the cartoonists themselves? What did they do when they were made redundant? They drew cartoons, of course. Spooner was glad that he had a creative way of channelling his emotions in his last week at *The Age*.

> My final cartoon was a desert island with one palm tree, the classic cartoonist's desert island. And I had [Malcolm] Turnbull and [Bill] Shorten on the beach as castaways, smiles on their faces. Behind them the Pope is holding a windmill, a jihadist

terrorist is going bananas, Donald Trump without any trousers is carrying on, and there are just signs of mayhem and it's stuff all over the island. In the background walking off the island is a cartoonist, and Turnbull's saying to Shorten, 'If the world's in such a God-awful mess, how come we're still laughing?' And Shorten says, 'Because another cartoonist just left.'[3]

Things were much more dramatic in Sydney, where reporters at *The Sydney Morning Herald* had revived an old printing ritual to farewell their colleagues. It stemmed from the days when typesetting was done on presses and printers used trays to collect the small metal letters ready for use by compositors. The printers would rattle the letters on the trays to make noise as a retiring colleague departed. By the time Matthew Moore left the *Herald*, this had become almost routine. But on this occasion, it was particularly difficult because as many as 50 people were leaving on the same day.[4] Everyone gathered in the newsroom. Speeches were given and personalised cards were handed out. And then the people who were staying started rattling whatever they could to make noise, as Moore and the others walked off the floor towards the lifts.

'I just remember getting in a lift with all these big blokes,' says Moore.

> There were blokes in their 50s and their 60s who were all sort of six foot or more. There were sports reporters, political reporters, finance reporters and there we were. We went downstairs and then as we got down to the ground floor, a couple of floors, we walked outside and you could just see tears running down people's faces. It was sad and many of them have not really recovered.

Debra Jopson left the *Herald* on the same day and also took part in the ritual, which she experienced as 'affirming your identity at the same time as you are losing a part of it'. She remembers 'going down this corridor with these echoes with all these colleagues and then we kind of went down in the lift and out, and it was this incredible feeling, like being reborn or something. Not being spat out. It's quite a strange thing, because I thought, "Ooh, we're going to feel like we're being spat out of the building," but it was more like a kind of a rebirth.'

Like Hugh Jones, Di Thomas had the job of managing other staff while coping with her own redundancy. She was busy reorganising *The Border Mail*'s newsgathering and publishing processes, while hiding the news that she had decided to go herself.

'I made that commitment that I wouldn't say anything until it was announced,' she says. However, the secrecy created difficulties until she could finally bring people 'into the loop'. The experience taught her that managing and experiencing retrenchment is 'really hard within the workplace because for some people it was a very straightforward decision to apply for redundancy and go and make plans for the next step. For other people it was more difficult … so this is why I say that everybody's journey is different.'[5]

Secrecy was also an issue for *The Australian*'s media writer, Amanda Meade. After hiding the truth of her redundancy from the news website *Crikey*, she did tell her story to the media. On her last day at work she pre-recorded an interview for *The Media Report* on Radio National.[6] After decades telling stories about the industry, she had become the reluctant subject of one.

Wheels editor Stephen Corby returned to Bauer Media after he signed off. Luckily his pass still worked so he could pack up his belongings. He distinctly remembers taking down the photos from the walls and feeling grateful he was there alone, away from the gaze of his former colleagues.

> I went in the day after and just cleared out the office on my own, because I didn't want anyone to be there, because I

thought it was too sad. I didn't want anyone to see me going through – like, I choke up thinking about it. Like, it was just awful. Packing all that up and just going … 'How did this happen? How did it all happen so quickly?'

Cate Swannell left the *Gold Coast Bulletin* in typically bold fashion. When her managers said they wanted her to keep working for a while before the redundancy took effect, she said, 'Fuck off, I'm not sitting around for three weeks, I'll leave next Tuesday thanks.' According to Swannell, the reaction of the bosses was, '"Oh yeah, righto" and not a word was said.'

Normally at the *Bulletin*, when someone leaves the newsroom, there'd be 'a little get-together and the editor talks shit about them for 20 minutes and you get a card and a present and a stupid free hat and you go out and have drinks with people'. But in Swannell's case, because she had been made redundant, she says she became 'one of the invisible' and the expectation was that she would 'just toddle off'. She wasn't happy about it. She had worked there for 23 years. As she was packing up her desk in readiness to leave, she logged on to her email, just to get a few things off her chest.

> I basically told them exactly what had happened and then I thanked quite a few people by name, Peter Wilcox and Pat McLeod and a few others who'd been really good mates and good mentors. Then I said, 'There's a bunch of you in here who are a pack of shit-stirring assholes, you know who you are, I don't need to name you, thanks for nothing.' It was along those lines. I can be quite funny when I want to be and I was. So I sent it out quickly before they signed me off the system.

As the staff in the newsroom were opening and reading her email she walked through the newsroom with her box of stuff and yelled out 'Bye everybody' and left the building. She says most of her colleagues 'thought it was hilarious, because I'd been there since God was a boy, they knew my sense of humour, they knew exactly how I felt. I don't hide my lamp under a bushel, so to speak. They've always known exactly how I was feeling about things … I'm amazed they didn't escort me from the building.'

For every dramatic departure there were others that were perfunctory and uneventful. Aleisha Orr remembers her last day at *WA Today* where she had some cake and was given a farewell card by the people remaining in the small newsroom. She didn't carry away a box of things because by the time she finished up she was only coming in one day a week, 'so I didn't really have a lot of stuff'.

Stephen Corby felt discarded on his final day as editor of *Wheels* magazine. He was hosting an annual event to select the winner of the prestigious Car of the Year award. It culminates in a tally of the votes, which are kept secret until an official announcement some days later. Corby had performed his last role as the editor and everyone was free to leave when Bauer Media's publisher stood up and gave a speech. First he thanked Corby for all his hard work and then he turned to someone standing in the crowd and declared, 'This is the new editor.' For Corby it was shocking. 'Everyone's clapping him on the back and stuff, and I'm sitting there going, "Did you have to do this in front of me? Like, did you have to do this now?" It was awful. I felt like bloody some Julius Caesar, Roman thing, I think, stabbed in front of everyone.'

Corby then 'went to the airport and left'. Although he was fuming about it, he had to 'play nice' because, like many of those facing redundancy, Corby was already focusing his attention on his future employment, and he had just accepted a small amount of work with Bauer on a regular retainer. 'I couldn't blow up about it,' he says. 'They're my new employer on a freelance basis, which is tricky because I'm redundant, so I can't earn too much, but there's still an arrangement that I will write a certain amount for them.'

For those seeking to reinvent themselves as freelancers, worries about future work were ever-present, even amid the celebrations and commiserations of their last day. Some of those about to depart were approached with work offers, even though these may have been tentative, and eventually came to nothing, On other occasions advances were made in the most public manner imaginable. Political journalist Michael Gordon was feted on the floor of the Commonwealth Parliament by both the Opposition leader and prime minister.[7] Matthew Franklin had a similar experience.

> When it emerged that I was going, a number of politicians from both sides of politics, at many different levels, said they wanted me to work for them. One of them, the day I finished, held a party in his office for me and I remember on the day I finished both [Julia] Gillard and Tony Abbott gave speeches in parliament about me saying what an ornament I was and blah, blah, blah.[8] It was very humbling, but they were also trying to butter me up to go and work for somebody. It wasn't all cynical. I had great relations with both of them. I had good relations with everybody I dealt with because I tried to be fair. People on both sides offered me jobs, but I just kept saying, 'I don't know what I'm doing and I'm not sure I'm ready for this. I've got to think about it.'

Tracee Hutchison says the experience was painful and that none of it helped give her a sense of closure. She describes it as 'just a punitive, targeted waste of expertise and a wholesale sort of destruction of people's lives'. She believes the decommissioning of the ABC's Asia-Pacific and specialist language services in radio and television meant that the ABC lost a generation of specialist multilingual broadcasters with in-depth cross-cultural expertise.

Stephen Corby is equally critical about his final days at *Wheels*.

Yes, that was an ugly, ugly way to end, and I've never been so depressed in my life as when that redundancy thing happened. I was like – I was just black. Like, it's this awful thing about having the carpet ripped out from under you. It was just so unexpected … you're just really, really, really down and, as great as it is now, when I look back on that time it was just really, really bad.

Perhaps it's not surprising then that the pub featured prominently during the last day for many people. Magazine editor Dean Mellor spent much of it at the Civic Hotel next door to Bauer Media's Sydney office. Usually the hotel, and the others nearby, were busy with staff from the publishing business. In fact, the whole neighbourhood was often buzzing with company staff, some of whom would be smoking outside the office, while mates greeted each other on the footpath. But on that day the area was quiet because so many people had already been retrenched. Mellor was drinking with just a few advertising managers and occasional drop-ins, including the man who was about to take over when the diminished business was relocated to a much smaller office in Melbourne after the Christmas break. He remembers the new guy was talking about how exciting things would be in Melbourne while Mellor just sat there, 'resigned to the fact that it's been over for quite a while now'. While Mellor took some comfort from knowing he never had to go back into the 'bloody depressing' office, he and his colleagues looked around at the nearly empty pub, saying, 'We can't believe it's over.' He says he drank 'thousands of beers' before picking up his backpack and catching the train home.

On Louise Graham's last day at *The Age* she said her farewells and got 'blind drunk' at a nearby pub with a bunch of colleagues. 'That's probably the drunkest I've ever been,' she says.

Some media outlets used their local pub to host farewell parties. Occasionally they were lavish and generous. Senior reporter Matthew Moore says that when he left *The Sydney Morning Herald* the company 'put 20 grand on the bar and had this wonderful party and off we went into the night'.

Di Thomas had a lot to contend with at her farewell party, which was also held at a pub, off site, after she had left her role as editor of *The Border Mail*. Her former colleagues had invited lots of notables from the local community, including two federal members of parliament. It came at the end of two very difficult weeks, in which she had not only overseen some of the company's restructure, while organising her own departure, but had also arranged the funeral of her father, who she had tended to during his last days. She would go to the palliative care unit to have breakfast with him each morning before going in to work. During these visits they often discussed whether she should leave the paper and she remembers his reaction when she told him that she had finally decided to take redundancy. 'He said, "I knew there was something going on." I said, "Why?" and he said, "You came in and you look like there'd been a weight lifted off your shoulders."' So, when Di Thomas rose to make her speech at her farewell, in that full Albury pub, she found it very difficult.

> I kind of got up to speak, and that's kind of where it hit. I cried at that because it was just the sort of culmination of everything. And you know the lovely thing is that the week before, the Friday before which had been Dad's funeral, you know, a good percentage of my colleagues had come and supported me at that, which was just so lovely.

Linda Hunt had sought voluntary redundancy, but the nature of her departure was forced upon her. She was winding up a shift in the ABC's Hobart newsroom, where she had worked for 30 years, when a woman from HR in Melbourne phoned and told her she would not be required the following day, or ever again, because her six-week redundancy period had effectively begun. She was meant to receive more notice and some time to consider her options. Instead, she was told she would be paid to leave immediately.

'I said, "So you're telling me 25 minutes before my shift ends that I'm no longer required? I've had no time to say goodbye to anyone … this is quite a shock. I would like to have actually been able to say goodbye to people."' She managed to negotiate one more day at work. So she came in early as usual and started counting down the day: 'This is my tenth last bulletin, this is my ninth last bulletin,' she said as the morning shift unfolded. As she was preparing the 8.30 am headlines, her boss asked her how she was. 'I said, "What do you mean how am I? What do you think?" The boss asked, "What do you mean?" I said, "Do you understand what actually happened in that office yesterday? I'm humiliated. I am devastated and humiliated and angry that I'm not able to leave this place on my terms."'

The lesson from these experiences of redundancy is that the last days at work are often painful and can expose those going through them to intense and raw emotion. It's a time when people's lives are so shaken by the rejection and confusion of redundancy that they become especially vulnerable to further acts of humiliation and indecency. This is not the moment to dishonour someone's service by failing to acknowledge their contribution and achievements. Nor is it the time to be punitive and dismissive. But unfortunately this is what sometimes happens in corporate settings, especially when the rates of redundancies reach industrial scale.

During their last days at work, people want compassion and recognition. They might not want a party or a long farewell speech, and they may feel there's little to celebrate, but they definitely want to know that their colleagues are not shunning or ignoring them as they leave. But just as they are especially vulnerable to slights and insults, those facing redundancy are also particularly receptive to acts of goodness and kindness, however small. Whether it's a bunch of hand-picked flowers or an offer of a cup of coffee, the thought behind each act is appreciated. What's possibly surprising is that, despite their supposed toughness, journalists are just like everyone else in valuing the empathy and humanity that each act of kindness represents.

Flip Prior

Interviewed by Penny O'Donnell, edited by Lawrie Zion

From small regional publications to metropolitan daily newspapers, and from embracing online media and training politicians how to use Twitter, Flip Prior has enjoyed a modern media career.

Growing up

I was born in 1978 in Basildon in the United Kingdom. I was three or four years old when we migrated to Perth. I only have very small snatches of memory from that time. I do remember just one thing, which was having to drink a small bottle of milk every day when I went to school. It was either icy cold in winter or quite warm in summer, and I just hated it, and you weren't allowed to go outside and play until you drank your milk. We didn't stay in Perth for very long. We ended up in Mount Newman in Western Australia. I've got quite a vivid memory of walking through a park near my house and just roasting: it's 45 degrees and it's dry and hot and dusty and red, and I think my young brain was a bit like 'what the hell's going on, where am I?' It was like an alien landscape.

You learn really quickly to lose your accent when you are a new migrant and you're very young. I remember two little Australian girls saying to me, 'You sound funny. We don't want to play with you,' and that sort of stuff sticks with you. And I thought all right, okay, I'd better sort that out. I certainly felt different when I arrived because I couldn't swim. I felt like I had to Australianise myself in a way, and I'm not exactly sure how I did that. Probably by eating sausage rolls and learning how to swim and all that sort of stuff, because you just don't want to be different at that age. You just want to slot right in.

I think I had trouble getting attention from my parents and so that's when I started to put effort into schooling. I was always good at school and I think I put a lot of pressure on myself as a child because that was the way I actually got some attention from people. That's my psychological reading of it now anyway: that if I did well then I would be acknowledged and I'd get a pat on the head, but otherwise there was no way to get positive affirmation.

After school

In 1997 I finished school and started to work and when I was 18 I bought a one-way ticket to London. I think all I wanted at that point was to get out of Perth – to get away from years of family conflict and stuff and start some other kind of life I suppose. I spent several years living in the UK. I didn't want to go to another country to hang out with Australian people; I wanted to meet locals. I lived all over Surrey and would hang out with British people and French people and I then moved to Edinburgh for two years and shared places with Swedes and Argentinians and Mexicans and Scottish people. People from all over the world and with really different life experiences.

I started writing long missives back home about the different places I was going and what I was doing with my life, and that's when I started to sit down and write in earnest I guess, though I had kept diaries sporadically over the years.

I remember being at a party once in London and I met someone who was a section editor for one of the newspapers. I think that must have been around the time people had been saying to me, you should think about being a journalist. I went up to him and I said, 'What does it take to get into journalism? I hear you're an editor', and he just looked at me and he said, 'Don't bother.' Even though I was a bit taken aback by how rude and dismissive he was, I wasn't deterred because I think at that stage I had only just started thinking about it and didn't really have any idea how to get in. But I got voraciously into newspapers. I would easily get through a bunch of newspapers a day. I just really loved reading them at that point.

Breaking into journalism

I ended up coming back to Australia because I wanted to go to university to study journalism, and I realised that I was not going to be able to do it over there and self-support. So I was a bit older when I started. I tried to get a job as a news captioner at Channel 9 in Perth and I flunked so badly on the current affairs test because I'd spent several years overseas. I don't think I'd ever done that badly in anything in my whole life and I was so embarrassed.

So that's when I thought, okay I'd better not be arrogant about my knowledge and start to become more aware of the world around me if I want to get in and start doing this sort of work. I studied journalism and professional writing at Curtin University in Perth and loved it.

I was really on top of things and took it very seriously and had some great lecturers. I got a Press Council commendation for an essay in my second year, and I was on the Vice Chancellor's list. Pretty much as soon as I started university, I also started to hear about things like the journalist union, so I got involved as a student with the local branch, just to help out with stuff like the media ball.

When I was at uni, I took to freelancing. I started off writing for free for various magazines, profiles and food stories and music reviews. I just tried to do everything I could get. I was just trying to get this broad experience and that was really helpful to get a sense of what editors actually wanted.

When I was close to graduating, I was keen to escape Perth again. I tried to get a *Herald Sun* cadetship twice and I got rejected both times. I got all the way through and then fell over on the local knowledge exam, which I thought was terribly unfair, and still do a bit, because I exceeded at every other part of it and got shortlisted which was unusual for someone outside Melbourne. They would hit you with a question like 'Which local council spent $1 million on a roundabout in July?' and I would go, 'Well I don't know that but of course if I lived here, I would know that' but they just said, 'We don't have to make concessions.'

I ended up taking a job as editor of ScienceNetwork WA, a science news website, which was all very new at the time. I wasn't writing anything, but I was helping to commission stories about science. It didn't feel like a forever job and I was still freelancing and getting stuff published and after about 18 months I finally thought 'I've really got to have a go at getting into newspapers.'

The West Australian didn't really take people unless you got a cadetship, which I kept missing out on; the other way in was to go to the regions. I was dreading that because I thought, they're going to send me out to sheep country and it's going to be boring. I finally sat down with the regional newspapers editor and asked for a job and I struck it lucky, because I got a job in Broome.

Within a short time I had packed my bags and started work at the *Broome Advertiser*, a small regional paper. There was an editor, two other young journalists, me, a sales team and the newsroom manager and a few graphics people.

I look back now and I think getting that newspaper out every week was a mammoth effort; it was just crazy. You had to fill a newspaper – if they sold lots of ads you had to fill it with copy and we all just wrote and wrote and wrote and just smashed out stories. But I loved it because Broome was such an interesting place. It's a coastal town, it's on the edge of the desert as well, it's artistic, it's got very mixed multicultural communities. It's beautiful.

A year later my editor told me that an opportunity had come up in Kalgoorlie. He presumed I didn't want to go because I loved Broome, loved the community and was very happy. But it meant going to work for a daily newspaper and from a town of 15 000 people to 30 000 people. As I was really ambitious I said, 'Yeah, I'll go', and he was so surprised.

And just in the same way that I'd known nothing about Broome before I moved, I really knew nothing about Kalgoorlie before I moved there. I was chasing opportunities that were being offered to me more than anything else. And I suppose I'd figured by that point that I'd survived a year in Broome and I'd made lots of friends, and so I could do the same thing again.

Kalgoorlie was a mining town and it was the boom years. There were lots of people who were flush with cash and industry was really going strong. The *Kalgoorlie Miner* building was on the main street next to the very famous Exchange Hotel, which had skimpies [topless waitresses] working in the bar. I think I probably had some regrets when I first arrived. I'd gone from a really beautiful place by the ocean to this land-locked town.

The newspaper was central to the town in the same way the *Broome Advertiser* had been. People really read the local paper. It's very much more a part of communities in those places than it might be in the big cities. You're constantly seeing people in the street that you write about. It's a different sort of vibe to being in a metro paper.

I'd been doing quite a bit of court reporting by then, and so I moved into doing more crime and police and courts, which I really enjoyed. And I was writing about Indigenous affairs. I felt like a grown up journalist because it was a daily newspaper, and the pressure was there every day, and I enjoyed the pressure. At that point it was all about learning the trade, because I was only a couple of years in and it was just learn, learn, learn and just keep pushing ahead. I think by then I'd graduated to about 50 grand and I felt so rich.

Obviously by then I knew I really wanted to do this for a job, so I really wanted to get into *The West* [*Australian*]. However, I didn't want to do a cadetship because I would have had to take a pay cut. By then I had won or come runner up in a couple of awards, so I begged for a shot, and they agreed to let me join the newsroom as long as I did shorthand with the cadets. I agreed to that and I had to do six months of Pitman shorthand, which was six months of hell. I hated it. I hated it with an abiding passion.

After I graduated finally with 120 words a minute I never touched it again really. I used to go and cry in the toilets because I would fail my 100 and my 110 and if you failed you were back in [shorthand classes]. It was hours a day, two hours of homework a night for months and months and months. And it was just horrendous.

But I think the worst part of the job at that point was the overnight police round. It was isolating, awful, just sitting in this small room and waiting for things to happen. You just sat there and scanned the death notices looking for interesting deaths and listened to the police radio trying to find snatches of interesting events. And then at the end of the night, they used to make you grab a stack of newspapers hot off the press, and drive out to the police command centre in Midland, about an hour's drive from Osborne Park. So your shift is about to finish, but then you had to wait for the newspaper to be printed, get in the car and do a two-hour round trip, and finish work in the wee hours of the morning. The next morning, you'd wake up and all your mates would be at work and you saw no one and then you went back to work at 3 or 4 in the afternoon, and did it all again.

In the first year I was at *The West* I did a three-month stint working back in Broome. And then the second year I did a four-month stint, and then I just wanted to move back there. It was an interesting time to be there.

Woodside wanted to build a big gas hub at James Price Point,

60 kilometres north of Broome in a very pristine part of the world, and people who live in Broome were understandably very upset about this. It became a much bigger story involving deals being done with Indigenous landowners. The government pitched it a bit as 'Do you want a future for your children or not?' And some people were absolutely like, Let's take the money. And others said, We won't sell off our land for that. And of course, there was plenty of opposition on the environmental front as well, and lots of arguments about the potential impacts on tourism and lifestyle and amenity.

The difficulty of being in the town then and being a reporter for *The West Australian* was there was disdain for the mainstream press. Both sides said I was biased so that was good. But the problem was that being that reporter and living in the town made it hard. I had to balance my work and friendship circles, and I look back now and I think it's a very unusual situation to be in. You're doing big city reporting, but you're trying to live in the community at the same time in a really visible way. And that's difficult. There were people who I probably would have been better friends with if I had had the opportunity, but I couldn't.

Beyond journalism

At that time I was still working in an analogue environment. But with the growth of online news and the advent of Facebook and Twitter, I slowly realised I had a distribution network for the stories that weren't deemed fit to print. That seemed especially significant when you are working in a regional bureau and trying to convince the chief of staff to run your story at the front of the paper. And I just thought, ah-hah, this is really interesting.

When I wrote my stories, I was thinking about who was going to be most impacted by the work and I knew it probably wasn't people in Perth. What seemed more important was to put stories where they mattered the most, and yeah, and suddenly, there was a mechanism to do that.

That was also when online news started to bite into newspaper profits in a big way. They must have had cuts before that, but there was a sense in the industry they were starting to become a bit more frequent. And at first, the old subs would go and the people who'd been in the game a long time would take their moment to retire, but then younger journos would leave as well. I don't know how much I was keeping up with industry news then, and certainly not to the extent that I am now, but I was aware that things were changing to a point where I needed to change what I was doing, otherwise I was going to get left behind really fast.

When *The West* put a call out for voluntary redundancies in 2012, I put up my hand. The editors by then had started trying to make me come back to Perth and I was reluctant to rejoin the newsroom. So I begged for a redundancy and to my relief, was given one. I had no idea at that point what I was going to do next. I'd had a holiday booked, and just as the redundancy was about to come through, I went to the Ubud Writers Festival in Bali. I snuck my way into some drinks put on by the Australian Embassy, and pretended to be an author.

When I was in there, I met Chris Warren, who was general secretary of the journalists' union, and Jacqui Park, his partner, who was chair of the Walkley Foundation. I didn't really know who they were at that point, but I got chatting to them. Jacqui said, 'We've got a position going at the Walkley Foundation for a communications person, are you interested?' And I said, 'Sure! In Sydney? I guess I can move to Sydney?' So, then I was moving to Sydney. It was a complete accident. I just thought it seemed a really good opportunity and I was ready to leave Broome.

But after writing, writing, writing my own stories, I just stopped dead. And I haven't really ever started again, though I have dabbled a little bit. When my deadlines were taken away, suddenly, the pressure came off and I just went, all right, I'm not doing that. I think maybe after stopping at *The West*, my brain took that as a sign to think 'you don't do that anymore'.

I do wonder now if I can find a way back to writing more frequently at some point in a way that's potentially not so stressful or deadline-dependent. I only stayed at the Walkley Foundation for 18 months.

I took a job at Twitter after I got a tap on the shoulder.

Danny Keens, who was at the time running the media partnerships team for Australia, was looking for someone to engage with journalists and politicians. I wasn't looking to shift necessarily, but I was really active in the industry by then and I knew lots of journalists, and I think because he'd struggled to find anyone who had that mix of skills, I kind of got fast-tracked through the system and then ended up getting the job. I loved working with Danny. He was a former *60 Minutes* producer and an all-round fantastic human being. He's now a vice president of a VR company in the US.

When I started that job, I really had no idea what to expect. It was a new role: I basically had to train myself how to use Twitter for news, and then I hit the road. I taught hundreds of Australian journalists and politicians how to use Twitter and – sorry, Australia, what can I say? Training all the different political parties and ministers and journalists and newsrooms was a lot of work over the next 15 months. I loved the work, even though at times it was extremely tiring. I probably felt more anxious in that job than in any other job because of that feeling, that inadequacy feeling. I felt like I was a couple of years behind. I was so smashed with work I didn't have the energy to keep up. There was the whole technology side to learn. And that's when I started to get overwhelmed.

Part of it was I was working for a company that just pinged messages at me constantly all day. That's when the notification era started, and it was full-on because your attention starts to get taken by these micro moments. And honestly, a few years down the track I feel like that is a detrimental thing: it has an effect on your deep focus, on your ability to really home in on one piece of information at a time. I think it's becoming a much wider problem; everyone is addicted to their phones and their devices and I do feel like Twitter has contributed to that in some way.

After just 15 months, I was let go from Twitter over a video call with the guy who was the Asia-Pacific news partnerships lead. I didn't know him very well. It was my second redundancy and this time very much involuntary. It was part of global cuts. It was an interesting and somewhat dehumanising experience: it goes from being showered with love and sunshine by your colleagues to cold-hearted efficiency: he actually used the word 'efficiency' several times in the call. And I was like, 'Stop, you're talking to a human being. What are you talking about, efficiency?' After the call, I just sat in my hotel room and cried. I was really shocked and embarrassed and felt like my world had collapsed.

That was on a Wednesday. I stayed the night in Canberra and the next morning posted about what had happened on social media – and ironically, my name started to trend on Twitter as all the journalists and politicians I'd trained expressed outrage on my behalf. The next morning, the phone started to ring and the job offers from news organisations and political parties started pouring in. After you work in tech and media, it turns out lots of people are keen to hire you.

By Friday, I was talking to the ABC about a job. I've been there ever since. My job has changed quite a lot at the ABC over the years. I started doing social media strategy and training journos, but it started veering more towards marketing, which wasn't my thing. I also got a bit sick of social media, to be honest. I'm still interested in it from a distribution perspective, but I don't really want to be in it all the time.

After a couple of years, I went to people around the organisation I'd worked with and asked them to tell me what they thought I'm good at. And then I wrote it all up, and took that to my director and I asked, 'Can I do this instead?'

And then I just moved back over into news. Since then, I've

helped to set up and execute a wide range of news innovation projects such as collaborative journalism investigations and more recently, I've become part of a team set up to improve representation of women across ABC News and to help produce more stories of interest to women – work which I really love. It's taken me almost five years, but I'm about to sign on to a permanent job after years of living contract to contract – a situation that has always made me feel a bit anxious and insecure in our precarious media environment.

I still don't like hierarchy or bureaucracy or moving too slowly. I'm lucky to have one of the few jobs at the ABC that involves working across lots of different teams. I'm always trying to push the ABC to be future-focused and experimental so we keep growing audiences and stay relevant. I've worked out over the last couple of years who are the go-getters, who are the really smart people – who get shit done basically – and try to work with those people as much as possible. As a result, I've landed in a good spot.

CHAPTER 16

What just happened? The days after redundancy

Penny O'Donnell
Timothy Marjoribanks

The morning after she took a redundancy, Gillian Lord walked up her home driveway to pick up a copy of the newspaper from the lawn. It wasn't there. As a staff member of *The Canberra Times* she had received free daily copies of the paper – a perk that ensured journalists arrived at work having read it. Though this delivery was becoming less necessary in the digital age, cutting it off placed a definite full stop on her association with Fairfax Media.

Lord remembers it as one of the 'classy things that you had to laugh at' post-redundancy. As she was long accustomed to starting each day with a scan of the news, it was also disconcerting. She had not anticipated needing new daily rhythms and rituals so quickly. But soon her morning routine included a walk to the nearby corner store, where she took pleasure in choosing her reading from the variety of newspapers on offer.

Lord was otherwise prepared for her new life. She had a book-editing job lined up before taking a voluntary redundancy. In early 2012, she had helped redesign the digital-first model for *The Canberra Times*, but it did not suit longform writing. A 24-hour news cycle demanded 'something new all the time'. Lord saw that as 'dumbing down the paper', a move she rejected. In her view, it was bad for readers and professionalism. She says, 'If you stayed there and thought like a proper thinking journalist, you would go mad. So you either had to drink the Kool-Aid or leave.' Lord felt resolved, not angry, when she left the paper in mid-September 2012. 'We all went through grief,' she says. 'But I'm not bitter, it's just what happened, and as journalists we're all used to the fact that things happen.' However, she adds, 'It could have been done differently.'

Despite this equanimity, the grieving was still difficult. Lord mentions sleepless nights, tears, and *Schadenfreude*. Life without newsroom adrenaline was another challenge. She says, 'It wasn't this feeling like you're an animal on the Serengeti with wild dogs tearing you apart piece by piece.' She slowed down by doing a lot of work in her garden. She also met other redundant journalists over lunch until the need tapered off. Lord says the experience was not all negative.

Most journalists become emotional when recalling life after redundancy. Job loss experiences varied; grieving was common, and many felt a new uncertainty. Many working part time or on contract realised journalism work was becoming more precarious. Anxiety is a natural response to such difficult circumstances. Most often people go through it in private, away from prying eyes. Moreover, journalists rarely talk about their personal feelings in public. Redundancy changed that, so that some now talk about feeling disoriented, traumatised, or afraid of the future. There is also anger and self-doubt. Some express anguish over the loss of their career, identity, income or purpose, while others show resilience and a determination to bounce back.[1]

Hugh Jones felt lost after his forced redundancy from The Herald and Weekly Times (HWT) in 2012, where he had worked for more than 20 years. He felt hurt when his 'little place in the grand network' vanished. Though he knew editorial resources were being rationalised across the country, he couldn't silence the 'gnawing voice' that said people at HWT had wanted him gone.

'There must have been a meeting,' he says. 'Did anyone say, "He might be the person who could help us do this job" or were people saying, "The bloke's a loser. Pay him out!"?' That doubt tormented Jones. The thought processes of management were opaque, even though he had recently been making difficult decisions to restructure parts of the same business. He had a recurring dream about people at work telling him, 'You're not supposed to be here'. He wondered whether those who managed redundancy processes ever thought about the human cost.

When he started feeling 'a bit screwed up' his wife suggested counselling. 'It was fabulous,' he says. The counsellor explained he was grieving and needed to process the sudden ending of his work. She advised him not to devalue what he'd created or the achievements he'd earned, even if others forgot. She encouraged him to reflect on what had been worthwhile to him. After a few more consultations, Jones felt relieved.

Cate Swannell found the employment advice provided by News Limited helpful, in practical matters such as CV preparation, but also in advising she not worry initially about finding a job, but take a holiday instead. What she found less helpful were her parents' continual questions about her situation. 'Have you found a job?' 'Are you looking for a job?' 'How's the job search going?' 'How are you going, how are you going?'

Jo Chandler did not dwell on her feelings about departing *The Age* in 2012. She did ask herself, 'Who am I without *The Age*?' but she found no ready answer. She had decided to freelance, focusing on 'hard-to-tell stories in hard-to-reach' places, but was 'panic stricken' about getting paid. She gave all her time and mental energy to setting up her own enterprise. She had not foreseen 'boring logistical things' taking so much time. 'Every minute, I am thinking I should be billing someone for this, and I can't,' she recalls.

To gain a higher profile, she pitched feature stories to reputable publishers. They took her on but paid by the word, not for her time, so she earned little for long hours. She remembers getting $3000 for a feature that took six or seven weeks to write.

Her plans stalled when, in early 2013, she was diagnosed with the deadly disease she had covered in Papua New Guinea, drug-resistant tuberculosis, and was unable to work for six months. As career and money worries deepened, Chandler wrestled with self-doubt: 'Can I do this? Was I only okay in the sheltered workshop of *The Age* where they held my hand? What if I am actually no good?'

Somehow, she managed to keep writing. Over the next five years, she freelanced for the ABC, *Griffith Review*, *The Guardian*, *The Monthly*, *The Global Mail*, *New Scientist* and others. She won half a dozen major awards, including a Walkley and a Quill. She recalls the stories from this time as the most ambitious and fulfilling of her career.

Press photographer Isabella Lettini could not pick up a camera for 12 months after her forced redundancy in 2012. She had loved working for Cumberland Newspapers covering the north-western beat, and often did six shoots a day, believing that dedication and good work would protect her from job loss. She didn't realise her job was precarious, or that she would feel so fragile when it was gone.

> I couldn't get myself out of bed. Nightmares and dreams about going back to work. There were others in the same situation. We all got together and had a beer about a week after. It was difficult. We were all bouncing off each other, what are you going to do? What are you going to do? It was horrible. All these wonderful people. And, it's the same in any job. There's so many people that lose their jobs and no one understands.

Lettini fretted that her photos had not been good enough. Management had told her being one of the ones to go was 'unfortunate'. Yet, all the others to go at that same time were older people, so why her? Had she done something wrong? She lost confidence and abandoned photography. To pay the rent, she worked in a pub pouring beers for 'all the old guys'. She could not shake off her anger.

> I was angry. I was disappointed, really disappointed. The guy who gave me the job at Cumberland Newspapers was the one that told me I was losing my job. Weeks before, he was telling me how his mother or wife had cancer, and I said, 'I feel so bad, we'll go out and have a coffee.' And he knew all along that I was going to lose my job. I felt cheated. You know when you're in a relationship and you find out that someone cheats behind your back? That's how I felt. With the knife in your heart. That's how I felt.

In time, the hurt healed and Lettini's passion for photography returned, but 'I've never bought a News Limited newspaper since I was made redundant in 2012.'

Every journalist experienced the aftermath of redundancy in their own way. Even those who welcomed redundancy (like people nearing retirement, or journos fed up with newsrooms) took time to adjust to their new life. The majority mourned the loss of their job, however. There were no set patterns of behaviour or common ways of coping. Some missed the sense of purpose their career had given them. Some looked for or tried other work. Some moved on with their lives while others felt stuck. Some took time to work through their feelings and adjust to new circumstances. Some believed journalism wasn't the same anymore. Some accepted that professional life might never be the same again. There was no right or wrong way to grieve, or move on.[2]

The variety of experiences shows up in what the journalists did next. For every Anne Davies who moved smoothly from a senior writing role at *The Sydney Morning Herald* to a similar perch at *Guardian Australia*, there were several who wrote a novel (or completed one in the case of Debra Jopson whose *Oliver of the Levant* was published in 2016). Others simply took a break. Jo Roberts did not want to be in Melbourne the Monday after leaving *The Age* so she took her family on a three-week holiday in Florida in the United States. Michael West wanted to set up his own website for investigative journalism, but first he burned through part of his payout on holidays in four countries, including skiing in Japan and surfing in Bali.

Matthew Franklin decompressed from political reporting in Canberra by renovating his garden. Tiring of that and wanting some pocket-money, he took a job at the local Hog's Breath Café (where his co-workers were all about 15 years of age), and lost a lot of weight because he was on his feet all the time. For others, such as Kate Mills, redundancy coincided with a major family event, in her case the illness and eventual death of her mother, for whom she cared. It was a time that was both draining and uplifting, as journalists adjusted to their new lives.

Veteran illustrator John Spooner had believed he could keep working until he was dead. Forced redundancy in 2016, a few months before his 70th birthday, was a shock, if not a surprise. Yet, that didn't make the immediate aftermath of redundancy easier. Spooner says, 'it was a huge struggle'. It was hard to adjust to change because his life had been 'wrapped up in that giant family', a newspaper that had become part of his identity. He says, 'I had hoped to make it to 70 before I got the nod. But I've gone out and bought one of those super-duper cricket bats with the thick sides. That's symbolising that I will be batting on!'

Kate Mills knew being editor of *Business Review Weekly* was not a 'forever job', but she did not expect a messy ending or the emotional turmoil that followed. It felt like a personal failure even when everyone was struggling with digital transformation. In hindsight, Mills believes her mistake was poor networking. After she persuaded Fairfax to invest $200 000 to revamp the *BRW* platform in 2012, she first focused on creating an atmosphere where people embraced change before working on the website itself. However, the CEO noticed the slow progress and appointed a new publisher above her. Mills felt devastated.

There were other opportunities at Fairfax, but Mills felt too hurt, angry and let down. Her ambition for managerial roles disappeared, but she agreed to stay on for four months and to work as a commercial editor on various projects. In 2013, she took a voluntary redundancy. The drawn-out leaving process was agonising. Mills says the 'tectonic plates' of her life 'completely shifted' and journalism moved away. She looked at the media landscape and thought 'everything's moved and you're going to have to move with it'. She forced herself to think about other careers, but nothing looked as good as being boss of *BRW*.

She says, 'It was a loss of identity and you grieve that loss of identity. I mean you grieve when you're no longer a daughter because your mother is dead. You grieve that sense of identity. And I didn't have an identity. I didn't know what to call myself.'

Charles Waterhouse, who had spent his working life in Tasmania with *The Examiner*, *The Advocate* and the *Mercury*, had no trouble calling himself 'an ex-journo'. He was contemplating a new career as a teacher in China and would later work in home and community care where he would routinely encounter people who appreciated what he did. But of the career he had just left, he concludes, 'I don't think journos have been highly respected. In fact [they are] very lowly respected in Australia.'

Ian McArthur had been in and out of newsroom jobs in Australia and Japan during his 30 years in journalism. He remembers the 'tap on the shoulder' that ended his career in 2013 because it still gives him pain. He had enjoyed three years' work as a sub-editor at News Corp's head office until he was 'no longer required' due to a restructure. Losing the job was a financial and psychological blow for him and his family. He says, 'It's unsettling to my wife in particular. She is Japanese. She comes from a culture where – for the most part – people have always had a lifetime job.' McArthur adds jobs in Australia can be precarious and the fact that he had been restructured out of a job was 'hard on her, and me'. Having gone through redundancy he realised he would never again have a full-time permanent job in journalism. He says, 'Knowing that and understanding it emotionally are two different things.' He has learned to live with employment insecurity, but is weary of 'the constant need to adjust'. He tries to keep positive.

Over time, people were able to think about other things, from home renovations and new hobbies (often funded by redundancy payouts) to gardening and uninterrupted family time. In the immediate aftermath of job loss, some felt like putting their personal as well as professional stories on the record. They wanted to talk openly. They wanted others to know.

Meredith Booth moved straight into public relations consulting after taking voluntary redundancy from *The Advertiser* in 2012. She felt jaded by change in journalism. She says, 'It wasn't the journalism that was there when I started in 1998.' Booth felt news reporting had become harder, with pressure to keep pace with new digital technology. Though she agreed that computers, voice recorders and smart phones had made it easier to get stories, her main concern was time spent on technology that meant less time with people.

She says, 'The basis of a journalist's career is relationships with the community they live in. That hasn't changed.'

Booth found PR work interesting and gave it 'a good go' for 14 months before admitting she was lonely. She says, 'I was in an office by myself most of the time. I was bored, no one to talk to. A friend suggested I should come back and work at *The Australian*. There was a job going and I jumped at it, because I was back in the newsroom, back in the game!'

Bart Sinclair went to New York with his wife after taking redundancy from *The Courier-Mail* in 2012. He describes the trip as 'wonderful' and 'euphoric'. He says, 'I didn't have to worry about what was happening and check in all the time.' Sinclair had worked as a racing writer with News Limited for 43 years. It was unrelenting, given that horse racing ran for 52 weeks of the year. After 40 years in the job, he was told he was a 'required person' and had no chance of redundancy. Although he says News was good to him, he felt they were waiting for him 'to give in and resign or die on the job'. So, he did some succession planning. He trained up a young colleague who could fill his position when he left.

When he finally found a way to go, he made 'a complete cut from the media' and enjoyed his holiday and time off. Yet, six months on, he was restless and looking for something to do. The Brisbane Racing Club offered him work as an advisor. He says, 'I just love the atmosphere of the racetrack. I've got a reason to be here at the moment.'

Rosslyn Beeby considered two options after she left *The Canberra Times* in 2012: to enrol in an environmental humanities doctorate or start blogging. The blog had more appeal as a way of maintaining her profile, but she was wary of getting trolled for her views on climate change, which had occurred frequently at *The Canberra Times*. She decided to build on her reputation for covering biodiversity research and launched her website, *The Hound*, in February 2015 after finding regular work with a global research news subscription service.

It was a slow start and involved posting the published blog on Twitter and Facebook. Her first post – on Australian scientists calling for a national bee pollination levy for crops – attracted around 30 views. But a month later, a post on the impact of commercial logging machinery on wildlife in Chile got hundreds of hits. She watched the blog's progress on the WordPress stats map, which showed it was being shared among forest ecologists across Latin America. It's still a popular post. 'I think every forest scientist in South America has read that piece by now.' Beeby says the response shows it's possible to build an international audience from a desk in the spare room, but 'you've got to put in the work'.

As we've seen, the immediate aftermath of job loss was, for many, accompanied by grief for all that had been lost, including the routine and regular income of steady employment and the identity and status that journalism had given them. That grief manifested in many forms, and for some took many months to resolve. Some sought solace in the company of others who had experienced redundancy, or in their garden, or on a holiday. Others found joy or peace by reconnecting with their family, and from the simple pleasures of parenthood, such as collecting their children from school or supporting their partners with their projects. Even those who welcomed redundancy faced challenges adjusting to a new life and changed circumstances. Some were advised to establish new careers quickly, while most found they needed time and space before they could properly reimagine their lives, either in another form of journalism or outside the industry. And with that came the prospect of new challenges, even rejuvenation. They felt re-energised in ways that would have seemed unimaginable in the throes of redundancy.

CHAPTER 17
Resilience and reinvention

Penny O'Donnell

After taking voluntary redundancy from News Corporation in July 2012, Maureen Shelley became a businesswoman. Though she had loved her job, she never assumed it would last a lifetime. In her role as national editorial development manager, she had been privy to frank talk about the 'catastrophic' decline in classified advertising revenue, and she had personally witnessed newsroom job shedding.

By mid-2012, *The Daily Telegraph*, where she worked, had just 80 staff where a dozen years earlier there had been 380. She'd spent a year as national technology writer for five metro dailies, which had given her insight into where the digital news business was heading. She found technological innovation exciting, and wanted to be more involved. It helped that she had given herself work options by using paid study to complete three postgraduate degrees – in business, intellectual property law, and equity and social administration.

'I was always a very unusual journalist, because I had qualifications in so many different areas,' she says. 'I was preparing myself for my next career.'

With her redundancy payout, she bought into The Copy Collective, a content marketing agency that business partner Dominique Antarakis had set up in 2008. 'It is a great adventure,' says Shelley. 'I know how to do this.'

Her expertise helped the business grow rapidly. Within five years, the agency had become a thriving global enterprise, operating in Australia, New Zealand, and Hong Kong, with a diversified suite of content marketing, fundraising and consultancy services. Shelley forged an 'encore career', giving her both fulfillment and financial reward.

Many journalists were over the age of 50 when their newsroom positions became redundant. Having held those jobs for 10, 20, 30, even 40 years, most had expected to 'see out' their working lives in newsroom employment. Doing something else was likely inconceivable because for many, journalism is a vocation, not just a job.[1] Few were prepared like Shelley to ride the wave of media transformation into another career. She was well ahead of the curve in reinventing herself as a digital entrepreneur.

Veronica Ridge and her two sons, Nick and Jay Cooper, co-founded a digital start-up, <issimo.io>, after she left *The Age* in October 2012. It was the boys' idea. They had the tech skills to set up an online business, but no idea how to engage users. They asked their mum for help. Ridge had always enjoyed crafting stories and knew how to attract audiences. She went to Google Trends, identified *Twilight* movies as a popular topic, set up a website for fans, and posted a heap of stories, which she also shared on Twitter.

'It went wild,' says Ridge. 'I remember the boys saying, "You've got eyeballs on this site when we couldn't get anyone to look at ours!"'

The family business was born. In their first venture, Ridge and her sons created an upmarket 'mobile first' digital magazine they called <issimomag.com>. That expanded into <issimo.io>, a subscription-based, digital self-publishing platform for journalists, which won a 2015 Walkley Foundation Innovation in Journalism Grant. The start-up has since morphed into operating a publishing and software company in the small business sector.

Ridge explains their survival in Silicon Valley terms, describing <issimo.io> as a 'cockroach' start-up. 'It's basically a start-up that is very lean,' she says. 'We own all this, and we stay completely lean, so nothing can kill us.' With her sons, Ridge learned to become agile in the face of relentless industry and technological change, and how to develop a viable digital business. Yet, she is more concerned with keeping 'the spirit of publishing and journalism alive' than claiming the title of successful digital entrepreneur. 'We still haven't found a solution for publishers and publishing,' she says.

'People probably think we're completely nuts, but journalism needs programmers and software engineers who are passionate about publishing. You need journalists and technicians to work together.'

Louise Graham had two business start-up options when she took voluntary redundancy from *The Age* in 2009. One was media recruitment, the other was home care for the elderly. In the spirit of making a fresh start, she registered an aged care company, called Happy at Home, and was about to hire a whole lot of people, but was deterred by the amount of paperwork required. Graham went back to doing something she knew well. In partnership with her sister, she set up The Media Gang, a job placement agency for media professionals. Her timing was impeccable. Antony Catalano, a former marketing director for *The Age*, had just launched Metro Media Publishing and was their first big client.

'That was a great project,' says Graham. 'They needed content, they needed staff, they needed photographers, journos and subs. And they were starting from scratch, it was perfect.'

Over time, the company grew into 'a reasonable sized business' by brokering jobs for redundant journalists who had 'no idea' how to sell themselves. Graham had found her groove.

In 2013, she looked around for new ventures. Three former *Age* colleagues, executive editor Rod Wiedermann, art director Bill Farr and senior journalist Ken Merrigan, decided to join her. Together they bought Clemson Text and Media, a content marketing agency, and transformed it into an end-to-end publishing company, called

MediaXpress. 'Bringing newsroom expertise to the corporate world' is their slogan. The business prospered.

'Like Media Gang, its timing was good,' she says. 'You're not dancing on people's redundancies, you're giving employment to people who otherwise probably wouldn't have it.'

In 2019 Graham sold her share and is now volunteering for Women and Mentoring in inner city Melbourne and Wellsprings for Women Inc in the outer south-eastern suburbs.

In 2016, Aleisha Orr set up a small online business, called Storyteller Services, after taking redundancy from Fairfax Media's Perth-based online news site, *WAtoday*. She collects people's life stories and photos and collates them into personal history books. 'We've got an ageing society, and lately people are really interested in nostalgia and stories from the good old days,' she says. Orr has a steady flow of jobs based on word-of-mouth recommendations, gets great feedback on her books, and believes there is a strong market for her services. On the other hand, she is still trying to figure out how a viable small business works when you do it all on your own. Her business development training provided some basics, but no blueprint.

'It has been a real learning process, how to make a product, and how to make money out of that, what the procedures are to sign people up and then interview them and get everything into a book.' The need to increase her marketing and promotion beyond her Facebook page has become more pressing, too.

Jane Hammond had well-honed digital media skills when she took voluntary redundancy from *The West Australian* in October 2012 and wanted to keep working in journalism. She was eager for a new challenge, but required additional audio-visual skills, so in 2013 Hammond enrolled in a postgraduate filmmaking degree to learn how to shoot and edit films. In 2014, after seeing an ad on <EthicalJobs.com.au>, she successfully applied for the job of national media coordinator of the Lock the Gate Alliance, a social movement fighting against excessive coal and gas extraction across regional and rural Australia. Hammond had returned to her roots in activism. She made eight short films about the Queensland gaslands, for online release, before her contract ended in 2015.

'I couldn't believe what we were doing to our farmers,' she says. 'I just found it astonishing. After so many years in journalism, you'd think I would be used to bad stuff, but this was on another scale.'

The experience accelerated Hammond's professional reinvention, and she began working as a videographer, relying on grants and philanthropy to fund her social and environmental documentary projects, and falling back on freelance journalism and media consultancy at other times.

'I've got half a dozen films that I'd like to make,' she says. 'It's an easy way to communicate a good story in an engaging way. You get people to speak for themselves, see the heart of the person, and can identify with them. It's fun.'

Many redundant journalists left their newsrooms without a job to go to and worried about their future. Decent redundancy payouts acted as a temporary safety net, allowing many to take a break from work or have a holiday. Many also used the time to consider their options. Some contemplated leaving their careers behind to drive a bus, or a truck, which is what Peter Hanlon and Campbell Cooney did respectively. Others wanted a chance to make a difference in their work. More than a few imagined a different kind of working life, with less stress and more mental space for personal projects. Sooner or later though, making wish-lists gave way to looking at job vacancies, updating CVs, writing applications, door knocking, or asking around for work. Everyone had to find a way to move on, and often that meant career change.

Steve Lewis, a former national political correspondent for News Corp Australia, moved into public relations, becoming a senior advisor at Newgate Communications in Canberra.

It's public relations, it's government relations, it's public affairs, it's media strategy, it's crisis management ...What I bring to the table is an understanding of Canberra and an understanding of the media, and that's essentially my value to a firm like Newgate, and that's why people engage me.

Lewis works four days a week and is happy in his new job. It leaves him with enough creative energy to do 'other stuff'. That includes co-writing three political thrillers with colleague Chris Uhlmann and turning them into well-received television series for Foxtel and Netflix. In addition, during his tenure as vice president of the National Press Club, Lewis wrote up the club's history, and, before that, he organised the first Midwinter Ball, raising funds for charity. Lewis 'occasionally' thinks about getting 'back into the game', but novel writing has become a passion. 'I'm trying to create a genre, "Canberra drama",' he says. 'I think there's huge potential!'

Dean Mellor adopted the moniker, 'Editorial Gun for Hire' after he left his job as editor of the Bauer Media magazine, *Australasian Dirt Bike*, in 2013. 'I don't know where I got that one from,' he says. 'I'm happy to do anything,' he says, before adding, 'as long as it's something that I want to do.' That has included photo shoots, camera work, product spruiking, and a tourism booklet. While his freelance work involves more content marketing than journalism, Mellor continues to write for editorial publications.

'Maybe I look at it through rose-coloured glasses,' he says. 'I've done more writing over the last three years than I had over the previous ten. It's been good to get back into writing. I really enjoy talking to people. I like doing interviews. I've done some fun stuff over the last three years that I might have otherwise not done, so it's been very good.'

Jo Roberts began reinventing herself as an online music magazine publisher post-redundancy, but the venture didn't work out. She turned to freelancing instead and did various 'really nice writing gigs' for the National Gallery Magazine, before a former colleague at *The Age*, Gabriella Coslovich, recommended she apply for an intriguing job at a health organisation.

'They were looking for someone with an arts background to edit medical content,' says Roberts. 'They wanted someone who would edit it in a way that "Joe Public" would understand. I took the job!'

It was good while it lasted, but within 18 months, the company's business model failed, and Roberts was out of work for the second time in three years. Fortunately, she quickly found re-employment as health content manager at the national non-profit organisation Jean Hailes for Women's Heath. She oversees printed material, web content and social media. 'It's not very rock and roll,' says Roberts. 'But I'm still using my journalism skills every day.' She still contributes to *Rhythms* magazine, and at *EG*, the entertainment section she used to edit at *The Age*.

Tom Arup has had three jobs in the four years since he left journalism in 2016.

'I felt like I was done with journalism,' he says. 'I'm a progressive person. I didn't want to work somewhere bland, and I didn't want to work somewhere evil. I didn't want to take a job for the sake of it. There were jobs out there where I could actually engage in a bit of politics without having to pretend.'

Initially, he worked in advocacy and fundraising for Save the Children Australia, and then campaigning for the Australian Conservation Foundation. For Arup, these jobs were 'liberating'. He was well-paid and doing something he cared about. Yet, he was also 'stuck in the fricking media cycle' and found it tiring.

'I've got 30 to 40 years of working life left,' he says. 'I don't want to be in media relations for the rest of that.'

In 2020, Arup was appointed as a director of two investment groups, one of which focused on climate change and Asia. He has moved into climate change advocacy and is leaving behind journalism and the 24/7 news-cycle.

Resilience and reinvention

Getting another decent job in journalism after redundancy was never going to be easy, given the continuing financial difficulties faced by media organisations, but many redundant journalists were determined to try. What they didn't anticipate were the various personal and professional challenges that accompanied job-seeking. Some didn't know where to start. Others struggled to get an interview. More than a few felt humiliated when their job applications were rejected. Many felt daunted by the media labour market, with its new job categories, short-term contracts and 'flexible' pay rates. Journalistic expertise and experience seemed to have lost value, leaving some to wonder whether re-employment might mean professional suicide.[2] Yet, they still had insider know-how *and* their contact books, so why not give it a go?

Lynne Dwyer got lucky. She was hired as a layout designer for News Limited one week after leaving *The Sydney Morning Herald*. It was an improbable switch. She had done a bit of layout over 23 years at *The Herald*, but not a lot. Her husband, who worked at News, heard of the vacancy, and put her name forward. When she got the job, he had to give her a weekend crash course on layout. 'That's totally journalism,' Dwyer says, 'you'd get thrown in, you've got to do it, so you learn.' Then, in a twist of fate, she faced an involuntary redundancy at News in 2018, but took up a role as desk editor back at *The Sydney Morning Herald*, just one week later.

Campbell Cooney seized the opportunity to work as chief of staff at the *Shepparton News* after a text message from a pal alerted him to the job opening. Cooney was a veteran ex-ABC broadcaster, who had never worked in newspapers, so did a month try-out before landing the position. The fresh start in journalism ended seven months of worrying about what to do post-redundancy. It was as welcome as unexpected.

'I'm learning a hell of a lot about a newspaper which I never knew before,' he says. 'It has certainly taught me there is resilience that I didn't know. I enjoy my job, even though it can be quite pressured as well, but I don't think I would ever rely on an employer like I did on the ABC.'

Peter Hanlon was told when he left *The Age* after 21 years as a sports journalist that it would take five years to establish what 'normal' looked like in the freelance world. The other takeaway message he gleaned from a Media, Entertainment and Arts Alliance briefing for redundant journalists was to take whatever work he could get. For Hanlon, that has meant writing human interest stories for the National Disability Insurance Scheme website, driving the Birregurra school bus, co-writing St Kilda footballer Nick Riewoldt's autobiography, and regular gigs from the ex-*Age* people at MediaXpress.

'Incredibly weird and wonderful stuff,' says Hanlon. 'But all the principles of journalism are there – knock it together quickly, make it understandable, a bit of fun as well, and write to deadline.'

In 2015, press photographer Isabella Lettini was 'called out of the blue', three years after a traumatic exit from her job at NewsLocal Newspapers. Fairfax Media had work going in north-west Sydney, and colleague Neoklis Bloukos had recommended her because she lived in the area. 'I was extremely grateful,' Lettini recalls, 'and I was going to give 2000 per cent, which I did.' In 2017 she won the PANPA Newspaper award for Community News. 'I wanted recognition,' she says. 'I achieved what I wanted to achieve.' However, in the same year she lost that job too, as Fairfax went through another round of redundancies.

Almost every redundant journalist has had to reinvent themselves in some way because media companies themselves are desperately trying to adapt to the collapse of their business models. Their digital business strategies focus on reader demand, and audience metrics drive their news selection, not editors' instincts and experience. Journalism skills still have wide industry currency, but journalism values seem to hold less sway. And, as journalists' working lives become more precarious, it is getting harder to do good journalism. Yet, among redundant journalists, there is no shortage of belief in the mission to interrogate and inform; no loss of will to scrutinise those in power and support democracy, no lack of interest in telling stories of heroic endeavours and everyday lives. Newsrooms may be dying, but the journalistic ethos is not.

Di Thomas's career in journalism started as a cadet journalist for the *Central Western Daily*, and she mostly worked in regional and rural media. Her passion is working closely with communities. When she left her job as editor of *The Border Mail* in 2015, after 17 years with the masthead, she published an article thanking the Albury-Wodonga readers for their trust. In 2016, Thomas successfully applied for work as chief of staff for Cathy McGowan, the Independent Member for Indi, and one of the crossbenchers who held the balance of power in Malcolm Turnbull's minority parliament. The successful pivot to politics relied on her community standing and understanding of local issues as much as her journalism skills. Three years of working with politicians refreshed her interest in public interest journalism.

Thomas says, 'The power of good journalism remains the power to hold officialdom to account and to address things like mental health issues, institutional child abuse … those things don't change because of what's happened with resources. That need remains.'

Matthew Franklin, who took a redundancy after many years as a respected political journalist with *The Australian*, got a late-night job offer from Kevin Rudd in June 2013. The Australian Labor Party had backflipped and made Rudd prime minister again, in what was widely seen as a desperate bid to hold on to government. Various politicians tried to recruit Franklin after he left the press gallery in 2012, but he opted for some time out. In a way, he had primed himself for a career change. Franklin recalls why he accepted Rudd's offer:

> I knew this is just a 10-week gig. I didn't think we were going to win. Although, for a while, it looked like we might. The way I viewed it was, 'I'm not going back to journalism. This is going to be a hell of an experience. And, finally, I'll get to answer to myself the question, Is this man a lunatic?' ... I wanted to see if all the terrible things people said about him were correct, and not all of them were. He was a very, very complex man whose experience, in terms of losing the prime ministership, had made him distrustful.

Franklin became Rudd's director of strategic communications. 'I had to communicate with the press gallery in an authentic way by telling them what particular announcements meant, and how that fitted into a broader narrative of what he stood for,' he recalls.

At the same time, Franklin set himself a professional challenge. 'I'd had years of unsatisfactory relationships with press secretaries and then this opportunity came up and I thought, "Well, if you think they're so hopeless why don't you see if you can do better?"'

Rudd lost the 2013 election, but Franklin remained on the politics side of the divide, picking up work as media adviser to former minister and later Opposition leader, Anthony Albanese.

Michael West is an independent media publisher who describes himself as a 'journalist covering the rising power of corporations over democracy'. He created <michaelwest.com.au>, a start-up for investigative reporting in 2016, specifically to focus on neglected stories of high public interest. The business model is lean: 'we are non-partisan, do not take advertising, and are funded by readers'. How does that work?

> Well, I decided that people aren't going to read it if they've got to pay for it. A few people will, but it's not going to pay its way. I stay alive basically by saying to people give me five dollars a month and I'll just do my best. We need somebody

out there to shine the spotlight on powerful vested interests and government. That's the spiel, which is true, because I don't want to put it behind a paywall. The first story was 20 000 audience!

West believes the media market is 'perfect' for his type of start-up.

'Look at Fairfax, look at News,' he says. 'They're either too agenda-driven or there are juniors writing copy. There's no longer people standing up to management, having blow-me-down arguments, saying "you've got to publish this story or you're a traitor to the public".'

West's website has become a sorting house for articles by other independent journalists, which attracts more users, but adds to his already exhausting workload and 'the constant pressure' this sort of journalism entails. For the moment, though, his expertise is in demand and West is optimistic about his new approach to investigative journalism. The next step is to secure funds to bring other like-minded journalists on board.

There are many more inspirational stories of redundant journalists reinventing themselves, and not just once, but again and again. Some are more adventurous than others. All of them have displayed grit and resilience.

Journalism gave them attributes and skills that translated into many other jobs and not just in public relations. They knew how to navigate in contested terrain. They knew how to ask for what they wanted. They understood pressure and could work quickly. They were also good communicators, and were also able to draw on well-established networks.

They fought to save their identity as journalists, despite that identity being taken from them. Some kept the central importance of journalism firmly in their sights, which sometimes meant they felt sadness for the state of the industry. For others, it meant they felt obliged to stay connected and even to attempt to fill gaps in the industry, sometimes at considerable financial cost to themselves.

As these accounts of post-redundancy ventures make clear, a good number of journalists have transferred the initiative and resourcefulness they used to deploy on stories into new enterprises. Some have enjoyed success beyond their imagining, while others have needed to adapt and then adapt again, as ventures folded. A number of journalists danced from one generous redundancy package to a new high-profile perch in the media. But others went backstage, so to speak, to public relations where they traded public recognition for influence, as Matthew Franklin and Matthew Moore did when they worked as press secretaries for Labor leader Anthony Albanese and Sydney Lord Mayor Clover Moore respectively. Moving back and forth between newsrooms and PR offices is a well-worn path for journalists. Not so well trodden is the riskier path to creating new businesses or reinventing journalism. But it is an important part and one that needs every encouragement.

CHAPTER 18
The wrap

Andrew Dodd
Matthew Ricketson

The upheaval of the last decade has separated two eras in journalism. In this chaotic period, people's lives have been as disrupted as much as the technology and business models of the media itself. The journalists who generously agreed to tell their stories in these pages predominantly worked in industrial newsrooms for wealthy, or at least stable organisations, and used well-honed skills to tell stories for loyal, consistent audiences. In their accounts we see commitment because their work mattered to them. They told us how they derived satisfaction from doing it well. It wasn't always fun and it wasn't without its frustrations, but it was usually interesting, often exhilarating, and it certainly defined them as people.

Just to capture these sentiments has been a valuable exercise. After all, many of our interviewees represent the last generation of reporters trained in analogue media. They used typewriters and knew about compositing and how to splice audio edits on quarter-inch tape. They worked alongside copy kids in highly structured, hierarchical newsrooms, where sub-editors wrote headlines and reporters didn't dare take photographs. They saw Saturday editions thick with classified ads and had travel budgets they were encouraged to spend. Some even worked where public relations operatives didn't block their access and politicians hadn't yet been media-trained to say nothing. Their stories might just be a testament to journalism's heyday.

And then it all changed.

Again, our interviewees have borne witness. They saw the collapse of the media's business model. At the time they didn't write much about what was happening, but now they have taken us inside their newsrooms and allowed us to see what media companies themselves kept opaque. We have seen what it was like to lose some of the very elements that defined journalism. We saw the effects of contraction and cost-cutting, and the ways stories and audiences suffered. We saw how some media companies struggled to understand new technology, and so lost opportunities, while others harnessed technology to save costs but reduce jobs. We also saw how the shock of sackings gave way to the pessimism and defeatism of sustained downsizing, as round after round of redundancies reduced newsrooms or closed them altogether.

The interviewees also revealed what it was like for them personally. The highs of journalism gave way to all sorts of hurt, whether it was anticipation at losing a job, or agony in deciding to go. Always, there was sadness at leaving behind longstanding colleagues. There was guilt at surviving in one round, and grief at succumbing in another. There was also anger over managerial indifference and relief, or even a sense of liberation, at leaving the stress behind. Some were just happy to leave. Whatever their reasons, we see their passion for storytelling and for the roles they played in animating democracy. We feel their loss, alongside the loss of the industry as we knew it. We share their fears for the future and wonder whether there's cause for hope.

Each year thousands of young people flock to university open days asking whether they should study journalism – for years one of the most popular courses in many institutions – or whether they should apply for buzz degrees like Digital Media. Accompanied by their sceptical HECS debt-conscious parents, they hear journalism academics acknowledge how the industry, at least legacy media, has been shedding jobs before adding that this is a time of great excitement and opportunity. Young graduates can be part of reinventing journalism. There are many more job opportunities in new fields because the barriers to entry have never been lower now that individuals and corporations have the means to build an audience and tell their own stories. And, they are told the world needs young people enthusiastic to learn and courageous to research, report and publish honest, reliable journalism.

If the presidency of Donald Trump taught us anything, the journalism academics say, it is the urgent need to counter toxic online trolling, prejudice-reinforcing algorithms, populist political hostility toward journalism and hyper-partisanship in the media itself. But the journalism academics do worry that they are preparing people for a diminishing pool of sustaining journalism jobs.

On the positive side, aspiring journalists can take comfort in knowing that audiences have not lost their appetite for good journalism in all its forms, including long reads, investigations and on-the-spot reportage. Journalists are excited about the potential of new technology which is now being realised, from data journalism, and story maps, to new ways of connecting with audiences and working with colleagues.

Look at how international collaborative projects are shaping global investigative reporting and connecting citizen journalists with mainstream media, and with each other. The Panama Papers, for instance, brought together 400 journalists across 80 countries who documented how the misuse of tax havens was not isolated to one or two countries but is a systemic global problem.[1]

There are new worries too. The ability of every organisation or company to produce their own media has further blurred lines between reportage and marketing, and Artificial Intelligence has emerged as the next disruptive threat.

But notice how so many more people are talking about journalism more now. That has to be one of the positive things to emerge from this upheaval. People feel genuine alarm about the state of our news media. It has permeated both public discussion and the chambers of federal parliament, resulting in policy interventions that would have seemed impossible even five years ago.

A conservative government has told Google and Facebook to pay for the news it has been taking and using to build audiences and attract advertising. The same government has subsidised journalists' jobs at regional media outlets, admittedly in part to win over its National Party colleagues as well as crossbench senators who allowed greater deregulation of media ownership. Perhaps most significantly, the large media companies have finally admitted they need help. They are more prepared to talk publicly about the effects of industry disruption, though, true to form, they have little interest in government supporting the entry into the media of any new, independent outlets.

There are legitimate fears that the federal government's News Media Bargaining Code, passed in early 2021, will primarily result in money being paid to larger media companies like News and Nine and with no guarantees the money will be spent on public interest journalism. This is what had originally been recommended by the Australian Competition and Consumer Commission (ACCC) in its Digital Platforms Inquiry Report in 2019.[2]

But back in the newsrooms, fewer journalists are pumping out more stories in less time with scarcer resources. They are connected to all manner of online or mobile devices that feed them much more information than journalists received in the past, but devices tend to tether them to their desk, limiting the serendipitous discoveries made when they get out of the office. Fewer old hands are imparting their wisdom, and some of their old practices, such as sub-editing, are disappearing.

As long ago as 1911, the editor of Baltimore's *Sun*, Charles H Grasty, described the production of his newspaper as a daily miracle.[3] Every day the team started with little more than blank pages, but by the nightly deadline managed to create a fully formed publication, packed with new information. The industry now needs another kind of miracle, a digital miracle perhaps, in which the news media itself is reshaped into something sustainable and whole.

Who knows? Perhaps it's already happening. Young journalists are up for the challenge of reporting in new ways for new audiences. They're keen and nimble enough to work across media forms and to adapt to new ones as they arise. And they also want to work in environments that are inclusive and fairer and more supportive. The voices in this book represent one generation of media workers talking to the next, offering their experiences, at times nostalgic, but mostly always passionate. They are voices from a time that, thanks to the impact of Covid-19, feels like it was decades ago. They are saying we gave it a go, it has changed and now we've largely left, although many of us still call ourselves journalists and desperately want the industry to survive. The interviewees are saying some elements have gone forever, but others remain. A story is still a story, although some are much easier to get and easier to tell today. Other kinds of stories, such as those that hold governments to account, remain as hard if not harder to deliver, let alone bring about lasting change. We don't have all the answers, the interviewees concede, but here are some insights you might find useful. We're here if you need us and most of all, we wish you well, because journalism really matters. Not just for us, but for everyone.

It is possible to harness the best from the past while rising to the new challenges of the present and the future. It is a cliché to say we need good journalism now more than ever but you can see why we've been hearing it a lot lately. Look at the events at the Capitol in Washington, DC, on 6 January 2021.[4] It is hard to fathom that so many Americans continue to believe the lies Donald Trump told about the presidential election result, and that some of them planned an assault that came close to lynching the Democrat speaker of the house, Nancy Pelosi, and the Republican vice-president Mike Pence.[5] We know this level of detail because journalists told us,[6] just as they informed us about the 30 000-plus lies Trump told during his presidency,[7] as well as his attacks on democratic institutions and failure to combat Covid-19. That many Americans did not see these stories, or chose to reject them has a lot to do with how social media has been used to distort and misinform.[8] This may help explain why 74 million Americans voted for Trump. But surely a key reason why more than 81 million voted for Joe Biden is the work reporters did to hold Trump's presidency to account. Journalism is central to a healthy democracy. That's why we need to keep saying it matters, now more than ever.

The roll call

Tom Arup grew up in Melbourne and started in journalism working on the University of Melbourne student paper, *Farrago*, which he later edited. He joined *The Age* in 2008 out of university, and after a shortened cadetship was sent by the paper to report on federal politics in the national press gallery later that year. In Canberra, he predominantly covered climate change and environmental policy, before returning to *The Age*'s Melbourne newsroom at the start of 2012. In Melbourne, he did stints as a state political correspondent and news desk editor, but worked largely as *The Age*'s environment editor, including covering the Paris climate change negotiations, until he took a voluntary redundancy in May 2016. Since leaving journalism, he has held senior roles in communications, strategy and investigations at Save the Children Australia, the Australian Conservation Foundation, the Investor Group on Climate Change and the Asia Investor Group on Climate Change. (Interviewed by Lawrie Zion on 3 April 2018.)

Rosslyn Beeby covered science, research policy and environmental news for more than 30 years. She grew up on a farm in East Gippsland, and started her journalism career with *Standard News*, a suburban media network in Melbourne. She had an Honours degree in English and American literature from Monash University and did her Master's thesis on Edgar Allan Poe's use of science in his horror fiction. She was a news reporter and feature writer at *The Age* for seven years, covering the Franklin river blockade in 1983. Beeby worked at Radio Australia as an editor and producer with its Pacific news service. She was science and environment reporter for

The Canberra Times from 2003 to 2012, when she took a voluntary redundancy. In 2013 she accepted a role as Australian and New Zealand news editor with Research Professional, a London-based subscription news service for universities. Beeby died in April 2021. (Interviewed by Matthew Ricketson on 15 December 2015.)

Meredith Booth has worked in newsrooms for more than 25 years as a business and general reporter, features editor and opinion editor. She began with Adelaide suburban group *The Messenger* in 1991, and later joined the metropolitan masthead *The Advertiser* and the Adelaide bureau of *The Australian*. She has worked in Melbourne with the Leader Group and experienced a bustling work environment at the *Daily Mail*, London. After volunteering for redundancy at *The Advertiser* in 2012, where she was a part-time business reporter, she worked as a public relations consultant and returned to news at *The Australian* before resigning to work as a freelance journalist and blogger for financial publications and companies. She is also an educator with the University of South Australia and the Google News Initiative/Walkley Foundation. She lives in Adelaide with her husband and three children. (Interviewed by Penny O'Donnell on 26 April 2019.)

Ross Brundrett began his career at *The Mail* in Footscray in 1975, covering general news and the Bulldogs for seven years before making the shift to sub-editor at Melbourne's afternoon daily, *The Herald*, for 12 months. He returned to the western suburbs as feature writer, columnist and sportswriter at the *Western Times* for three years before joining the *Sunday Press* as a general reporter in 1986 until its demise in 1989. He then moved to *The Sun News-Pictorial* (which became the *Herald Sun* soon after). For 24 years he remained at the paper, although his role fluctuated between feature writer, columnist and 'colour writer'. He took voluntary redundancy from the paper in 2013. (Interviewed by Andrew Dodd on 6 September 2015.)

Jo Chandler started out as a school-leaver cadet on her hometown masthead, *The Kyneton Guardian*, in 1984. She then worked for various Leader suburban titles until a fellowship to study journalism took her to the US. Returning in late 1989, she was offered a position on *The Age* where she remained for 23 years. As a senior writer and roving correspondent, she reported from Antarctica, Afghanistan, Africa, remote Australia and Papua New Guinea. She volunteered for redundancy in 2012, aiming to pursue neglected hard-to-tell stories from hard-to-reach places as a freelancer. Her work on climate, human rights, health, environment and women's issues has appeared internationally in *The New York Times*, *The Guardian* and *The Atlantic* among others, and domestically in *The Monthly*, *Griffith Review*, *Good Weekend* and ABC Radio National. She has earned numerous commendations including Walkley and Quill awards. Today a senior lecturer in journalism at the University of Melbourne, she continues to produce longform reportage. (Interviewed by Matthew Ricketson on 21 January 2018.)

Tim Colebatch is unusual in having spent his entire newspaper career on one paper, *The Age*, working as a journalist from 1971 to 2013. He counts himself lucky to have worked in a politically independent, warm-hearted media outlet; a team enterprise committed to the welfare of the many, not the few. His first formal role there was as an environment writer, then he went on the Insight investigative team, and had four-year stints as an editorial writer and Washington correspondent before settling in Canberra, first as economics writer and then, from 1993 to 2013, as economics editor. Less formally, he was also a weekly columnist for most of the years from 1985 on, and his role as numbers man included the election numbers. He has three degrees acquired in different decades, in Arts, Commerce and Asian studies. In semi-retirement, he now writes for the website *Inside Story* <www.insidestory.org.au>. (Interviewed by Matthew Ricketson on 14 August 2019.)

Campbell Cooney started his working life in Western Queensland, working various jobs ranging from station hand to auctioneer, before studying journalism in the 1990s. In 1997 he joined the ABC in Tasmania as a rural reporter based in Launceston and over 17 years worked in a range of roles including news reporter, station manager and executive producer of *Victorian Country Hour*. In 2007 he was appointed as one of the ABC's Pacific correspondents, a role he held until 2014 when he took redundancy after the Abbott government cut the ABC's funding. Since then, he's been chief of staff and the editor of newspapers in Shepparton and Sydney, and in the corporate communications sector. He has also worked in freelance communications, delivered rental cars and worked in a whiskey distillery. Since 2019 Cooney has been national beef and cattle writer covering southern Australia for Australian Community Media's agricultural papers. He lives in Melbourne with his family. (Interviewed by Lawrie Zion on 16 October 2015.)

Stephen Corby grew up in Canberra and gained his dream job of a cadetship at *The Canberra Times* in 1993, at age 22. He covered various rounds, writing news, music, technology, cars, politics and everything in between, until 1997, when he moved to London and worked on the *Evening Standard*, the *Sunday Mail* and *Daily Mail*. Returning in 2000 in time for the Sydney Olympics, he took a casual job on *The Daily Telegraph* and was soon made chief sub-editor of Features, but resigned to focus on writing in 2002. After freelancing internationally for two years, he was offered a job as feature writer for *The Sunday Telegraph* in 2004. In 2008, he was poached to become launch editor of *Top Gear Australia* magazine. He was asked to take the reins of *Wheels* magazine in 2012. One year later, he was made redundant, and has been working as a freelancer ever since. (Interviewed by Andrew Dodd on 9 August 2017.)

The roll call

Anne Davies began her career at *The Australian Financial Review* in 1984 as a cadet after working briefly as a lawyer. However, she spent most of her professional life at *The Sydney Morning Herald*, where she worked in a number of roles including urban affairs editor, state political editor, Washington correspondent for *The Herald* and *The Age*, news editor and investigations editor. In 2002 she won the Gold Walkley Award with Kate McClymont for coverage of the Canterbury Bulldogs rugby league salary cap scandal. She was also director of the Communications Law Centre for three years. In 2016 she took redundancy from Fairfax, but returned quickly to journalism at *Guardian Australia*, where she is currently investigations editor. (Interviewed by Matthew Ricketson on 21 September 2018.)

Lynne Dwyer grew up in Sydney and completed a Bachelor of Arts (Communications) in Print Journalism at Charles Sturt University, Bathurst, in 1984. She started work as a journalist in 1985 at ESN (Eastern Suburbs Newspapers), followed by *The Bankstown Express* (part of the Cumberland Group), where while chief reporter the paper won Best Suburban Newspaper. In late 1988, she was hired as a sub-editor on the news desk of *The Sydney Morning Herald*, and over the following 23 years she took up a variety of posts, chiefly in production. In 2012, while was working as an Arts writer for Spectrum, she took a voluntary redundancy along with some 80 fellow *Herald* journalists. A week later, she started work part-time at News Limited as a layout sub for *The Australian* and *The Daily Telegraph*, along with stints at Bauer Media on *Gourmet Traveller* and Pagemasters. In June 2014, she took up a full-time production position at *The Daily Telegraph* including regular night editor, letters editor, relief chief sub and relief masthead chief for *The Sunday Telegraph*. In November 2018, she was made redundant (forced), then a week later, took up a desk editor role on *The Sydney Morning Herald* where she is today. (Interviewed by Andrew Dodd on 26 March 2018.)

Bruce Elder started in journalism while he was studying at the University of New England. He was a regular contributor – writing about popular music – for the student newspaper. In 1974, having published a successful text book for School Certificate English students, he travelled to England where he worked as a freelance music journalist (1974–1981) writing for all the major British music papers, regularly contributing to *Nation Review*, and being the London correspondent for *Bunte* in Germany and *Rolling Stone* and 2JJ in Australia. In 1987 he became the popular music concerts and music reviewer for *The Sydney Morning Herald* and subsequently became a full-time member of the Fairfax staff in 1996. As a senior journalist working predominantly in music, television and travel he took redundancy in 2013. Since then, he has created and developed a detailed internet guide to Australian towns <aussietowns.com.au>. (Interviewed by Penny O'Donnell on 9 April 2018.)

Rocco Fazzari is a graduate of the South Australian School of Art. He first started in newspapers as an illustrator in 1986 at *The Canberra Times*. In 1988 he moved to *The Sydney Morning Herald* where he was recognised for his acerbic black-and-white illustrations. He accumulated numerous awards and became known as a leader and innovator in his craft. Later years saw him embracing digital media, successfully creating a portfolio of contemporary cross-platform images and video published across the Fairfax titles. Fazzari's 28-year career at Fairfax ended in May 2016 when he was unexpectedly made redundant. He now runs a thriving multimedia practice and has collaborated with the ABC, the University of Technology, Sydney, the International Consortium of Investigative Journalists, the Asia Society, Facebook, the Art Gallery Society of NSW and the Law Society of New South Wales, to name a few. He is also a painter who regularly exhibits. (Interviewed by Penny O'Donnell on 9 March 2018.)

Matthew Franklin was born in Sydney, but grew up in Redcliffe, north of Brisbane. After studying at the University of Queensland, he completed a cadetship at *The Chronicle* in Toowoomba in 1986 before moving to the *Townsville Bulletin*, then *The Courier-Mail* where he spent 19 years as a general reporter, council roundsman, state political editor and national political editor based in Canberra. During this period, he was also Tokyo correspondent for News Limited. In 2005 he joined *The Australian* where he served as bureau chief and chief political correspondent. He took a voluntary redundancy in 2012 after 29 years' work for News Limited mastheads. He is currently head of media for the leader of the Labor Party, Anthony Albanese. (Interviewed by Matthew Ricketson on 24 September 2015.)

Louise Graham started her career as a cadet photographer at *The Herald* in Melbourne. After completing her cadetship, she was the first female photographer on the News Limited photography staff. In 1984 she was appointed deputy picture editor of *The Herald* and shortly after was promoted to picture editor at the age of 24. She was the first female picture editor in the state, as well as nationally. From then she moved between News and Fairfax a number of times, taking on picture editor positions as well as senior management roles. During that time, she managed photographic departments at *The Age, The Sunday Age*, the colour magazine for *The Sunday Herald* and the *Herald Sun*. In 2009, when she was editorial operations manager of *The Age*, she took a redundancy package to start her own media recruitment business (The Media Gang), which placed unemployed journalists and photographers in permanent, contract and contributor positions. (Interviewed by Matthew Ricketson on 11 December 2017.)

Jane Hammond started working as a journalist/editor and photographer in 1985 on the *Merredin Telegraph* in Western Australia's wheatbelt. She later took up a position with the *Northam*

Telegraph and then the *Albany Advertiser*. She moved to Sydney in 1988 to work with Fairfax Community Newspapers. Hammond joined *The Australian* in 1989 and eventually moved back to Perth to work as a state political reporter with the paper. She left in 1993 and took up freelancing full time while also working as a casual for AAP and later CSIRO. After raising three children, Jane returned to work on a daily newspaper, joining *The West Australian* in 2007. She was social affairs reporter when she took voluntary redundancy in 2012. Hammond then went back to university to complete a Master's in Film and Video, and now works as an independent documentary filmmaker. She specialises in stories of environmental justice and human rights. (Interviewed by Andrew Dodd on 5 September 2017.)

Peter Hanlon has worked in journalism for more than 30 years, initially at the *Colac Herald* and then *The Sun News-Pictorial* and *Herald Sun*. After two years sub-editing on various titles in London, including *The Times*, *The Sunday Times* and *Daily Express*, he was appointed deputy sports editor of *The Age*. This led to an 18-month exchange posting at *The Guardian*, and upon return he had stints as sports editor of *The Sunday Age* and *The Saturday Age* and also covered the 2001 Ashes in England. He was a senior sportswriter during the last 10 of his 21 years at *The Age*, covering the Beijing and London Olympics and Delhi Commonwealth Games and winning major feature writing awards for his work on AFL, cricket and horse racing. Since taking redundancy in May 2016, he has freelanced for a variety of publications, and has worked with footballers Nick Riewoldt, Bob Murphy and Jarryd Roughead on their autobiographies. (Interviewed by Matthew Ricketson on 24 January 2018.)

Wendy Hargreaves grew up in Colac, Victoria and started work as a cadet at the *Geelong Advertiser* in 1986 (a few days after completing Orientation Week at Deakin University). She later worked briefly at The Herald and Weekly Times. She moved to Tokyo in 1992, freelance writing and teaching English for 18 months. On her return to Melbourne, she joined the *Herald Sun* as a reporter, covering health, education and politics before several years as deputy chief of staff. Wendy switched to freelance life when her children were small, returning to the *Sunday Herald Sun* in 2009 as online editor before becoming the masthead's first food editor in 2010, creating its most popular section, apart from the sport liftout. When News Corp decided to run its food coverage from Sydney, Wendy took a redundancy in 2012. Since then, she has become a regular broadcaster on 3AW and launched her own online magazine. She has also freelanced for newspapers and magazines and, in the middle of the Covid-19 lockdown, launched a TV show on Ticker about the food and drink business called *Bread + Butter*. (Interviewed by Lawrie Zion on 18 September 2017.)

Samela Harris grew up in the modernist arts world of Adelaide and from childhood reviewed and wrote articles. Her election as editor of Adelaide University's *On Dit* newspaper launched her in 1965 into full-time journalism at *The News* where she became the first female general reporter and the country's first female Australian rules football columnist. She worked at AAP Reuters' London bureau and *The Edinburgh Evening News* before returning to Adelaide in 1980. She was a stringer for *The Australian* before joining *The Advertiser* in 1985. For nine years she was a daily gossip columnist and thereafter, Arts editor, issues and opinions writer, Features writer and theatre critic. Her popular cookery column *On a Shoestring, Recipes from the House of the Raising Sons* was made into a book. As an early adopter of technology, she created the first internet columns and became the paper's inaugural online editor. Accepting redundancy in 2013, she went freelance. She was inaugural chair of the Adelaide Critics Circle, remains the Media, Entertainment and Arts Alliance president of journalists for South Australia and the

Northern Territory and is a member of the Journalism Hall of Fame. (Interviewed by Penny O'Donnell on 7 June 2019.)

Linda Hunt was 17 years old and fresh out of school when she started her journalism career at ABC News in Hobart in 1988. Three decades later in 2018, she was working in the same newsroom when she was made redundant. During those years, Hunt led a varied media career, which included work in publishing, communications, PR and events, mostly in Victoria. Hunt worked as a journalist across television, radio, print and digital; presented news on television and radio; covered major news events from state elections to natural disasters; and won numerous awards. Two reporting assignments to Antarctica were the highlights. She was regularly presenting the morning news on ABC Radio in Hobart, with stints as a reporter chasing her own yarns, when she was made redundant. She is now a lecturer at the Media School at the University of Tasmania and researching her PhD thesis on news media representations of Antarctica. (Interviewed by Matthew Ricketson on 5 December 2018.)

Tracee Hutchison's media career spans 30-plus years in national and international radio and television. She got her start at the ABC's youth station, Triple J, where she launched the national network. Her on-air roles include: ABC TV's *7.30 Report*, SBS *World News*, ABC NewsRadio, ABC Local Radio (Melbourne/Sydney/Darwin/Lismore), Radio Australia and 3RRR.FM. She is a former op/ed columnist for *The Saturday Age*, the author of three books and the subject of the Australian power-pop song, Tracee Lee, by The Chevelles. As former program director and board member at 3RRR.FM, she has served on the board of Music Victoria and as inaugural head of journalism at the Australian College of Arts. Production credits include music shows *RocKwiz*, *nomad*, *DIG TV* and network executive producer ABC Australia Network. Hutchison was made redundant, involuntarily, in 2014 when the ABC shut down its Asia–Pacific TV service, the Australia Network. (Interviewed by Lawrie Zion on 24 November 2015.)

Tom Hyland grew up in Tasmania and started work as a journalist on *The North West Star*, a daily newspaper in Mount Isa, Queensland, in 1979. After a stint as a reporter and sub-editor on *The Cairns Post*, he moved to Sydney where he worked for AAP, mainly as a news editor. He spent 1983–1984 overseas, where he worked as a sub-editor with the BBC World Service in London. On his return to Australia he joined Radio Australia and then AAP in Melbourne. From 1989–1991 he was AAP's Southeast Asia correspondent, based in Jakarta, before becoming AAP's Melbourne bureau chief. In 1997 he joined *The Age*, where he held a series of senior editing positions, including foreign editor. In 2006 he moved to *The Sunday Age*, where he was a senior writer and international editor, a position he held until he took a redundancy in 2012. (Interviewed by Andrew Dodd on 25 July 2015.)

Hugh Jones went to school in Melbourne, then university in Hobart until he joined Launceston's *The Examiner* in 1980 as its first graduate cadet. After four years he joined *The Herald* in Melbourne as a sub-editor. In mid-1985 he went to the UK, working as sports editor of the *Oxford Star* for nine months, then freelancing as a sub-editor for national newspapers including *Today, The Times* and *The Sunday Times*. He returned to *The Herald* in 1988, and was deputy chief of staff when the paper merged with *The Sun* in 1990. He spent the next eight years with *The Weekly Times*, including as editor from 1994–98, then moved to the *Herald Sun* to manage a range of one-off publishing projects and inserts. He was editorial business manager of the Herald & Weekly Times (HWT) from 2003 to 2010, then managing editor of News Central Victoria, The HWT subs hub, until being made redundant by News Limited in 2012.

He has since worked in public relations and corporate communications. (Interviewed by Andrew Dodd on 13 December 2015.)

Debra Jopson joined *The Sunday Australian* as a cadet journalist in 1971 in her hometown, Sydney. During her 20s, she worked as a feature writer in Hong Kong and London. From 1980 to 1986, she contributed regularly to *The National Times* on the arts and social issues. She had stints on *The Sun-Herald* and *The Times on Sunday*, but inadequate childcare drove her back to freelancing. She campaigned to improve conditions for freelancers and became the New South Wales Journalists' Union's first freelance organiser. In 1994, she joined *The Sydney Morning Herald*, where she pioneered the Indigenous affairs round, breaking many stories over six years. During four years as a senior reporter on the investigations team, she won a 2004 Walkley Award with Gerard Ryle. She was *The Herald*'s regional affairs reporter when she took voluntary redundancy in 2012. She became the 2014 Walkley Freelance Journalist of the Year and is now a novelist. (Interviewed by Penny O'Donnell on 27 March 2018.)

Phil Kafcaloudes started his career with Sydney radio station 2KY as a producer for John Singleton and Ita Buttrose, eventually becoming the station's only reporter. He covered federal elections, crime, courts and arts before moving to the ABC, where he became a long-term legal reporter, even publishing a text on court reporting for ABC Books. Over the next 26 years he worked in 12 countries, and hosted the ABC's first English language program from China. In 2014 he was highly commended as International Radio Personality (Asian Broadcasting Awards) and was shortlisted in AIB awards in 2007. His experience at the ABC was very wide, being a TV political reporter, Arts editor for NewsRadio, and finally the breakfast presenter on Radio Australia for nine years. His program was made redundant in the Abbott government cuts of 2014. He has lectured in journalism at La Trobe and RMIT universities. (Interviewed by Lawrie Zion on 13 July 2015.)

Christian Kerr was born in Adelaide, the child of three generations of journalists. After doing some writing at university, he began work as an editorial assistant on the independent arts and issues monthly the *Sydney Review* in 1988. He spent most of the '90s as a political or media adviser to a string of Liberal parliamentarians, including two of John Howard's cabinet members and a state premier, then joined construction giant Baulderstone Hornibrook as corporate affairs manager in 1999. A chance encounter led to involvement in the founding of *Crikey* the following year, which he joined full time in 2002, remaining until he left for *The Australian* in 2008. He worked for the national broadsheet, helped found *The Spectator Australia* and acted as a regular commentator on ABC Radio and television, Sky News Australia and various commercial and overseas outlets including the BBC World Service from Canberra and Melbourne until made compulsorily redundant in 2016. He now works in strategic communications in the Catholic school sector. (Interviewed by Lawrie Zion on 19 January 2019.)

Antoinette Lattouf grew up in western Sydney and was raised by refugee parents who initially opposed her career choice. She got her first job in journalism while still at university in 2004, taking on a role as researcher then producer/reporter at SBS's *Insight*. Lattouf then joined the ABC and worked on a range of television and radio programs and wore many hats, including researcher, reporter and presenter. In 2011 Lattouf joined Network Ten as a reporter and took a voluntary redundancy four years later while she was pregnant with her second child. Lattouf co-founded Media Diversity Australia, a not-for-profit organisation that seeks to increase cultural and linguistic diversity in newsrooms. She was named among *The Australian Financial Review*'s Women of Infuence in

2019. She returned to Network 10 as a senior journalist in 2018. In May 2020, she survived another round of redundancies at Ten that claimed around 20 of her colleagues in digital. (Interviewed by Penny O'Donnell on 9 October 2017.)

Isabella Lettini grew up in Sydney. She fell in love with photography at 15 when she received her first camera, a Kodak Ektra 100. She started working at News Limited in 2004 in the newsphotos department. In 2006 she commenced as a press photographer for Cumberland Newspapers (now NewsLocal) based in Parramatta, covering the north-west region of Sydney. In 2012 she received her first redundancy. She freelanced for three years, then in 2015 commenced at Fairfax Media based in Bella Vista. In September 2017 she won the PANPA Photography of the Year Award for best news photo and she received her second redundancy, from Fairfax Media, the same year. Since 2016 she has been working for Corrective Services NSW, running rehabilitation programs and looking after the welfare needs of inmates in a maximum security prison. (Interviewed by Penny O'Donnell on 9 March 2019.)

Steve Lewis was born in Sydney in 1960 and left school aged 15 to become an apprentice butcher before working in the music industry for several years. He did a Communications degree at the University of Technology Sydney before gaining a cadetship at *The Australian Financial Review* in 1989. He moved to Canberra in 1992 where for the next 21 years he was a member of the Canberra press gallery, initially for *The Fin Review*, then for *The Australian* from 2002 to 2007 and finally for News Corporation Australia's tabloid newspapers. In 2013 he took a redundancy package, though he continued to serve as a vice-president of the National Press Club. Since leaving News Corp, Lewis has divided his time between government relations and media training work for Newgate Communications and co-authoring with Chris Uhlmann three political thrillers, two of which were adapted for television in a program called *Secret City* (2016). (Interviewed by Matthew Ricketson on 5 April 2017.)

Gillian Lord grew up in South Africa, obtained a journalism degree at Rhodes University and started out on suburban papers in Cape Town before moving to *The Argus*, an afternoon broadsheet. There she worked as a feature writer, critic and columnist before immigrating to Australia in 1998. After a brief stint with News Limited's *Daily Telegraph* in Sydney, she edited a section part time for Fairfax Community Newspapers and freelanced extensively for a variety of magazines. She moved to Canberra in 2003, where she became the Features editor of *The Canberra Times* before taking voluntary redundancy in 2012. She then worked as a sessional tutor at the University of Canberra and as deputy editor of the Policy Forum website of the Crawford School at the Australian National University. She also edited books and did some freelance writing. She moved to Scotland in 2016 and is now the Features editor of DC Thomson's 200-year-old newspaper, *The Courier*. (Interviewed by Matthew Ricketson on 13 August 2018.)

Simon Mann got his first taste of journalism in 1980 working for $15 a day on the *Coastal Telegraph*, a free weekly paper covering the Otway Ranges and Victoria's south-west coast. After brief stints on the *Geelong Advertiser* and Melbourne's *Sun News-Pictorial*, and a year studying journalism in the UK, he joined *The Age* as a business reporter in 1984. Over the course of the next 28 years, he held a wide range of senior writing and editing positions (except a year spent overseas working for London's *Independent* from 1989 to 1990) and was the paper's acting editor for much of 2004. He was Europe correspondent for *The Age* and *The Sydney Morning Herald* (1999–2002) and won the Walkley Award for International Journalism in 1999. He was US correspondent from 2010–2012 and then senior writer until taking a redundancy in 2012. (Interviewed by Matthew Ricketson on 23 January 2018.)

David Marr is a journalist, broadcaster and biographer who spent most of his career working for Fairfax and the ABC. He has written a number of books including biographies of Patrick White and Garfield Barwick. With his *Sydney Morning Herald* colleague Marian Wilkinson, he wrote *Dark Victory*, an account of the Tampa crisis of 2001. He presented *Media Watch* for some years and has appeared often on *Q&A* and *Insiders*. His half dozen *Quarterly Essays* include *The Prince: Faith, Abuse and George Pell*. Marr was at *The Sydney Morning Herald* in 2012 when he took redundancy on the eve of his 65th birthday. He has written since for *Guardian Australia* and published *My Country*, stories, speeches and essays about the Australia he has been exploring over 45 years in journalism. (Interviewed by Matthew Ricketson on 24 August 2017.)

Ian McArthur is bilingual in Japanese and English. His first job was scriptwriting for ABC radio's *Nihon Shokai* for school learners of Japanese (1975–1981). In 1979, he joined *The Courier-Mail*, moving to *The Daily Yomiuri* in Tokyo in 1981, and becoming The Herald and Weekly Times Tokyo bureau chief (1982–1985). After working in Sydney with Japanese documentary makers, he returned to Tokyo in 1989 as a reporter at *Kyodo News*, specialising in environmental stories, including the 1992 UN Earth Summit in Brazil. After completing a PhD in Japanese studies at Sydney University (1996), he taught Japanese and media in Asia courses at Sydney universities and published *Henry Black: On Stage in Meiji Japan* (2013). In 2010, he became a sub-editor at News Corp until retrenchment in 2014. He moved to Pagemasters, but in 2014 when his name fell off the roster he reverted to English teaching. He is writing two novels. (Interviewed by Penny O'Donnell on 19 February 2019.)

The roll call

Amanda Meade is *Guardian Australia's* media correspondent and writes the Friday media diary the Weekly Beast. Meade has been writing general media news and features for *Guardian Australia* since 2013. She has been a journalist since 1989, when she got a graduate cadetship on *The Sydney Morning Herald* after post-graduate study in journalism at University of Technology Sydney and an Honours degree in English literature from the University of Sydney. Meade spent five years on *The Herald* in Sydney and Canberra, covering general news, local and federal politics and health. An offer from *The Australian* saw her move to the national broadsheet's Canberra bureau in 1995 and then back to Sydney to cover the Wood Royal Commission into police corruption. Meade became a media specialist after covering the 'cash for comment' inquiry in 1999. She joined *The Australian's* new media section as a diarist in 2000, editing the Media Diary for 10 years, as well as writing media news and features, before taking redundancy from News Corp in November 2012. (Interviewed by Penny O'Donnell on 9 September 2017.)

George Megalogenis grew up in Melbourne, the local born son of Greek migrants. He entered journalism in 1986, as a graduate cadet with *The Sun News-Pictorial*. After a six-month stint on the subs desk writing captions, and a summer on police rounds, he joined the paper's state rounds bureau at Victoria's parliament house in 1987. He was posted to the federal parliamentary press gallery in 1988 as economics writer for the News Limited group. When *The Sun News-Pictorial* merged with *The Herald* in October 1990, he became economics writer for the *Herald Sun*. He left the paper the following year and joined *The Australian's* Canberra bureau. He moved to *The Australian's* Melbourne bureau at the end of 1999, where he remained until he took redundancy in 2012. He is the author of five books and two *Quarterly Essays*. *The Australian Moment* (2013) formed the basis for his three-part ABC documentary series *Making Australia Great*, which aired in 2015. He also wrote and presented the documentary tribute to former Australian prime minister Malcolm Fraser, *Life Wasn't Meant To Be Easy*, which aired in the same year. (Interviewed by Lawrie Zion on 17 June 2016.)

Dean Mellor's career in automotive journalism has spanned 25 years, starting with a five-year stint at four-wheel drive and travel publication *Overlander 4WD* magazine. Dean left what was then the Federal Publishing Company to head up Universal Magazines' automotive titles in 1999, including *New Car Buyer's Guide*, *New 4WD Buyer's Guide* and *4WD Australia*. In 2000 Mellor left Universal and freelanced for 12 months before landing a job with ACP as deputy editor of *4X4 Australia*; he was soon appointed editor, a position he held for eight years. Mellor then did a three-year stint as deputy editor of *Australian Motor Cycle News* before being appointed editor of *Australasian Dirt Bike* magazine. He was then made redundant in 2013 and successfully freelanced for various print and digital titles for the next five years. He recently returned to a familiar full-time role as deputy editor of *4X4 Australia* before becoming editor of *Unsealed 4X4* in 2020. (Interviewed by Andrew Dodd on 8 August 2017.)

Kate Mills grew up in Scotland and Africa and started work as a journalist in London on a legal magazine in 1995. After a few years she moved to Scotland to work on *The Scotsman* before moving to Australia in 2002. In Australia, she worked on a series of business magazines including *Investor Weekly* and *Australian Legal Business*, before moving to Fairfax in 2007 and working as the editor of *CFO Magazine*. In 2010 she became the deputy-editor of *Business Review Weekly* and then the editor. She left in 2013 to set up <ProfessionalMums.net>, an online job site for women returning to the workplace. She now works in the for-purpose sector, and still spends the first hour of the day reading the news. (Interviewed by Penny O'Donnell on 3 March 2019.)

Matthew Moore started at *The Sydney Morning Herald* in 1983 after completing a journalism degree in Bathurst. His first round was in Melbourne during the Hawke government era, reporting on wages policy and the Australian Council of Trade Unions. Four years later he returned to Sydney as the state political correspondent covering the Greiner government. Moore worked as Olympics editor in the lead up to the Sydney Games before three busy years in Jakarta covering the Bali bombing, the tsunami in Aceh, and the arrests and trials of Schapelle Corby and the Bali Nine. He was chief of staff, national editor and news editor, ran the investigations team and, as Freedom of Information editor, campaigned successfully for changes to New South Wales and federal Freedom of Information laws. For much of nearly three decades at *The Herald*, he organised and represented journalists, especially in public campaigns to preserve the paper's editorial independence. He'd been urban affairs editor for several years when he was part of a major redundancy round in September 2012. (Interviewed by Matthew Ricketson on 26 July 2017.)

Sophie Morris studied political science and languages in Brisbane and Germany before moving to Sydney in 2000 to start as a copykid at *The Australian*. After completing a cadetship, she was posted in 2002 to the newspaper's Canberra bureau. She joined *The Australian Financial Review*'s press gallery bureau in 2004, covering a range of rounds across federal politics and winning several prestigious journalism awards. She met and married journalist Nick Butterly in Canberra and was on maternity leave with their second daughter in late 2013 when she took a voluntary redundancy from *The Fin Review*. When *The Saturday Paper* launched in 2014, Morris was inaugural chief political correspondent, a position she held for two years. Morris and her family moved to Perth in 2016, where she worked briefly at *The West Australian*, before leaving journalism for a corporate speechwriting role. (Interviewed by Matthew Ricketson on 2 November 2015.)

Aleisha Orr's first role in journalism in 2006 took her back to the West Australian goldfields where she'd spent much of her youth. After a year at the *Golden Mail* newspaper in Kalgoorlie, in 2007 she moved to another inland mining town, this time in Queensland. In Mount Isa, she was a journalist at daily newspaper, *The North West Star*, for another year before spending almost a year backpacking overseas. Upon returning to Western Australia, Orr worked at Examiner Newspapers, writing across a handful of weekly suburban papers in Perth for 18 months. Next came a six-month sojourn in the Solomon Islands volunteering in the newsroom of daily newspaper, the *Solomon Star*. Upon returning to Perth in 2011, Orr worked as a journalist for Community Newspaper Group. She joined Fairfax-owned online news site *WAtoday* as a general news reporter in 2012 and in 2016 took a voluntary redundancy. (Interviewed by Andrew Dodd on 7 September 2017.)

Flip Prior was born in the UK, spent her early childhood in Perth and the dusty 'up north' of Newman. She completed university at Curtin in Perth after another stint living overseas. She was a cub reporter on the *Broome Advertiser* in 2006 and moved to the *Kalgoorlie Miner* in 2007, before returning to Perth as a general reporter with *The West Australian* in 2009. The lure of the north proved too great, so she spent several years moving back and forth before returning to Broome full time in 2011 to become the north-west bureau reporter, working across the Pilbara and Kimberley regions in a patch that spanned almost a million square kilometres. In 2013, she took a voluntary redundancy and moved to Sydney. (Interviewed by Penny O'Donnell on 7 April 2018.)

Veronica Ridge grew up in Melbourne and started work in journalism at 18 as a cadet on afternoon broadsheet *The Herald* in 1973. Early in her career, she specialised in arts and showbusiness on The Herald and Weekly Times' publication *TV Scene*, the ABC's *TV Times* and

The roll call

Woman's Day. After the birth of her two sons, Ridge was a freelance writer for eight years before joining *The Age* in 1992 as a property writer. During her 20 years at *The Age*, she held senior positions such as supplements editor, senior editor of *The Sunday Age*, the culture deputy editor, education editor, epicure editor and senior editor of *The Saturday Age*. Ridge took a voluntary redundancy from *The Age* in 2012. (Interviewed by Andrew Dodd on 12 April 2018.)

Jo Roberts started her career in Melbourne's suburban papers after completing a Bachelor of Arts in Journalism at Deakin University in Geelong. From 1991 she worked as a reporter for Leader Newspapers across several mastheads, including the *Doncaster-Templestowe News*, *Ringwood-Croydon Mail* and *Progress Press*. In 1995 Roberts became a sub-editor at Leader and, two years later, landed a casual subbing gig at *The Age*. There she held various sub-editing and production roles until 2000 when she was made deputy Arts editor, a position she held for eight years. In 2008, Roberts was appointed editor of the EG section, remaining in that role until taking a voluntary redundancy from *The Age* in October 2012. She has since worked as a freelance writer and editor, university tutor and online magazine founder. She now works full-time as a content manager, but keeps a hand in writing, still contributing the odd yarn to *The Age*. (Interviewed by Lawrie Zion on 29 March 2018.)

Russell Robinson began as a copy boy with *The Herald* in 1969. In 1976 he worked for Australian Associated Press in London. In 1977, Robinson went to Hong Kong, spending three years on the *South China Morning Post*, including as chief of staff. In 1979 he joined *The Sun News-Pictorial* in Melbourne, becoming deputy chief of staff, then sports editor. In 1990, he took voluntary redundancy after the merger of *The Sun* and *The Herald*, later joining the Leader Community Newspaper group where he became editor-in-chief, overseeing 30 newspapers. Six years later he joined the *Sunday Herald*

Sun as senior writer and chief of staff before returning to the *Herald Sun* as an investigative reporter. Robinson won three Melbourne Press Club Quills and two Walkley award commendations. He took voluntary redundancy in 2012. Robinson is an Industry Panel Member of the Australian Press Council, author of *Khaki Crims and Desperadoes* (2014) and co-author of *Shotgun and Standover: The Story of the Painters and Dockers* (2010). (Interviewed by Matthew Ricketson on 9 December 2015.)

Michael Sainsbury grew up in Goulburn, New South Wales, and worked in politics and business before journalism. He started at *The Australian*, where he was a senior business reporter from 2002 to 2009, before moving to Beijing as the paper's China correspondent. He left *The Australian* at the end of 2012, choosing to remain in Asia where he has been regional correspondent for *Nikkei Asian Review* and editorial director at Union of Catholic Asian News <ucanews.com>. He is now a freelance journalist based in Southeast Asia with 25 years' experience. He has been based in Asia for a decade, writing for publications across Australia and internationally. In 2015 Sainsbury won the award for excellence in environmental reporting from the Society of Publishers in Asia awards in Hong Kong, writing for NAR, and has been nominated for a Walkley Award. (Interviewed by Lawrie Zion on 21 March 2019.)

Maureen Shelley gained a degree in journalism at the Western Australian Institute of Technology, now Curtin University. She worked on *The Southern Focus*, a paper produced on campus and as a copy kid at *The Sunday Independent*, and as a producer at Radio 6PR in 1978 and 1979. Moving to Sydney, after a 17-year diversion into equal opportunity, Shelley was a freelancer, sub-editor and editor at *Business Sydney* 1997–1998. She moved to *The Australian Financial Review* as a sub-editor in 1998. After 18 months on three Fairfax titles, Shelley left for *The Daily Telegraph* in 2000, remaining for 12 years, also working for <news.com.au> and in management as national editorial development manager. She was editor of *The Tele*'s business pages and took the role of national technology writer for News Corp in 2010, which she held until accepting voluntary redundancy in 2012. (Interviewed by Penny O'Donnell on 10 March 2018.)

Michael Shmith was born in Melbourne in 1949 and educated at Wesley College. He was a cadet journalist at *The Herald*, Melbourne, from 1969 to 1972, when he moved to London. He worked as a Features production journalist and writer for the *Daily Express* from 1972 to 1981, when he returned to Australia to work for *The Age*. He was editor of its television supplement, the *Green Guide*, from 1982 to 1985, when he was appointed Arts editor, a position he held until 1992. He then became a full-time writer for the paper, contributing columns, editorials, book reviews and interviews. He was *The Age*'s national culture correspondent from 1994 to 1995, when he was appointed director of communications for The Australian Ballet. In 1999, after a brief return to London, during which he wrote a biography of the composer Gustav Mahler, he rejoined *The Age*, also writing a weekly column for *The Sunday Age*. He was travel editor from 2005 to 2007, after which he wrote editorials until taking redundancy in 2016. Shmith is now a full-time author, and his books include *Cranlana: The First One Hundred Years* (2019). (Interviewed by Lawrie Zion on 8 April 2016.)

Bart Sinclair was born into a racing family. His father Bart Snr was a successful jockey and trainer who had success at the top level in both endeavours in Brisbane, Sydney and Melbourne. After a two-year flirtation with a tertiary degree in Business Communications, Sinclair gained employment as a cadet sports reporter at *The Australian*'s Brisbane bureau. He started work on January 1, 1970, and worked continuously for News Limited as a journalist until November 2012. Sinclair also worked in electronic media. He was employed in radio at Brisbane AM station 4BC – later RadioTAB – from 1972 until 2012. He also worked in television at Channel 0 (now Ten) and Channel Seven. For many years he also provided expert comments and interviews for Sky Channel. Sinclair retired from print journalism in late 2012, but since then has been a consultant to the Brisbane Racing Club. In June 2018 Sinclair was awarded an Order of Australia for his services to racing and charity. (Interviewed by Lawrie Zion on 8 October 2018.)

John Spooner first started submitting cartoons to the *Sunday Press* in 1974 and then some caricatures to *The Age* during a year's articles and another three as a solicitor with Archer Shulman and Co. During that period, he obtained regular illustration work with *The National Times*. In 1977 Spooner quit the law and began editorial illustration work with *The Age*. He continued in that role until becoming a staff member in 1981. For the next 36 years Spooner developed his interest in editorial cartooning culminating in Spooner's View in *The Saturday Age*. Spooner received the Graham Perkin Australian Journalist of the Year Award in 2003 and has also won five Stanleys and three Walkleys. On 13 June 2016, Spooner's last cartoon was published following his involuntary redundancy. He joined *The Australian* three years later where he now contributes one editorial cartoon, one business cartoon and two business illustrations over a four-day week. (Interviewed by Andrew Dodd on 7 August 2016.)

Cate Swannell grew up in Brisbane and patched together an Arts degree from sticky tape, Blu-Tack and a couple of journalism subjects before ending up as a reporter with the *Whitsunday Times* in Airlie Beach in 1987–1988. She joined the *Gold Coast Bulletin* as a sports reporter the day after the Seoul Olympics finished and spent the next 14 years covering sport, including one memorable Christmas Day at the Maccabi Games. She then moved into layout design, production editor, chief subeditor and finally she was <goldcoast.com.au>'s online editor before being made redundant in July 2012. Since 2013 she has been the news and online editor for the *Medical Journal of Australia*, and editor of the journal's weekly online news magazine, *InSight+*. (Interviewed by Andrew Dodd on 27 September 2015.)

Sophie Tedmanson grew up in Adelaide and started her media career in 1993 at the age of 17 as an editorial assistant in *The Australian*'s Adelaide bureau. She then moved to Sydney with News Limited and began a three-year non-graduate cadetship working on *The Australian*, *The Daily Telegraph* and *The Sunday Telegraph* newspapers. After completing her cadetship in 1998 she joined the News Limited Olympics bureau as an Olympics reporter and covered the Sydney 2000 Games. She then became the national entertainment reporter for *The Australian* until 2006 when she moved to London and joined *The Times*. During two years in London she worked as an online reporter, layout designer and sub-editor before returning to Sydney and becoming *The Times*' deputy Southeast Asia editor. Duties included running the Australia bureau, commissioning foreign correspondents, being an Australian correspondent for both print and online, and editing <thetimes.co.uk> during the British evening. In 2013 she took a redundancy from *The Times*. Since then she has spent five years as deputy editor at *Vogue Australia*, worked as executive editor at *Qantas Magazine* and in 2020 joined the National Gallery of Australia as its first chief content officer. (Interviewed by Lawrie Zion on 11 May 2018.)

Di Thomas grew up in Sydney and moved to Orange in New South Wales in 1985 to begin her journalism career at the *Central Western Daily*. Thomas returned to Sydney in 1987 as a sub-editor and reporter with weekly rural publication *The Land* before being appointed as chief sub-editor in 1991, managing the newspaper's transition to full pagination in 1992; and production editor/chief sub-editor in 1996. In 1998, Thomas moved to Albury on the New

South Wales–Victorian border to edit the *Countrymail* lift-out in *The Border Mail* and its weekly sister publication *The Twin Cities Post*. She transferred to *The Border Mail* in 2001, serving as chief of staff, sub-editor and senior reporter before being appointed deputy editor in 2008. Thomas was appointed editor of *The Border Mail* in 2012 before taking redundancy in 2015. (Interviewed by Lawrie Zion on 27 September 2017.)

Gary Tippet was born in Footscray, Victoria and started work as a cadet journalist at Melbourne's *Sun News-Pictorial*, straight out of high school, in 1972. Between then and 1998, he worked as a general reporter, court reporter, feature writer, TV columnist and film critic, sports reporter, ghost writer for football personality Lou Richards, and had a year as the first male writer in the paper's women's section. After four years in the Victorian government media unit, including as press secretary to Premier Joan Kirner, he returned to journalism at *The Sunday Age* and *The Age*, where he happily remained as a senior writer/reporter until taking redundancy in 2012. He won a Walkley for feature writing in 1997; four Quill awards; and four Victorian Law Foundation Legal Reporting Awards. He was the first Australasian named Ochberg Fellow by the Dart Center for Journalism and Trauma. After freelancing for some years, he is now effectively retired. (Interviewed by Andrew Dodd on 15 September 2015.)

Tony Walker joined the ABC in 1971 as a specialist trainee. In 1974 he became Radio Australia's first Canberra correspondent. He joined *The Age* in 1976 and in 1979 was posted to Beijing for *The Age* and *The Sydney Morning Herald*, also serving there as *The Financial Times* correspondent. In 1984 he went to Cairo as Middle East correspondent for Fairfax newspapers and *The Financial Times*. In 1993 he returned to China for *The Financial Times*, then in 1998 went to the United States for the same publication. In 2000 he joined *The Australian Financial Review* as political editor in Canberra. In

2003 he went to Washington, DC, as its correspondent. He returned to Australia in 2010 as international editor before taking a voluntary redundancy in 2016. Since then, he has written columns for *The Age* and *The Sydney Morning Herald*. He is an editorial board member for *The Conversation* and has won awards, including two Walkleys for Commentary and the Paul Lyneham Award for Excellence in Press Gallery Journalism. (Interviewed by Lawrie Zion on 19 May 2018.)

Charles Waterhouse began at *The Examiner* newspaper in Launceston, Tasmania, as a cadet journalist, as a career in journalism offered reasonable pay without requiring a university degree. He worked at the paper for six years in Launceston, Devonport and Hobart, then for *The Advocate* in Burnie for almost 10 years, followed by 23 years working for the *Mercury*, mainly in Hobart covering general news and local issues before receiving a voluntary redundancy in mid-2012. He mainly covered police rounds, courts and general news. On the weekend following Waterhouse's last day, the *Mercury* relocated from its long-time Hobart offices in Macquarie Street to Salamanca Square. Since leaving journalism he worked for short periods in China teaching English and for the last few years has worked as a community support worker in Hobart and then in Melbourne. (Interviewed by Lawrie Zion on 16 October 2017.)

Alysson Watson grew up in Maitland in the New South Wales Hunter Valley. She took up a cadetship with the *Newcastle Herald* after finishing school and worked there for 30 years. Beginning as a reporter on the *Herald* and its free paper, the *Newcastle and Lake Macquarie Post*, Watson then became a sub-editor on the *Herald* in news, and then Features. She worked part-time as a Features writer and sub-editor while studying law and raising her children. When she returned to work full-time, Watson became property editor, Features editor and Features director, managing 20 writers and sub-editors to produce Features content and magazines. After a restructure following mass redundancies in 2012, Watson became news director, but returned to the Features director role after a year. She was made redundant in 2015 and has since worked as a media advisor to two federal members of parliament and as a casual journalism academic. She is now a PhD candidate. (Interviewed by Lawrie Zion on 25 October 2018.)

Liz Wells fell in love with the media in 1986 while working in admin at ABC Radio in Sydney. After completing a journalism degree, she joined *The Land* newspaper. Based at North Richmond, then Young and Grenfell, she wrote news, magazine and on-farm stories before becoming the Australian agricultural commodities correspondent for US-based newswire Knight-Ridder/Bridge, which was wound up and gave Wells her first redundancy. Wells became a sub-editor at *The Chronicle* in Toowoomba, then joined its Features department. She left to write for the short-lived *Toowoomba Telegraph*, which went into receivership and gave Wells her second redundancy. This prompted her return to agricultural journalism with the *Queensland Country Life* prior to a stint in corporate communications at the University of Southern Queensland while also writing for the national farming magazine *GroundCover*. Wells now writes online news for Nascon Media's Grain Central and associated websites and freelances for Coretext's client publications. (Interviewed by Penny O'Donnell on 30 March 2019.)

Michael West has spent two decades working as a journalist, stockbroker, editor and finance commentator before striking out on his own in July 2016. He started his career in 1989 as a cadet at *The Australian Financial Review*. In 1991 he moved to *The Sydney Morning Herald* as a reporter on the business desk, followed by three years as a stockbroker with Hartley Poynton Ltd. He joined *The Australian* as a columnist in 1999. After eight years with *The Australian* and another eight years with *The Sydney Morning Herald* as a journalist and business editor, West found himself obliged to take a redundancy in May 2016. He then founded Michael West Media (MWM) to focus on journalism of high public interest. MWM now does production for John Menadue's blog *Pearls and Irritations*. Both websites have no paywall, accept no advertising, are funded by community donations and are experiencing rapid growth in audience traffic. West is a Walkley-Award winner and adjunct professor at the University of Sydney's School of Social and Political Sciences. (Interviewed by Andrew Dodd on 27 March 2018.)

The redundancy timeline: Media coverage of job losses

Date	Media coverage
June 18, 2012	Fairfax Media announces to the Australian Stock Exchange that 1900 jobs will be cut across the company. 380 are expected to be editorial roles. Sources: <theage.com.au>; <smh.com.au>
June 20, 2012	Days after the Fairfax announcement, the then chief executive of News Corp Australia, Kim Williams, announces sweeping changes including centralising newsrooms but a continuing commitment to print media. He says there will be job cuts but does not specify how many. There is speculation in the media that the number could be 1000. Two years later, on 20 August 2014, *Crikey* receives leaked News 2012–13 financial statements revealing the scale of the job cuts. In the 2012–13 period, one in eight of its metropolitan newsroom staff have left, been axed or not replaced. *The Australian* lost 54 staff, *The Daily Telegraph* 167, *The Courier-Mail* 295, the *Herald Sun* 241 and *The Advertiser* in Adelaide 195. Further cuts were made to suburban papers and the digital desks, as well as regional mastheads. Sources: <10play.com.au>, <abc.net.au>; <crikey.com.au>

The redundancy timeline: Media coverage of job losses

Date	Media coverage
September 2012	700 jobs, or one in seven journalism positions in the two major press companies, have disappeared in the last few months, according to Chris Warren, the federal secretary of the Media, Entertainment and Arts Alliance (MEAA). This includes up to 270 from Fairfax, 300 from News Ltd, and casuals and contributors from both companies. Source: <theaustralian.com.au>
September 2012	Seven West Media offers redundancies to 15 staff at *The West Australian* Source: <abc.net.au>
November 2, 2012	Network Ten, after posting an annual loss of close to $13 million, shuts down its Breakfast program and sacks six newsreaders and presenters, as well as 10 senior journalists from its newsroom in Queensland. Back in October, the MEAA had speculated that the network was planning to sack 100 journalists. Sources: <news.com.au>; <smh.com.au>
December 2012	After less than a year of operation, *The Global Mail* announces it will cut seven jobs, including those of four local staff members and three correspondents, in New York, the Middle East and Latin America. The investigative journalism site would close permanently in February 2014, less than two years after its launch. Source: <mumbrella.com.au>
February 2013	Nine Network staff receive emails calling for an unspecified number of voluntary redundancies. Source: <news.com.au>
February 2013	Regional newspaper company APN News & Media reveals it will cut 12 jobs in central and northern Queensland over the next two months. Source: <abc.net.au>
June 4, 2013	Seven newspapers owned by Metro Media Publishing in Melbourne's south-eastern and bayside suburbs are to be shut down with the loss of 32 jobs. Metro Media blames News Ltd rivals, accused of offering kickbacks to real estate agents in return for exclusive advertising rights. Sources: <abc.net.au>; <crikey.com.au>

Date	Media coverage
June 11, 2013	Up to 100 jobs to be cut at West Australian Newspapers (WAN) through voluntary or involuntary redundancies. Source: <abc.net.au>
July 2, 2013	WIN TV Ballarat's news director, Steve Marshall, is made redundant after 11 years in the role. Several production staff at the Ballarat office, including one member from the IT department, are made redundant. Source: <thecourier.com.au>
July 11, 2013	One year after 50 jobs were cut at the *Newcastle Herald* and *Illawarra Mercury*, Fairfax reveals another 15 jobs will go because operations are being shifted to New Zealand. Meanwhile, key positions at News Ltd remain unoccupied following a restructure. Sources: <crikey.com.au>; <abc.net.au>
October 1, 2013	Fairfax ceases publication of its glossy magazines, *the (Sydney) magazine* and *the (Melbourne) magazine*, with at least 45 jobs expected to be cut, although some employees may be redeployed within the organisation. Source: <smh.com.au>
November 14, 2013	*The Australian Financial Review* is facing another round of redundancies, according to *The Australian*, with the loss of 30 staff, including many senior reporters. Source: <theaustralian.com.au>
May 7, 2014	Fairfax announces it will dismiss 30 of its 45 metro photographers and rely more on Getty Images, prompting staff at *The Sydney Morning Herald* and *The Age* to go on strike. Also 35 sub-editors and 15 lifestyle reporters' jobs are in jeopardy. Fairfax staff strike for 24 hours. Source: <mumbrella.com.au>

The redundancy timeline: Media coverage of job losses

Date	Media coverage
June 2014	A special 'Perth edition' of Channel Ten's weekend news bulletin is being replaced by a national news edition on two hours' delay, as veteran political reporter Paul Bongiorno, at the station for 36 years, announces he is going into retirement in the belief it will 'save a few other jobs'. These moves follow announcements that the network will be axing 150 jobs nationwide, its news staff bearing the brunt of these losses. Sources: <tvtonight.com.au>; <smh.com.au>; <news.com.au>
November 25, 2014	Federal budget cuts are blamed for the ABC's plan to shed 400 jobs, lopping off 10 per cent of the national broadcaster's entire workforce at a stroke, including 100 from the news division. Some regional bureaus will also close. Source: <abc.net.au>
March 12, 2015	Fairfax Media announces it will seek 80 voluntary redundancies from its newsrooms while trying to revitalise its regional Victorian outlets and ready them to deal with increasing demand for online content. Three dominant regional dailies – the *Bendigo Advertiser*, *Warrnambool Standard* and Albury-Wodonga's *Border Morning Mail*, are set to lose 20 staff apiece. Source: <abc.net.au>
April 2015	Macquarie Radio's merger with Fairfax costs nearly 50 staff at 2UE, 4BC, Magic 1278 and Magic 882 their jobs. Source: <smh.com.au>
May 14, 2015	More than half the editorial staff on the *Illawarra Mercury* are among 50 casualties of cuts on the Wollongong paper and other South Coast newspapers in the Fairfax Media group. Source: <illawarramercury.com.au>

Date	Media coverage
May 21, 2015	Seven's investigative news team loses executive producer Max Uechtritz, believed to be on a salary of $500 000 a year, but the network plays down rumours of up to 15 cuts, vowing staff will be redeployed. This news comes the day before staff at WIN TV learn, with little or no notice, that their Mildura and Mackay offices are to close. The CEO echoes Seven in trying to soften the blow by saying staff across the network will be deployed in other roles. Sources: <mumbrella.com.au>; <tvtonight.com.au>
May 28, 2015	Evening rail commuters in Melbourne, Sydney and Brisbane will no longer be able to catch the afternoon freebie *mX* before they catch their train, a routine familiar to them since 2001. Thirty fulltime staff are expected to be affected by the paper's demise, but management says it will try to redeploy some. Source: <smh.com.au>
July 2, 2015	South Australian rural and regional newspapers are to be bled of 35 staff, most of them holding down editorial positions, their Fairfax owners have announced. One of the papers, the *Roxby Downs Sun*, will cease publication. Source: <abc.net.au>
August 2015	The equivalent of 41 full-time editorial positions are to go, and some valuable properties will be sold off, at Fairfax Sydney suburban newspapers as well as the publisher's rural flagship, *The Land*. A week after these announcements, Fairfax announces 69 jobs will become redundant in the Hunter Valley region, including 37 full-time positions at the *Newcastle Herald*. Source: <mumbrella.com.au>
September 18, 2015	Three regional West Australian newspapers – *The Wagin Argus*, the *Merredin Wheatbelt Mercury* and *Central Midlands & Coastal Advocate* – will close due to a restructure at Fairfax Media, which states its regional newsrooms will adopt a 'digital-first' approach from now on. Source: <abc.net.au>

The redundancy timeline: Media coverage of job losses

Date	Media coverage
September 21, 2015	Senior editorial positions in Wagga Wagga, Tamworth and Canberra have been abolished by Prime Media Group. CEO Ian Audsley warns that regional voices are 'under threat' in Australia's evolving media landscape. Source: <mumbrella.com.au>
September 22, 2015	Northern NSW radio newsreader John Shaw refuses to go quietly: after he speaks out against plans to replace Glen Innes' local news service, his bosses at 2NZ and GEM FM issue him four weeks' notice. Not easily cowed into silence, Shaw blasts the decision, saying there'll be 'bugger all' local coverage. Source: <gleninnesexaminer.com.au>
September 23, 2015	Journalists in the country's three biggest cities are made redundant as Southern Cross Austereo says it is 'streamlining' its news services. For Geoff Field, newsreader for Kyle and Jackie O in the Sydney market, and later Hamish and Andy in Melbourne, it's the end of the road after 18 years on air. Source: <mumbrella.com.au>
September 24, 2015	Editorial heads roll at *The Examiner* in Launceston and *The Advocate* in Burnie as Fairfax reveals up to 13 staff will lose their jobs under a major restructure. Source: <abc.net.au>
October 28, 2015	WIN TV's half-hour nightly Victorian news bulletins, long produced in Ballarat, will from next February be brought to them from the network's head office in Wollongong, New South Wales. Source: <abc.net.au>
November 2015	News Corp Australia's announcement that it will retrench 55 journalistic roles across the range of its newspaper titles earns a sharp rebuke from the MEAA. In the same week, reports emerge that Fairfax plans to do away with 150 jobs in its Metro Media division over the next six months, a much bigger round of cuts than originally expected. Sources: <theaustralian.com.au>; <theaustralian.com.au/weekend-australian-magazine>

Date	Media coverage
April 21, 2016	A Fairfax Media plan to cut the 'equivalent of 120 full-time jobs' from News and Business sections at *The Sydney Morning Herald* and *The Age* has now reduced that number to 100, management has announced. Source: <mumbrella.com.au>
April 28, 2016	A dozen positions at *The Canberra Times* are threatened as the newspaper looks to transform itself to a quality compact print format, but management says this is only one-third as many as originally contemplated. On the same day, after nearly two decades as an independent, Scoop Publishing, based in Western Australia, is shutting down publication of its nine niche magazines. Sources: <canberratimes.com.au>; <watoday.com.au>
May 5, 2016	After 134 years of publication, the *Cooma-Monaro Express* puts out its final edition, farewelled by editor Lee Evans, while in nearby Jindabyne, as part of a Fairfax restructuring initiative, the *Summit Sun* also publishes for the last time. Source: <abc.net.au>
May 9, 2016	Up to 30 more redundancies, many of them involuntary according to a spokesperson from the MEAA, have taken place at Fairfax in Sydney and Melbourne. Fairfax had called for 120 voluntary redundancies months ago but this was later negotiated down to 82, making today's move all the more of a shock. Source: <abc.net.au>
August 2, 2016	Faced with a 25 per cent fall in profits over the past year, *The West Australian* – which is the only daily newspaper in the entire state – shows a number of senior journalists the door, as morale at the paper is said to be at an all-time low. Source: <watoday.com.au>
September 12, 2016	News Corp Australia's acquisition of Australian Regional Media (ARM) News and Media will cost 300 staff jobs as the company pursues 'back-office synergies'. *The Australian* insists there are no plans afoot to shut ARM titles 'provided they remain profitable'. Source: <mumbrella.com.au>

The redundancy timeline: Media coverage of job losses

Date	Media coverage
October 14, 2016	Sixteen journalists, more than half the staff complement at the suburban newspaper group that publishes *The Weekly Review*, are out of a job as management shifts from a local news focus to a preference for national news. Source: <crikey.com.au>
November 3, 2016	A new format of ABC science program *Catalyst* is announced and staff are told their positions are being made redundant. Source: <theaustralian.com.au>
November 16, 2016	The ABC imposes a new round of cuts at its flagship national radio network, Radio National, where eight staff and a slew of programs, including John Cleary's long-running Sunday night program on religion, are removed from the schedule for 2017. Source: <theguardian.com/au>
December 2, 2016	Seven West Media embarks on a program of voluntary redundancies as the media company grapples with a tight advertising market. Jobs in its television holdings will be where the company aims to find the most savings after a warning that next year its earnings could decline by up to 20 per cent. Source: <mumbrella.com.au>
December 7, 2016	News Corp Australia says it needs to cut costs by $40 million and has a target of reducing 42 fulltime positions, which it will achieve by forced redundancies if necessary. Journalists, artists and photographers will be the likeliest to go. Source: <theguardian.com>
March 8, 2017	The ABC's managing director, Michelle Guthrie, says up to 85 staff have been told they will be made redundant. Many have been working on the leading current-affairs programs *Foreign Correspondent* and *7.30*. Source: <theguardian.com>

Date	Media coverage
April 5, 2017	Close to $30 million will be cut from Fairfax Media's editorial budget, predominantly affecting staff at *The Age* and *The Sydney Morning Herald* though it is not clear how many jobs will vanish. Source: <abc.net.au>
April 11, 2017	After posting a $287 million loss in the second quarter of the financial year, News Corp Australia has issued redundancy notices to most of its photographers and sub-editors at *The Daily Telegraph*, *Herald Sun* and *The Courier-Mail*. Source: <theguardian.com>
May 3, 2017	For the first time a figure is put on the number of newsroom staff being let go to attain the $30 million in budget cuts announced a month ago. The loss of 125 journalists at *The Age*, *The Sydney Morning Herald* and *The Australian Financial Review* will make all three titles more dependent on contributors. Source: <theguardian.com>
May 5, 2017	Both *The Sydney Morning Herald* and *The Age* plan to cut their arts editorial staff so that a single editor or journalist will now be covering the arts at each of those titles. Journalists at both declare a seven-day strike in protest. Source: <dailyreview.com.au>
May 26, 2017	Staff in the ABC Radio division have been told nine jobs will go as part of the latest round of redundancies at the public broadcaster. Source: <theguardian.com>
June 6 & 8, 2017	Among senior figures to be leaving Fairfax Media in its latest round of redundancies are a former editor of *The Sydney Morning Herald*, Alan Stokes, long-time AFL writer Rohan Connolly and environment journalist Adam Morton. Sources: <mumbrella.com.au>; <smh.com.au>

The redundancy timeline: Media coverage of job losses

Date	Media coverage
June 9, 2017	Further turmoil is revealed at the ABC in South Australia after interstate-based management decides to axe Leigh Radford, a respected staff veteran and leading voice on rural and national programs for the regional service. Source: <indaily.com.au>
June 20, 2017	Before the financial year ends, Pacific Magazines is set to reduce costs by declaring 11 sub-editing positions redundant across all magazines and sending their work to the external sub-editing business Pagemasters. Source: <mumbrella.com.au>
July 11, 2017	Nine News in Darwin will terminate its standalone commercial news bulletin as the company announces sweeping cuts, at the cost of a dozen or so jobs. Source: <abc.net.au>
July 28, 2017	Dozens of editorial staff at the News Corp Australia-owned Brisbane newspaper *The Courier-Mail* are given their marching orders in the latest wave of job cuts. On the same day, chief executive of Bauer Media Paul Dykzeul tells the eight staff of *Good Health* that their services will no longer be required as the magazine is going to be produced in New Zealand in future. Source: <theguardian.com>
September 12, 2017	Effective immediately, the short-lived start-up *Newcastle Sunday* is closed down, putting all staff out of a job. Source: <mumbrella.com.au>
November 3, 2017	The journalists' union, the MEAA, fears for the future of the *Sunday Times* newspaper in Western Australia as Seven West Media employees brace themselves for big staff cuts, including at *The West Australian*, likely to be announced soon. The company says it's looking for $125 million in savings over two years. Source: <abc.net.au>

Date	Media coverage
November 9, 2017	A single magazine servicing north-west Sydney is to be launched in 2018, replacing six Australian Community Media mastheads that will be retired: *Hills News*, *Rouse Hill Courier*, *Penrith City Gazette*, *St Marys and Mt Druitt Star*, *Blacktown Sun* and *Parramatta Holroyd Sun*. Source: <thinknewsbrands.com.au>
November 29, 2017	Fairfax Media and HuffPost's business partnership has ended in divorce. Fairfax Media will move the 30-plus affected staff members into the company's metro business, but others will be jobless as the local team for the US-based online media outlet is tipped to shrink to a handful of contractors. Source: <mumbrella.com.au>
December 4, 2017	A piece of Australian literary history, *The Western Herald* – which published the early writings of Henry Lawson and the poems of 'Breaker' Morant – is being mourned in the far western New South Wales city of Bourke. Last week the paper's three staff were handed redundancy notices. Simultaneously Bauer Media's *Australian Women's Weekly* reveals up to 15 jobs, including senior roles such as chief sub-editor and art director, are to go. Sources: <theaustralian.com.au>; <crikey.com.au>
December 21, 2017	Bauer Media has ended a difficult year of publishing by shuttering another magazine, *Men's Style*, less than a week before Christmas. Source: <mumbrella.com.au>
February 15, 2018	A restructure of online media company Yahoo7 has wiped out the positions of eight fulltime staff in the television team including that of head of TV Homaira Razi. Source: <mumbrella.com.au>
February 28, 2018	Seven West Media's management told around 150 staff yesterday at Broadcast Centre in Melbourne that most of their jobs would be outsourced next year. Source: <tvtonight.com.au>

The redundancy timeline: Media coverage of job losses

Date	Media coverage
April 5, 2018	Blitz Publications and Multimedia Group went into liquidation on March 1, sounding the death knell for the following publications: *Women's Health and Fitness, Nourish, Australian Natural Health, Muse, Gluten-Free Heaven, Natural Vegan* and *Blitz Martial Arts Magazine*. Source: <mumbrella.com.au>
April 6, 2018	Trent Casson, general manager for the national magazine publisher *Domain*, is set to leave as the company launches a quest for 'operational and business efficiencies' following its separation from Fairfax Media. Source: <mumbrella.com.au>
April 30, 2018	ABC announces it will cut 20 capital city newsroom positions as it tries to adjust to a digital media environment. But the broadcaster says after this is carried out there will be the same number of employees as before. Source: <mumbrella.com.au>
June 5, 2018	Bauer Media confirms it will restructure the editorial departments at *Woman's Day, NW* and *OK Magazine*, with the axe falling on 11 staff in all. Source: <mumbrella.com.au>
June 5, 2018	Wire agency Australian Associated Press has cited weaker market demand for its determination to cut 20 to 25 staff positions. Source: <mumbrella.com.au>
June 6, 2018	Pacific Magazines will dispense with three fulltime journalist roles, amounting to six staff positions, on the editorial teams of *Who* and *New Idea*. Source: <mumbrella.com.au>
August 8, 2018	WIN TV's weeknight news bulletins are to be presented from the network's Wollongong studios, rendering nine Tasmanian staff unemployed. Source: <illawarramercury.com.au>
August 9, 2018	Community Newspaper Group in Perth has announced it is closing 17 of its titles which served readers in the Darling Range and along Perth's northern coastal strip. Source: <watoday.com.au>

Date	Media coverage
September 14, 2018	News Corp is eliminating up to 30 newsroom roles at *The Australian*, *The Daily Telegraph* and *Herald Sun*. Source: <mumbrella.com.au>
December 6, 2018	Staff on six of Bauer Media's magazine titles and staff have been given less than a week to decide whether they will reapply for their jobs. Source: <crikey.com.au>
December 11, 2018	Journalists' union the MEAA has issued a statement of solidarity with 26 journalists and other staff retrenched by Nine-owned (formerly Fairfax-owned) Allure Media. Source: <meaa.org>
January 29, 2019	All staff members at *BuzzFeed* Australia have been told the online media company will do away with 11 positions. Two weeks later, several senior editors and reporters announce their departure on Twitter. Source: <theguardian.com>
April 18, 2019	More than 30 journalists face the loss of their jobs at *The West Australian* and *The Sunday Times*, raising the spectre of a 'denuded' newsroom. Source: <abc.net.au>
April 26, 2019	*The Courier-Mail* has sacked all its casuals plus 10 full-time staff in the middle of a federal election in which Queensland seats are crucial. Source: <theguardian.com>
June 7, 2019	Several senior journalists have accepted redundancies after News Corp announced this week it wanted to lay off 55 journalists and many more non-editorial employees across Australia. Among those leaving are *The Courier-Mail*'s political commentator Dennis Atkins, football writer for *The Australian* Ray Gatt and senior writer Paul Toohey. Source: <theguardian.com>
June 20, 2019	WIN News is terminating 30 jobs and shutting down four regional bureaus at Orange, Wagga Wagga, Albury and Bundaberg. Management pledges to try reassigning staff to the network's remaining offices. Source: <abc.net.au>

The redundancy timeline: Media coverage of job losses

Date	Media coverage
March 3, 2020	After 85 years, AAP is no more. The demise of the Australian Associated Press entails the loss of 500 jobs at the newswire service. Source: <abc.net.au>
April 9, 2020	Mumbrella reports that Foxtel will lay off 200 workers and stand down an additional 140 until the end of June as it attempts to survive the Covid-19 pandemic. Source: <mumbrella.com.au>
April 29, 2020	Bauer Media has suspended publication of its magazines *Take 5*, *Australian Women's Weekly*, *TV Week* and *NW*, leaving 70 staff without a job. Source: <mumbrella.com.au>
April 30, 2020	Foxtel is to further restructure its business, claiming the jobs of an extra 70 staff, as it seeks to compete more aggressively with international streaming platforms. Source: <smh.com.au>
May 14, 2020	*BuzzFeed* will shut down its UK and Australian news outfits to refocus on big-hitting news in the US as a result of shrinking advertising revenue. Source: <theguardian.com>
May 18, 2020	Almost exactly two years since its launch in 2018, Network Ten's online news and short-video site *10 Daily* will cease operations on Friday. Source: <mumbrella.com.au>
May 28, 2020	News Corp will cease printing more than 100 regional and suburban titles. Source: <crikey.com.au>
June 5, 2020	A conglomerate of investors led by former News Corp chief executive Peter Tonagh has saved AAP from complete shutdown. However, jobs will still be cut in a new slimmed-down operation. The move will save up to 95 of the original 500 positions expected to be lost. Source: <theguardian.com>

Date	Media coverage
June 24, 2020	The ABC is to slash 250 jobs, axe its 7.45 am radio news bulletin and terminate the *ABC Life* brand. From now on, the broadcaster will make fewer *Foreign Correspondent* and *Australian Story* episodes each year. Source: <theguardian.com>
July 10, 2020	Newspaper publisher Australian Community Media announces it is considering shutting down four printing sites which would result in 200 job losses. Source: <abc.net.au>
November 27, 2020	News Corp Australia axes 16 more photographers from *The Courier-Mail* after previously sacking 200 journalists and photographers from numerous outlets. Source: <theguardian.com>

CONTRIBUTORS

Lawrie Zion is a professor of Journalism at La Trobe University and associate provost (Research and Industry Engagement) for the College of Arts, Social Sciences and Commerce. Prior to joining La Trobe in 2006, he worked as a broadcaster at ABC Radio and a journalist for several newspapers, principally covering film. He wrote the 2007 documentary, *The Sounds of Aus*, which told the story of the Australian accent, and is the author of *The Weather Obsession* (Melbourne University Publishing, 2017) and co-editor of *Ethics for Digital Journalists: Emerging Best Practices* (Routledge, 2014). Since 2014, he has led the New Beats project.

Brad Buller has been interested in journalism issues for over a decade. He is a research assistant with the Centre for Advancing Journalism, University of Melbourne, where he works on the New Beats project and is writing a history of the AN Smith Memorial Lecture in Journalism with Andrew Dodd. Previously, Buller assisted journalist and academic Margaret Simons with the research for her biography of Kerry Stokes. Buller has a particular interest in the history of *The Age* newspaper, having written a postgraduate diploma thesis examining its editorial culture between 1966 and 1997, and he is finishing a PhD thesis on the life and legacy of Graham Perkin.

Andrew Dodd is the director of the Centre for Advancing Journalism and an associate professor of Journalism at the University of Melbourne. He was a broadcaster at ABC Radio National, where he presented several programs and launched the Media Report. He was a journalist at ABC TV's *7.30 Report* and *The Australian* newspaper, where he covered media and business. He is the founding editor of

The Junction, which connects over 25 university journalism programs across Australia and the Pacific to produce collaborative journalism. He is the author of one book and the co-editor of another.

Timothy Marjoribanks is dean (Research and Development), in Business and Law, and professor of Management, at Swinburne University of Technology, Melbourne. His research has been funded by the Australian Research Council and engages with managing organisational innovation and transformation in the media industry, in particular in the context of technological change, as well as media representations of social relations, and the relationship between media and sport. Among his books are *News Corporation, Technology and the Workplace* (Cambridge, 2000), and *Australian Media and the Politics of Belonging* (Anthem, 2018), co-edited with David Nolan and Karen Farquharson.

Penny O'Donnell is senior lecturer in International Media and Journalism at the University of Sydney, and research director of the Department of Media and Communications. In the 1990s she worked as a journalist at ABC Radio National (Sydney) and Notimex (Mexico City). Her research has been funded by the Australian Research Council, and currently focuses on precarious work in journalism and the future of news. She is the co-author of *Journalism at the Speed of Bytes* (Walkley Foundation, 2012) and *Australians Against Racism* (Pluto Press, 1995). Recent academic journal articles appear in *Journalism Practice, Journalism Studies* and *Media International Australia*.

Matthew Ricketson has worked as an academic and journalist for four decades. He has worked on staff at *The Age*, *The Australian* and *Time Australia* magazine, among others. He has run journalism programs in three universities – RMIT, University of Canberra and now Deakin University, where he is a professor of Communications.

He is a chief investigator on three Australian Research Council grants about the state of journalism in Australia. He is the author of three books and editor of two. In 2011 he was appointed by the federal government to assist Ray Finkelstein QC in an independent inquiry into the media and media regulation.

Merryn Sherwood is a senior lecturer and convener of the Bachelor of Media and Communication at La Trobe University. She was a newspaper sports journalist at *The Canberra Times* and communications manager for the International Triathlon Union, before she completed a PhD thesis that explored how digital technology is transforming sports media. Her research has been funded by the Australian Research Council, and focuses primarily on disruption and change in media work. She is a co-author of *Sport and the Media: Managing the Nexus* (Routledge, 2015).

Acknowledgments

This book originated in an academic project called New Beats, which was set up in the months immediately after Fairfax Media's announcement in June 2012 that it was laying off 1900 staff members across the company. From the outset we could see that Fairfax's news, followed swiftly by News Corp's announcements of sizeable but unspecified redundancies, marked an important shift in the Australian media that clearly merited further investigation. A team of researchers was assembled and we applied successfully for an Australian Research Council Linkage Projects grant and an Australian Research Council Discovery Program grant. These were aimed at charting the impact of the large-scale redundancy rounds in Australian newsrooms on those who were leaving them and, more broadly, on the future of journalism in Australia. The team has been led by Professor Lawrie Zion of La Trobe University and includes Associate Professor Andrew Dodd (Melbourne University), Professor Timothy Marjoribanks (Swinburne University), Dr Penny O'Donnell (Sydney University), Professor Matthew Ricketson (Deakin University) and Dr Merryn Sherwood (La Trobe University).

Under the Linkage grant the New Beats team created partnerships with three key organisations. The Media, Entertainment and Arts Alliance (MEAA) helped us connect with journalists who had taken redundancies. The Australian Broadcasting Corporation (ABC) was interested in developing programs about the media and job loss, and the National Library of Australia (NLA) supported our plan to conduct what the library calls 'whole of life' interviews with 60 journalists who had taken redundancy. (The impact of

Acknowledgments

Covid-19 prevented us from completing the final two interviews before the deadline for this book. And we have not drawn on one of the interviews which is unavailable for public access at present.) Under the Discovery grant the New Beats team created partnerships with academic researchers in Brazil, Canada, Finland, Indonesia, the Netherlands, South Africa, the United Kingdom and the United States. These connections proved there were many similarities, and some differences, in the ways digital disruption was reshaping the industry globally.

The New Beats team has produced two books, this one and an academic monograph, *Journalists and Job Loss*, which takes a global perspective on journalism and downsizing and will be published later in 2021. The project has also generated numerous academic articles, an industry report, conference presentations, submissions to parliamentary inquiries, media interviews and podcasts.

It's fair to say that *Upheaval* has been probably the most complicated editing task we've done. We wanted to ensure that unlike many edited books containing numerous authors, the tone and style of the chapters is consistent, as the book's focus is on the journalists' stories rather than the authors' individual voices. As much if not more demanding than the editing has been the logistics of the project, including but not limited to, as lawyers like to say: compiling research briefs for the interviews, wrangling the journalists to provide pocket-bios, overseeing the 'chunking' of the 4885 pages of interview transcript into files for the authors to work on, ensuring all of the interviewees' quotes were checked with them for accuracy and context, managing the masses of files and versions of chapters, overseeing endnotes and running down stray references. This work and no doubt much more has been done by one person, Brad Buller, and done while he has been working on his PhD about former editor of *The Age*, Graham Perkin. The term 'research assistant' doesn't begin to describe Brad's contribution to this book. He is the first person we want to acknowledge.

Second, we want to acknowledge our colleagues in the New Beats team who contributed chapters and – again under deadline pressure – had to endure editing interventions that may have reminded them of earlier newsroom editing experiences. That this book has come together owes a lot to the collegiality of the New Beats team and to the democratic leadership of Lawrie Zion. Others contributed to various parts of the New Beats project, including Jai Denham, who transcribed interviews and produced timed summaries for the NLA, Steinar Ellingsen, who designed the redundancy timeline for the New Beats blog, Greg Flynn, who worked with Brad on the 'chunking' of transcripts, Callum Glennen, who compiled the initial research dossiers for the interviews, Robin Harper, who dealt with all the team's administrative needs, Monika Winarnita, who worked on the redundancy timeline (as did Robin), and Ken Haley, who proofread the final pages. Many others helped us along the way. For example, Craig Butt and Jake Niall helped with access to *The Age*, while countless others gave us research tips and helped with contacts and fact checking. Michelle Stillman in *The Age* editorial library helped us track down a couple of hard-to-find articles. We thank you all.

We'd like to thank the New Beats project's partners, in particular Michelle Rayner at the ABC, Mike Dobbie, Paul Murphy, Mark Phillips and Marcus Strom at the MEAA and Kevin Bradley, Shelly Grant, Mark Piva and Shirleene Robinson at the NLA.

This book would not have been possible without the 58 journalists who generously agreed to be interviewed by either Lawrie, Matthew, Penny or Andrew from the New Beats team. By journalistic standards these were alarmingly long – between four and eight hours – but for us the opportunity to interview so many people at length about their working lives has been one of the great rewards of the project. We also thank the interviewees for responding to further requests for information. We only hope we have done justice to your honest and powerful stories. One story that we feel sure would have been a fine

Acknowledgments

addition was Michael Gordon's, who was going to be interviewed but sadly died shortly before that could happen, in 2018.

At NewSouth we'd like to thank Phillipa McGuinness who was the first to show interest, but who moved on to her own writing work before our manuscript was submitted. We are grateful for her early suggestions, which helped shape the book. We've valued too working with Kathy Bail, Emma Hutchinson, Harriet McInerney, Elspeth Menzies and Jessica Perini. We'd like to thank the external readers who provided thoughtful responses to the manuscript.

And there are some personal thank yous too:

From Brad: February 2018. I was in Melbourne University's Baillieu Library working on my PhD when by chance I ran into Andrew Dodd who had recently joined the Centre for Advancing Journalism. That encounter triggered the start of my work with the New Beats project, initially on a three-month contract, but three years later I'm still here. Thank you, Andrew, for bringing me onto this project and for trusting me to deliver on its outputs. I'd also like to thank Matthew, who provided much encouragement and support. It's been a wild ride but their larrikin humour and devotion to telling journalists' stories (and telling them well) has made this project a pleasure. Special thanks to Lawrie, Penny, Tim, Merryn, Robin and Jai for their collegiality. And of course, then there's family. To Beate, you have been there for me even when I have let you down. My sincere thanks. Without you, my part in this book would not exist.

From Andrew: The title, *Upheaval*, could describe more than the book's subject matter. Heather, thank you for pretty well everything really, but especially for your graceful generosity and acceptance. To our children, Lucy and Tim, thank you for all the ways you reach out to find connection. To Anna, thank you for your abundant hospitality and for never saying 'no' to anything, except for regret of course. To Maryanne, and my brothers, Martin and Simon, you have been here for me when I had no right to expect it. My sincere thanks. And a big thank you to my colleagues at the Centre for Advancing Journalism.

From Matthew: I'd like to thank my family. Gemma and Josh, as always, showed keen interest in the book throughout even though they're no longer living at home. Hayley is, having been forced to stay in Australia in 2020 when she should have been in London overseeing staging of her play *Graceful*. The pandemic cruelled that plan. Gill was also working from home during the gestation of this book. Otto von Bismarck once remarked that 'Laws are like sausages; it is better not to see them being made'. To that advice Gill would probably add 'books'. This didn't stop her of course from providing wonderful food when Andrew and Brad and I worked on the manuscript around the family dining table for a couple of weeks just before lockdown in Melbourne. She has also been enormously patient while we inched along what the Chemical Brothers called the 'supposed golden path' toward finishing. Thank you darling. Hopefully I am forgiven.

Notes

Chapter 1 – The precede
1. Rachel Buchanan, *Stop Press: The Last Days of Newspapers* (Melbourne: Scribe, 2013), 95.
2. Media, Entertainment and Arts Alliance, Submission to the Senate Inquiry into Media Diversity, December 2020, 3, <aph.gov.au/Parliamentary_Business/Committees/Senate/Environment_and_Communications/Mediadiversity/Submissions> (accessed 12 February 2021).
3. Joel Deane, 'Drinking in the sun: Media before Murdoch', *Meanjin*, 6 October 2020, <meanjin.com.au/blog/drinking-in-the-sun-media-before-murdoch> (accessed 19 January 2021).
4. Jan McGuinness, 'HWT memories', Melbourne Press Club, 17 February 2016, <melbournepressclub.com/article/back-to-the-herald---the-class-of--66> (accessed 19 January 2021).
5. Matthew Ricketson, 'Newspaper Feature Writing in Australia 1956–1966,' in *Journalism: Print, Politics and Popular Culture*, eds. Ann Curthoys and Julianne Schultz (Brisbane: University of Queensland Press, 1999), 178–179.
6. Ray Finkelstein, assisted by Matthew Ricketson, *Report of the Independent Inquiry into the Media and Media Regulation* (Canberra: Department of Broadband, Communications and the Digital Economy, 2012).
7. Chris Zappone, 'Fairfax to shed 1900 jobs, erect paywalls', *The Sydney Morning Herald*, 18 June 2012, <smh.com.au/business/fairfax-to-shed-1900-staff-erect-paywalls-20120618-20ix1.html> (accessed 19 January 2021).
8. Anne Hyland, 'Mark Scott's ABC exit interview: "I had no idea the scale of the challenge"', *The AFR Magazine*, 27 November 2015, <afr.com/life-and-luxury/abcs-mark-scott-on-success-and-his-legacy-20151019-gkcgi8> (accessed 19 January 2021).
9. Andrew Dodd, 'Game of sabotage: The culture war for the ABC', *Australian Quarterly*, vol 9, no 4 (October–December 2020): 3–9.
10. Roger McNamee in *The Social Dilemma* (2020), directed by Jeff Orlowski, written by Jeff Orlowski, Davis Coombe, and Vickie Curtis.
11. Jennifer Martin, *Emotions and Virtues in Feature Writing: The Alchemy of Creating Prize-winning Stories* (London: Palgrave Macmillan, London, 2021).

Chapter 2 – Where do journalists come from?
1. For more on the West Gate Bridge disaster, see Tim Callanan, 'West Gate Bridge disaster still haunts the men who were there, 50 years on', ABC News, 11 October 2020, <abc.net.au/news/2020-10-11/west-gate-bridge-collapse-haunts-survivors-50-years-on/12739324> (accessed 11 February 2021).
2. Numerous memoirs have been written by journalists exploring the factors that led them to pursuing journalism as a career. Some include Phillip Knightley,

A Hack's Progress (London: Jonathan Cape, 1997), 10–11; Shaun Carney, *Press Escape* (Melbourne: Melbourne University Press, 2016); Mark Colvin, *Light and Shadow: Memoirs of a Spy's Son* (Melbourne: Melbourne University Press, 2016).

Chapter 3 – Many roads to journalism

1. Matthew Ricketson, 'How to school a scribe', *The Australian*, Media supplement, 31 May 2001.
2. Phillip Knightley, *A Hack's Progress* (London: Jonathan Cape, 1997), 10–11; Ian Milne, 'Gender, hierarchies and change: An oral history of independent newspapers since the 1960s', *Saothar*, vol 39 (2014): 55–61.
3. Matthew Ricketson, *Writing Feature Stories* (Sydney: Allen & Unwin, 2004), 3.
4. David Conley and Stephen Lamble, *The Daily Miracle* (Melbourne: Oxford University Press, 2006), 9.
5. Lindsay Revill and Colin Roderick (eds), *The Journalist's Craft: A Guide to Modern Practice* (Sydney: Angus and Robertson, 1965), 41–42.
6. Bridget Griffin-Foley and Stephanie Walker, 'Student Newspapers', in *A Companion to the Australian Media*, ed. Bridget Griffen-Foley (Melbourne: Australian Scholarly Publishing, 2014), 442–444.
7. Media, Entertainment and Arts Alliance, 'New guidelines to define what is an ethical media internship', 14 April 2016, <meaa.org/mediaroom/new-guidelines-to-define-what-is-an-ethical-media-internship> (accessed 9 February 2021).
8. Melville J Davies, 'Hancock, Langley Frederick (Lang) (1909–1992)', *Australian Dictionary of Biography*, National Centre of Biography, Australian National University, <adb.anu.edu.au/biography/hancock-langley-frederick-lang-17492/text29181> (accessed 9 February 2021).
9. Andrew Dodd, 'Web of intrigue, by *Crikey*', *The Australian*, Media supplement, 10 January 2000.

Chapter 4 – The first byline: Early careers

1. According to *Oxford English Dictionary* contributor Barry Popik, in 1911 Baltimore *Sun* editor Charles H Grasty called the modern metropolitan newspaper 'a daily miracle'; also, the movie *He Said, She Said* (1991) contained the line 'A newspaper is a daily miracle'. See Barry Popik, 'The Big Apple Blog', 5 January 2016, <barrypopik.com/index.php/new_york_city/entry/a_newspaper_is_a_daily_miracle> (accessed 9 February 2021).
2. John Henningham, 'Characteristics and attitudes of Australian journalists', *Electronic Journal of Communication*, vol 4, no 3 (1993): np; John Henningham, 'Australian journalists' attitudes to education', *Australian Journalism Review*, vol 15, no 2 (July 1993): 77–90.
3. Folker Hanusch, 'Journalists in times of change: Evidence from a new survey of Australia's journalistic workforce', *Australian Journalism Review*, vol 35, no 1 (2013): 33.

Chapter 5 – Copy copy copy! Newsroom culture

1. James Fairfax, *My Regards to Broadway: A Memoir* (Sydney: Angus & Robertson, 1992).
2. Bridget Griffen-Foley, *Sir Frank Packer: A Biography* (Sydney: Sydney University Press, 2014); Paul Barry, *The Rise and Rise of Kerry Packer Uncut* (Sydney: Bantam

Australia, 2008); Gerald Stone, *Who Killed Channel 9: The Death of Kerry Packer's Mighty Dream Machine* (Sydney: Macmillan Australia, 2007).
3   Rodney Tiffen, *Rupert Murdoch: A Reassessment* (Sydney: NewSouth, 2014).
4   Gavin Souter, *A Company of Heralds: A Century and a Half of Australian Publishing by John Fairfax Limited and its Predecessors, 1831–1981* (Melbourne: Melbourne University Press, 1981); Phillip Knightley, *A Hack's Progress* (London: Jonathan Cape, 1997), 24–36.
5   Colleen Ryan and Glenn Burge, *Corporate Cannibals: The Taking of Fairfax* (Melbourne: William Heinemann Australia, 1992), 277–303.
6   Mike Smith, personal communication, 3 February 2021.

Chapter 6 – The constant undercurrent: Sexual harassment and discrimination

1   Media, Entertainment and Arts Alliance and International Federation of Journalists, *Women in the Media: Participation and Portrayal* (Sydney: MEAA, 1996); Louise North, '"Just a little bit of cheeky ribaldry": Newsroom discourses of sexually harassing behaviour', *Feminist Media Studies*, vol 7, no 1 (2007): 81–96.
2   Louise North, 'Still a "blokes club": The motherhood dilemma in journalism', *Journalism: Theory, Practice & Criticism*, vol 17, no 3 (2016): 315–330.
3   Louise North, 'Damaging and daunting: Female journalists; Experiences of sexual harassment in the newsroom', *Feminist Media Studies*, vol 16, no 3 (2016): 495–510.
4   As historians Fay Anderson and Sally Young have shown, initiations and inappropriate behaviour were a feature of darkrooms at many newspapers. Although they tend to be romanticised in the memories of some photographers, darkrooms were not always welcoming or inclusive places in which to work. See Fay Anderson and Sally Young, *Shooting the Picture: Press Photography in Australia* (Melbourne: Miegunyah Press, 2016), 30.
5   According to Anderson and Young, the first female photographer at The Herald and Weekly Times was hired in 1977. See *Shooting the Picture*, 15.
6   Ben Hills, *Breaking News: The Golden Age of Graham Perkin* (Melbourne: Scribe, 2010), 351.
7   Michelle Grattan, interviewed by Brad Buller, 8 December 2017.
8   Laurie Oakes, 'Michelle Grattan', The Australian Media Hall of Fame, <halloffame.melbournepressclub.com/article/michelle-grattan> (accessed 20 January 2021).
9   Patricia Clarke, 'Women in the Media,' in *A Companion to the Australian Media*, ed. Bridget Griffen-Foley (Melbourne: Australian Scholarly Publishing, 2014), 497.
10 See Rosalind Smallwood, 'Guts and Substance: The Work and Influence of Journalist Nancy Dexter,' BA Hons thesis (Royal Melbourne Institute of Technology, 1985); Sybil Nolan, 'Dexter, Nancy Nugent (1923–1983)', *Australian Dictionary of Biography*, National Centre of Biography, Australian National University, <adb.anu.edu.au/biography/dexter-nancy-nugent-12416/text22321> (accessed 20 January 2021).
11 'Women in the Media,' 497.
12 Marie Hardin and Erin Whiteside, 'Token responses to gendered newsrooms: Factors in the career-related decisions of female newspaper sports journalists', *Journalism*, vol 10, no 5 (2009): 627–646.
13 There were some exceptions. Margaret Jones became *The Sydney Morning Herald*'s first Washington correspondent in 1966 and was also appointed foreign editor in

the 1970s. Yvonne Preston was China correspondent for *The Sydney Morning Herald* from 1975–1978. Colleen Ryan was Papua New Guinea correspondent for *The Australian Financial Review* from 1976–1978. See Barbara Lemon, 'Jones, Margaret Mary (1923–2006)', *The Australian Women's Register*, 12 April 2019, <womenaustralia.info/biogs/AWE2175b.htm> (accessed 20 January 2021); Nikki Henningham, 'Ryan, Colleen', *The Australian Women's Register*, 5 September 2012, <womenaustralia.info/biogs/AWE2797b.htm> (accessed 20 January 2021); Anne Summers, *Unfettered and Alive: A Memoir* (Sydney: Allen & Unwin, 2018), 14.

14   On Robert Haupt's career see Robert Haupt, *Last Boat to Astrakhan: A Russian Memoir* (Sydney: Random House Australia, 1998).
15   For further detail regarding the career of Piers Akerman see Caroline Wilson, 'The power of a Murdoch man', *The Sunday Age*, 8 December 1991, 1, 4.
16   On the career of Chris Copas see Danielle Blewett, 'Chris Copas remembered as music man, respected journalist', *The Examiner*, 31 January 2018, 12, <examiner.com.au/story/5199881/chris-copas-remembered-as-music-man-respected-journalist> (accessed 20 January 2021).
17   Margaret Simons, 'Phillip Chubb', *Australian Journalism Review* vol. 39, no. 2 (Dec 2017): 5-7.
18   Paula Hamilton, 'Journalists, Gender and Workplace Culture 1900–194,' in *Journalism: Print, Politics and Popular Culture*, eds. Ann Curthoys and Julianne Schultz (Brisbane: University of Queensland Press, 1999), 97–116.
19   Trevor Grant, 'Learning on the job … my life and the booze', *Drink Tank*, 2 July 2013, <drinktank.org.au/2013/07/learning-on-the-job> (accessed 20 January 2021).
20   Andrew Stephens, 'Ink in the Blood: The life of Melbourne's newspapers,' Exhibition Catalogue (Melbourne: City of Melbourne, 2017), <citycollection.melbourne.vic.gov.au/city-gallery-catalogues> (accessed 20 January 2021).
21   Pamela Bone was also *The Age*'s first female associate editor. See Iola Mathews, *Winning for Women: A Personal Story* (Melbourne: Monash University Publishing, 2019), 93.
22   'Women in the Media,' 497.
23   Kate Jenkins, *Respect@Work: National Inquiry into Sexual Harassment in Australian Workplaces*, Australian Human Rights Commission, https://humanrights.gov.au/our-work/sex-discrimination/publications, 218–224.

Chapter 7 – The thrill of the chase: Memorable stories
1   The full quote, attributed to celebrated American war correspondent HR Knickerbocker, is: 'Whenever you find hundreds of thousands of sane people trying to get out of a place and a little bunch of madmen struggling to get in, you know the latter are newspapermen.' See Giovanna Dell'Orto, *AP Foreign Correspondence in Action: World War II to the Present* (New York: Cambridge University Press, 2016), 167.
2   Sophie Morris, 'You're terrible Muir et al …', *The Saturday Paper*, 12–18 July 2014, <thesaturdaypaper.com.au/news/politics/2014/07/12/youre-terrible-muir-et-al/1405087200> (accessed 9 February 2021).
3   Denis Muller, *Journalism Ethics for the Digital Age* (Melbourne: Scribe, 2014).
4   Ian Richards, *Quagmires and Quandaries: Exploring Journalism Ethics* (Sydney: UNSW Press, 2005).

5 David Garrett, 'Challender, Stuart David (1947–1991)', *Australian Dictionary of Biography*, National Centre of Biography, Australian National University, <adb.anu.edu.au/biography/challender-stuart-david-29678/text36690> (accessed 9 February 2021).
6 Tom Stoppard, *Night and Day* (London: Faber, 1978), 48.

Chapter 8 – Errors and regrets
1 Martin Toseland, *A Steroid Hit the Earth: A Celebration of Misprints, Typos and Other Howlers* (London: Portico, 2008).
2 Dan Froomkin, 'George W Bush was AWOL but what's "truth" got to do with it?', *The Intercept*, 28 October 2015, <theintercept.com/2015/10/27/george-w-bush-was-awol-but-whats-truth-got-to-do-with-it> (accessed 20 January 2021).
3 Walter Robinson, 'One-year gap in Bush's National Guard duty', *The Boston Globe*, 23 May 2000, <web.archive.org/web/20000619121358/www.boston.com/news/politics/campaign2000/news/One_year_gap_in_Bush_s_Guard_duty+.shtml> (accessed 20 January 2021).
4 Malcolm Turnbull, *A Bigger Picture* (Melbourne: Hardie Grant, 2020), 153–156.
5 Kate Legge, '1997: Lowitja O'Donoghue, Indigenous leader', *The Weekend Australian Magazine*, 21 September 2013, <theaustralian.com.au/life/weekend-australian-magazine/lowitja-odonoghue-indigenous-leader/news-story/0cde724bda964be3e3d2101a7fe543e0> (accessed 20 January 2021).
6 Matthew Ricketson, 'Racism is more than "hurt feelings": We've already had an inquiry to prove it', *Guardian Australia*, 10 June 2014, <theguardian.com/commentisfree/2014/jun/10/racism-is-more-than-hurt-feelings-weve-already-had-an-inquiry-to-prove-it> (accessed 20 January 2021).

Chapter 9 – Knocking on grass: Reporting trauma
1 Gretchen Dworznik, 'Journalism and trauma: How reporters and photographers make sense of what they see', *Journalism Studies*, vol 7, no 4 (2006): 534–553.
2 According to Gary Tippet, his story was published as Fatalities #74 and Fatalities #75, *The Sunday Age*, 3 March 1996; Email correspondence between Gary Tippet and Matthew Ricketson, 13 October 2020.
3 Anthony Feinstein, *Journalists Under Fire: The Psychological Hazards of Covering War* (Baltimore: The Johns Hopkins University Press, 2006).
4 Kate Adie, *The Kindness of Strangers* (London: Hodder & Stoughton, 2002).
5 Marie Brenner, *A Private War: Marie Colvin and Other Tales of Heroes, Scoundrels and Renegades* (London: Simon & Schuster, 2018). See especially Ch 1, 'Marie Colvin's Private War', 21–52. Peter Greste, *The First Casualty: A Memoir from the Front Lines of the Global War on Journalism* (Sydney: Penguin, 2017).
6 Marla Buchanan and Patrice Keats, 'Coping with traumatic stress in journalism: A critical ethnographic study', *International Journal of Psychology*, vol 46, no 2 (2011): 127–135.
7 Personal communication between Matthew Ricketson and Lisa Millar, 16 October 2020.
8 Jonas Osmann, Jeffrey Dvorkin, Yoel Inbar, Elizabeth Page-Gould and Anthony Feinstein, 'The emotional well-being of journalists exposed to traumatic events: A mapping review', *Media, War and Conflict* (2020), <journals.sagepub.com/doi/abs/10.1177/1750635219895998?journalCode=mwca> (accessed 20 January 2021). Yuta Aoki, Estelle Malcolm, Sosei Yamaguchi, Graham Thornicroft

and Claire Henderson, 'Mental illness among journalists: A systematic review', *International Journal of Social Psychiatry*, vol 59, no 4 (2013): 377–390.
9   Kimina Lyall, 'Covering Traumatic Events Without Traumatising Yourself or Others,' in *Australian Journalism Today*, ed. Matthew Ricketson (Melbourne: Palgrave Macmillan, 2012), 33.
10 Matthew Ricketson and Alexandra Wake, 'Media companies on notice over traumatised journalists after landmark court decision', *The Conversation*, 6 March, 2019, <theconversation.com/media-companies-on-notice-over-traumatised-journalists-after-landmark-court-decision-112766> (accessed 20 January 2021); Damien Carrick, 'Trauma of news journalism in focus after *The Age* found responsible for reporter's PTSD', *The Law Report*, ABC Radio National, 22 March 2019, <abc.net.au/news/2019-03-22/ex-age-journalist-awarded-damages-for-ptsd-world-first/10896382> (accessed 20 January 2021).

Chapter 10 – Work-life imbalance
1   Bill Birnbauer, 'The Power of Investigative Journalism and Why It Is Needed More Than Ever,' in *Australian Journalism Today*, ed. Matthew Ricketson (Melbourne: Palgrave Macmillan, 2012), 81.
2   This claim has been made by John Tidey and John Larkin who were the first Insight reporters. See Ben Hills, *Breaking News: The Golden Age of Graham Perkin* (Melbourne: Scribe, 2010), 295; John Tidey, *Stories from a Bygone Age: A Newspaper Memoir* (Melbourne: Arcadia, 2018), 45.
3   Although Insight was first established by *The Age*'s reforming editor Graham Perkin in 1967, he did not formalise it as a full-time, permanent team of three reporters until November 1973. See Memorandum from Graham Perkin to *Age* Executives, 8 November 1973, Graham Perkin Papers, Folder 8, National Library of Australia, Canberra.
4   For Insight's long history of exposing wrongdoing see *Breaking News*, 291–313, 324–327, 441, 457–461.
5   *The Age*'s 'Minus Children' campaign exposed appalling conditions at Kew Cottages, an institution for intellectually disabled children. The Victorian land scandal stories of 1973–1982 involved corrupt housing commission land deals. *The Age* Tapes stories documented links between organised crime in New South Wales, police and government and resulted in corruption allegations against High Court justice Lionel Murphy.
6   Although many journalists think of *The Age* Tapes story as a landmark example of investigative journalism, in fact it was not flawless. As historian Jenny Hocking has argued, 'The paper's coverage avoided any distinction between tape, transcripts and summaries, compressed several conversations over different years into one, and established a tone of sinister intrigue, double dealing, sexual profligacy and dissolute corruption.' See Jenny Hocking, *Lionel Murphy: A Political Biography* (Melbourne: Cambridge University Press, 1997), 289.
7   For the full story see Jo Chandler, '$100m ANZ loan bungle', *The Age*, 29 January 1992, 1.
8   See David Wilson and Jo Chandler, 'Investigation on Mr Fixit tapes', *The Age*, 13 June 1992, 1; Jo Chandler and David Wilson, 'Police inquiry rejected', *The Age*, 15 June 1992, 1.
9   As Chris Masters has shown, for each investigative story that is published there are dozens that never see the light of day – perhaps due to a fact that could not be

checked, or an unreliable source, or because they are replaced by something more urgent. Yet these untold stories are often the most intriguing. See Chris Masters, *Not for Publication* (Sydney: ABC Books, 2002).

10   Louise North, 'Still a "blokes club": The motherhood dilemma in journalism', *Journalism: Theory, Practice & Criticism*, vol 17, no 3 (2016): 315–330.

11   For example, Graham Perkin was notorious for his workaholism, which led to his untimely death at age 45. Similarly, the then editor of *The Sunday Age* turned down the editorship of *The Sydney Morning Herald* because in his words: 'weekly publications allowed you a life outside journalism, daily papers didn't'. See Bruce Guthrie, *Man Bites Murdoch: Four Decades in Print, Six Days in Court* (Melbourne: Melbourne University Press, 2010), 136. Women's experience of working long hours and drinking shared elements with men's experiences and were also inflected by their gender. For discussion of various aspects of this issue, see Channel Seven journalist and tv newsreader Talitha Cummins's account of her struggle with alcohol in 'The Big Dry', *Australian Story*, ABC TV, 10 October 2016. See also Rosie Boycott, *A Nice Girl Like Me: A Story of the Seventies*, (London: Penguin, 2nd edition, 1984) and Jill Stark, *High Sobriety: My Year Without Booze*, (Brunswick: Scribe, 2013).

12   Garry Barker, a former Southeast Asia and New York correspondent for The Herald and Weekly Times, says being appointed to a foreign posting is a lot like being 'knighted in their profession'. See Garry Barker, 'The Foreign Correspondent,' in *Reporting for Work: A Guide to Daily Journalism*, ed. Robert Coleman (Melbourne: The Herald and Weekly Times, 1970), 171.

13   Laurie Oakes, 'Michelle Grattan', The Australian Media Hall of Fame, <halloffame.melbournepressclub.com/article/michelle-grattan> (accessed 20 January 2021).

14   Iola Mathews, *Winning for Women: A Personal Story* (Melbourne: Monash University Publishing, 2019).

Profile – David Marr

1   See Joseph Dowling, 'Buthelezi, Packer link', *The Australian Financial Review*, 29 July 1991, <afr.com/politics/buthelezi-packer-link-19910729-k4gdj> (accessed 10 February 2021).

2   Craig Munro, *Inky Stephensen: Wild Man of Letters* (St Lucia: University of Queensland Press, 1992).

Chapter 11 – Chasing clicks: Changing technology

1   Clem Lloyd, *Profession: Journalist: A History of the Australian Journalists' Association* (Sydney: Hale & Iremonger, 1985): 275–282.

2   Sybil Nolan, 'Born Outside the Newsroom: The Creation of The Age Online', in *Web 25: Histories from the First 25 Years of the World Wide Web*, ed. Niels Brügger, (DOI: 10.3726/b11492: Peter Lang, 2017).

3   Vittoria Sacco and Diana Bossio, 'Don't Tweet this!: How journalists and media organizations negotiate tensions emerging from the implementation of social media policy in newsrooms', *Digital Journalism*, vol 5, no 2 (2017): 177–193.

4   Julie Posetti, *Time to Step Away from the 'Bright, Shiny Things'? Towards a Sustainable Model of Journalism Innovation in an Era of Perpetual Change* (Oxford: Reuters Institute for the Study of Journalism, 2018).

5   Steen Steensen, 'Online journalism and the promises of new technology: A critical review and look ahead', *Journalism Studies*, vol 12, no 3 (2011): 311–327; An Nguyen, 'Facing "the fabulous monster": The traditional media's fear-driven innovation culture in the development of online news', *Journalism Studies*, vol 9, no 1(2008): 91–104.
6   Helen Caple, 'Anyone can take a photo, but: Is there space for the professional photographer in the twenty-first century newsroom?', *Digital Journalism*, vol 2, no 3 (2014): 355–365.
7   Tim Burrowes, 'Why sub-editors matter', *Mumbrella*, 3 May 2011, <mumbrella.com.au/why-sub-editors-matter-45414> (accessed 20 January 2021).
8   Folker Hanusch, 'Transformative times: Australian journalists' perceptions of changes', *Media International Australia, Incorporating Culture & Policy*, vol 155, no 1 (May 2015): 38–53; Penny O'Donnell, David McKnight and Jonathan Este, *Journalism at the Speed of Bytes: Australian Newspapers in the 21st Century* (Sydney: Media, Entertainment and Arts Alliance, 2012).

Chapter 12 – Should I stay or should I go now?
1   Tim Elliott, 'How a German media company brought Australia's greatest magazine to its knees', *The Sydney Morning Herald*, Good Weekend, 4 July 2020, <smh.com.au/national/how-a-german-media-company-brought-australia-s-greatest-magazine-empire-to-its-knees-20200622-p5551c.html> (accessed 10 February 2021).
2   Colleen Ryan, *Fairfax: The Rise and Fall* (Melbourne: Miegunyah Press, 2013); Pamela Williams, *Killing Fairfax: Packer, Murdoch and The Ultimate Revenge* (Sydney: HarperCollins, 2013).
3   Mitchell Stephens, *A History of News* (New York: Oxford University Press, 2007), 8.
4   Lawrie Zion, Merryn Sherwood, Penny O'Donnell, Tim Marjoribanks, Matthew Ricketson, Andrew Dodd and Monika Winarnita, *New Beats Report: Mass Redundancies and Career Change in Australian Journalism* (Melbourne: New Beats Team, 2018), <newbeatsblog.com/wp-content/uploads/2016/12/New_Beats_Report.pdf> (accessed 20 January 2021).
5   The Walkley Foundation, 'Walkley Winners Archive', <walkleys.com/awards/walkley-winners-archive> (accessed 20 January 2021).
6   Margaret Simons, *The Content Makers: Understanding the Media in Australia* (Melbourne: Penguin, 2007), 14–18.
7   Jo Chandler, *Feeling the Heat* (Melbourne: Melbourne University Publishing, 2011).
8   Nielsen BookScan figures show *The Australian Moment* was the 43rd best-selling non-fiction book in Australia in 2012, whether originating from overseas or published locally.
9   Matthew Ricketson, 'Media news: The dearth estate: A question of quality', *The Age*, 6 September 2008.
10 Rachel Buchanan, *Stop Press: The Last Days of Newspapers* (Melbourne: Scribe, 2013).
11 Bianca Hall, '*SMH* and *Age* editors to quit Fairfax', *The Sydney Morning Herald*, 25 June 2012, <smh.com.au/politics/federal/smh-and-age-editors-quit-fairfax-20120625-20xnx.html> (accessed 20 January 2021).
12 For analysis of Fairfax Media chief executive Greg Hywood's stance on quality

journalism, see Matthew Ricketson, 'A broken record of quality journalism', *Inside Story*, 15 November 2018, <insidestory.org.au/a-broken-record-of-quality-journalism> (accessed 20 January 2021).

Chapter 13 – Pickets and payouts: Unions in the newsroom
1. 'A proud history at the forefront of journalism', Media, Entertainment and Arts Alliance, 8 December 2017, <meaa.org/news/meaa-media-aja-history> (accessed 20 January 2021).
2. Personal communication with Chris Warren, 8 July 2020.
3. Paul Chadwick, *Media Mates: Carving up Australia's Media* (Melbourne: Macmillan, 1989).
4. Matthew Ricketson, Andrew Dodd, Lawrie Zion and Monika Winarnita, '"Like being shot in the face" or "I'm glad I'm out": Journalists' experiences of job loss in the Australian media industry 2012–2014', *Journalism Studies*, vol 21, no 1 (2020): 63.
5. Lawrie Zion, Merryn Sherwood, Penny O'Donnell, Tim Marjoribanks, Matthew Ricketson, Andrew Dodd and Monika Winarnita, *New Beats Report: Mass Redundancies and Career Change in Australian Journalism* (Melbourne: New Beats Project, 2018), <newbeatsblog.com/wp-content/uploads/2016/12/New_Beats_Report.pdf> (accessed 20 January 2021).
6. Amanda Meade, 'Union passes no confidence vote in Fairfax after 30 forced redundancies', *Guardian Australia*, 10 May 2016, <theguardian.com/media/2016/may/10/fairfax-staff-stop-work-forcible-redundancies> (accessed 20 January 2021).
7. Rodney Tiffen, *Rupert Murdoch: A Reassessment* (Sydney: NewSouth, 2014), 32.
8. Margaret Van Heekeren, 'Stop the presses: Strikes in the Australian news media', *Media International Australia*, 2014, vol 150, no 1, 41–46.
9. See for example Richard Aedy, *The Media Report*, ABC Radio National, 20 November 2008, <abc.net.au/radionational/programs/archived/mediareport-1999/melbourne-future-of-journalism-summit/3162030> (accessed 20 January 2021).

Chapter 14 – Mate, this gives me absolutely no pleasure, but …
1. Matthew Ricketson, Andrew Dodd, Lawrie Zion and Monika Winarnita, '"Like being shot in the face" or "I'm glad I'm out": Journalists' experiences of job loss in the Australian media industry 2012–2014', *Journalism Studies*, vol 21, no 1 (2020): 54–71.
2. Colleen Ryan, *Fairfax: The Rise and Fall* (Melbourne: Miegunyah Press, 2013).
3. Katharine Murphy, *On Disruption* (Melbourne: Melbourne University Press, 2018).
4. Tim Elliott, 'How a German media company brought Australia's greatest magazine to its knees', *The Sydney Morning Herald*, Good Weekend, 4 July 2020, <smh.com.au/national/how-a-german-media-company-brought-australia-s-greatest-magazine-empire-to-its-knees-20200622-p5551c.html> (accessed 10 February 2021).
5. Nic Maclellan, 'The gutting of Radio Australia', *Inside Story*, 22 July 2014, <insidestory.org.au/the-gutting-of-radio-australia> (accessed 10 February 2021).
6. Anne Davies, Lisa Cox and Latika Bourke, 'ABC staff await a "Hunger Games" battle for their jobs', *The Sydney Morning Herald*, 25 November 2014, <smh.com.au/national/abc-staff-await-a-hunger-games-battle-for-their-jobs-20141125-11tsay.html> (accessed 10 February 2021).

7   Miranda Ward, 'Axed Fairfax journalist Michael West to launch own investigative journalism website', *Mumbrella*, 31 May 2016, <mumbrella.com.au/sacked-fairfax-journalist-michael-west-launch-investigative-journalism-website-370181> (accessed 10 February 2021).
8   Lawrie Zion, Andrew Dodd, Merryn Sherwood, Penny O'Donnell, Tim Marjoribanks and Matthew Ricketson, 'Working for less: The aftermath for journalists made redundant in Australia between 2012 and 2014', *Communication Research and Practice*, vol 2, no 2 (2016): 117–136.

Chapter 15 – The walk to the lift: Last days at work

1   Matthew Ricketson, Andrew Dodd, Lawrie Zion and Monika Winarnita, '"Like being shot in the face" or "I'm glad I'm out": Journalists' experiences of job loss in the Australian media industry 2012–2014', *Journalism Studies*, vol 21, no 1 (2020): 54–71.
2   Merryn Sherwood and Penny O'Donnell, 'Once a journalist, always a journalist? Industry restructure, job loss and professional identity', *Journalism Studies*, vol 19, no 7 (2018): 1021–1038.
3   Spooner's last *Age* cartoon, published on 14 May 2016, is no longer on *The Age*'s website, but has been subsequently published by the ABC: 'John Spooner's last cartoon for *The Age*', ABC News, 11 August 2017, <mobile.abc.net.au/news/2017-08-11/john-spooners-last-cartoon-for-the-age/8798670?nw=0> (accessed 11 February 2021).
4   'A man of his word', *Australian Story*, ABC TV, 29 October 2012, <abc.net.au/austory/a-man-of-his-word/9170166> (accessed 10 February 2021).
5   Lawrie Zion, Merryn Sherwood, Penny O'Donnell, Andrew Dodd, Matthew Ricketson and Tim Marjoribanks, '"It has a bleak future": The effects of job loss on regional and rural journalism in Australia', *Australian Journalism Review*, vol 38, no 1 (2016): 115–128.
6   Amanda Meade, interview by Richard Aedy, *The Media Report*, ABC Radio National, 16 November 2012, <abc.net.au/radionational/programs/archived/mediareport/amanda-meade-takes-redundancy/4374414#transcript> (accessed 20 January 2021).
7   Tony Wright, 'Tributes flow as Michael Gordon, a giant of journalism and the most decent of men, departs *The Age*', *The Age*, 15 June 2017, <smh.com.au/politics/federal/tributes-flow-as-michael-gordon-a-giant-of-journalism-and-the-most-decent-of-men-departs-the-age-20170614-gwqoyy.html> (accessed 10 February 2021).
8   Australia, House of Representatives, *Parliamentary Debates*, 16 August 2012, Julia Gillard, <parlinfo.aph.gov.au/parlInfo/genpdf/chamber/hansardr/a8785071-a01e-4d0b-bf4e-9e6ea9104940/0125/hansard_frag.pdf;fileType=application%2Fpdf> (accessed 10 February 2021); Australia, House of Representatives, *Parliamentary Debates*, 16 August 2012, Tony Abbott, <parlinfo.aph.gov.au/parlInfo/genpdf/chamber/hansardr/a8785071-a01e-4d0b-bf4e-9e6ea9104940/0126/hansard_frag.pdf;fileType=application%2Fpdf> (accessed 10 February 2021).

Chapter 16 – What just happened? The days after redundancy

1   Nicole S Cohen, Andrea Hunter and Penny O'Donnell, 'Bearing the burden of corporate restructuring: Job loss and precarious employment in Canadian journalism', *Journalism Practice*, vol 13, no 7 (2019): 817–833; Lawrie Zion,

Merryn Sherwood, Penny O'Donnell, Tim Marjoribanks, Matthew Ricketson, Andrew Dodd and Monika Winarnita, *New Beats Report: Mass Redundancies and Career Change in Australian Journalism* (Melbourne: New Beats Team, 2018), <newbeatsblog.com/wp-content/uploads/2016/12/New_Beats_Report.pdf> (accessed 20 January 2021).

2 Penny O'Donnell, 'Beyond newsrooms: Younger journalists talk about job loss and reemployment in Australian journalism', *Australian Journalism Review*, vol 39, no 2 (2017): 163–175; Penny O'Donnell, Lawrie Zion and Merryn Sherwood, 'Where do journalists go after newsroom job cuts?', *Journalism Practice*, vol 10, no 1 (2016): 35–51.

Chapter 17 – Resilience and reinvention

1 Penny O'Donnell and Lawrie Zion, 'Precarity in Media Work,' in *Making Media: Production, Practices and Professions*, eds. Mark Deuze and Mirjam Prenger (Amsterdam: Amsterdam University Press, 2019), 223–234; Penny O'Donnell, 'Australian Journalists at Work: Their Views on Employment, Unionisation and Professional Identity,' in *Critical Perspectives on Journalistic Beliefs and Actions: Global Experiences*, eds. Eric Freeman, Robyn S Goodman and Elanie Steyn (New York: Routledge, 2018), 24–34.

2 Merryn Sherwood and Penny O'Donnell, 'Once a journalist, always a journalist? Industry restructure, job loss and professional identity', *Journalism Studies*, vol 19, no 7 (2018): 1021–1038.

Chapter 18 – The wrap

1 Bastian Obermayer and Frederik Obermaier, *The Panama Papers: Breaking the Story of How the Rich and Powerful Hide their Money* (London: Oneworld, 2016).

2 Bernard Keene, 'Australian Media Policy: Of the Mates, By the Mates, For the Mates', *Crikey*, 26 February 2021, https://protect-au.mimecast.com/s/38q9C Gvmpxh1GpL0pIKAm5r?domain=crikey.com.au" https://www.crikey.com.au/2021/02/26/media-policy-tradition/, accessed 19 March 2021.

3 See Barry Popik, 'The Big Apple Blog', 5 January 2016, <barrypopik.com/index.php/new_york_city/entry/a_newspaper_is_a_daily_miracle> (accessed 10 February 2021).

4 Dalton Bennett, Emma Brown, Atthar Mirza, Sarah Cahlan, Joyce Sohyun Lee, Meg Kelly, Elyse Samuels and Jon Swaine, '41 minutes of fear: A video timeline from inside the Capitol siege', *The Washington Post*, 16 January 2021, <washingtonpost.com/investigations/2021/01/16/video-timeline-capitol-siege/?arc404=true> (accessed 10 February 2021).

5 Sarah Ferguson and Tony Jones, 'Downfall: The last days of President Trump', *Four Corners*, ABC Television, 1 February 2021, <abc.net.au/4corners/downfall:-the-last-days-of-president-trump/13110382> (accessed 10 February 2021).

6 Luke Mogelson, 'Among the insurrectionists', *The New Yorker*, 15 January 2021, <newyorker.com/magazine/2021/01/25/among-the-insurrectionists?utm_source=onsite-share&utm_medium=email&utm_campaign=onsite-share&utm_brand=the-new-yorker> (accessed 10 February 2021).

7 Glenn Kessler, Salvador Rizzo and Meg Kelly, 'Trump's false or misleading claims total 30,573 over 4 years', *The Washington Post*, 24 January 2021, <washingtonpost.com/politics/2021/01/24/trumps-false-or-misleading-claims-total-30573-over-four-years> (accessed 10 February 2021).

Note to page 282

8   Andrew Marantz, 'The importance and incoherence of Twitter's Trump ban', *The New Yorker*, 15 January 2021, <newyorker.com/news/daily-comment/the-importance-and-incoherence-of-twitters-trump-ban> (accessed 10 February 2021).

Bibliography

Adie, Kate. *The Kindness of Strangers*. London: Hodder & Stoughton, 2002.
Anderson, Fay, and Sally Young. *Shooting the Picture: Press Photography in Australia*. Melbourne: Miegunyah Press, 2016.
Behr, Edward. *Anyone Here Been Raped and Speaks English? A Foreign Correspondent's Life Behind the Lines*. New York: Viking Press, 1978.
Birnbauer, Bill. 'The Power of Investigative Journalism and Why It Is Needed More Than Ever.' In *Australian Journalism Today*, edited by Matthew Ricketson, 78–92. Melbourne: Palgrave Macmillan, 2012.
Brenner, Marie. *A Private War*. London: Simon & Schuster, 2018.
Buchanan, Rachel. *Stop Press: The Last Days of Newspapers*. Melbourne: Scribe, 2013.
Chadwick, Paul. *Media Mates: Carving up Australia's Media*. Melbourne: Macmillan, 1989.
Chandler, Jo. *Feeling the Heat*. Carlton: Melbourne University Publishing, 2011.
Grabosky, Peter N. *Wayward Governance: Illegality and its Control in the Public Sector*. Canberra: Australian Institute of Criminology, 1989.
Greste, Peter. *The First Casualty: A Memoir from the Front Lines of the Global War on Journalism*. Melbourne: Penguin, 2017.
Hanusch, Folker. 'Journalists in times of change: Evidence from a new survey of Australia's journalistic workforce'. *Australian Journalism Review*, vol 35, no 1 (2013): 29–42.
Haupt, Robert. *Last Boat to Astrakhan: A Russian Memoir*. Sydney: Random House, 1998.
Henningham, John. 'Australian journalists' attitudes to education'. *Australian Journalism Review*, vol 15, no 2 (July 1993): 77–90.
Henningham, John. 'Characteristics and attitudes of Australian journalists'. *Electronic Journal of Communication*, vol 4, no 3 (1993): np.
Hills, Ben. *Breaking News: The Golden Age of Graham Perkin*. Melbourne: Scribe, 2010.
Lyall, Kimina. 'Covering Traumatic Events Without Traumatising Yourself or Others.' In *Australian Journalism Today*, edited by Matthew Ricketson, 28–44. Melbourne: Palgrave, 2012.
Mathews, Iola, *Winning for Women: A Personal Story*. Melbourne: Monash University Publishing, 2019.
O'Donnell, Penny, McKnight, David and Este, Jonathan. *Journalism at the Speed of Bytes: Australian Newspapers in the 21st Century*. Sydney: Media, Entertainment and Arts Alliance, 2012.
Ricketson, Matthew. 'Newspaper Feature Writing in Australia 1956–1966.' In *Journalism: Print Politics and Popular Culture*, edited by Ann Curthoys and Julianne Schultz. Brisbane: University of Queensland Press, 1999.
Ryan, Colleen. *Fairfax: The Rise and Fall*. Melbourne: Miegunyah Press, 2013.

Simons, Margaret. *The Content Makers: Understanding the Media in Australia*.
    Melbourne: Penguin, 2007.
Summers, Anne. *Unfettered and Alive: A Memoir*. Sydney: *Allen* & Unwin, 2018.
Tidey, John. *Stories from a Bygone Age: A Newspaper Memoir*. Melbourne: Arcadia, 2018.
Tiffen, Rodney. *Rupert Murdoch: A Reassessment*. Sydney: NewSouth, 2014.
Van Heekeren, Margaret. 'Stop the presses: Strikes in the Australian news media'.
    Media International Australia, vol 150, no 1 (2014): 41–46.
Williams, Pamela. *Killing Fairfax: Packer, Murdoch and the Ultimate Revenge*. Sydney:
    HarperCollins, 2013.

Index

Abbott government 221
Abbott, Tony 166
ABC 7, 87, 292, 294
   Behind the News 21
   funding cuts 7
   Hack 149
   Hobart 240–1, 292
   Hunger Games 222
   Media Watch 82, 165, 298
   News Corp and 82–83, 165
   Radio Australia 60, 232, 283, 294
   Radio National 235, 285
   redundancies 221–22
   7.30 Report and *7:30* 292, 317
   TV Times 302
   Victorian Country Hour 286
Ablett Snr, Gary 52
abusive emails 89–90
Adelaide University *On Dit* 291
Adie, Kate 137
The Advertiser 284, 291, 309
The Advocate 20, 260
The Age 6, 15, 21, 52–53, 60, 67, 93–94, 96, 97, 136, 187, 193, 211, 265, 266, 270, 272, 283, 285, 287, 289, 290, 293, 297, 303, 305, 306, 308, 309
   '*The Age* Tapes' 145
   Bog Bar 99
   childcare facilities 151
   digital innovation, lack of 172, 181–82
   editorial choices 111–12
   Editorial Independence Committee 189–90
   errors 119, 130
   first female editor 100
   first female leader writer 100
   first website 169
   foreign correspondents 139–40, 148
   Insight investigations team 145, 153, 285
   Money Extra 58
   newsroom then and now 1–3, 61, 75, 175–76
   occupational post-traumatic disorder cases 144
   redundancies 192, 194–97, 225, 229, 231, 233, 239, 256–57, 259 *see also* redundancies
   sister papers, helping 114–15
   'women's pages' 95
   work-life imbalance 150, 151, 153, 154
Akerman, Piers 97–98
Albanese, Anthony 274, 276
Albany Advertiser 97, 290
Alcorn, Gay 100
Alexander, John 71, 164, 192
Allan, Col 64
Allen, Allen & Helmsley 157, 159
Allen, David 157
Antarakis, Dominique 264
ANZ Bank lending practices 146
The Argus 21, 297
Armsden, Alan 219–20
Arnold, Bob 70–71
Arup, Tom 52, 61, 111–12, 154, 196–97, 208, 225, 270, 283
Askin, Bob 160
The Atlantic 285
Austin, Peter 55
Australia Council 161
The Australian 6, 17, 18, 19, 35, 44, 54, 86, 87, 107, 109, 111, 121, 147, 193, 261, 273, 284, 287, 289, 290, 291, 295, 296, 299, 301, 304, 305, 306, 307, 310
   newsroom culture 49, 63–64, 80–85
   perspective and focus 187–88, 225

redundancies 191, 235
technology and 83–84, 169, 174, 190–91
union hostility 205–206
Australian Associated Press (AAP) 59, 147, 303
Australian Bureau of Statistics 27, 109
Australian Conservation Foundation 270
Australian Competition and Consumer Commission (ACCC) 280
Australian Consolidated Press 172, 184–85, 300
The Australian Financial Review 1–3, 35, 53–54, 71, 72, 100, 107, 136, 152, 187, 223, 287, 295, 296, 301, 304, 308, 310
Australian Journalists' Association (AJA) see Media, Entertainment and Arts Alliance (MEAA)
Australian Legal Business 300
Australian Press Council 83, 304

Bacon, Wendy 101
Baker, Don 74
Baker, Suzanne 95
The Bankstown Express 287
Bannon, John 37
Barwick, Chief Justice Sir Garfield 160, 161
Battersby, Lucy 61
Bauer Media 185, 210, 217, 237, 239, 269, 287
BBC 19, 126, 293, 295
Beeby, Rosslyn 89–90, 96–97, 194–95, 230–31, 262, 283–84
Biden, Joe 282
Black, Conrad 74
Black Saturday bushfires 111, 166
Bloukos, Neoklis 272
Blunden, Peter 129–30
Boland, Ron 37
Bolt, Andrew 128
Bond, Alan 57
Bondi Girls 101
Bone, Pamela 100
Booth, Meredith 153–54, 171, 226, 261, 284
The Border Mail 210, 235, 240, 273, 308
Brenner, Marie 137–38

Broome Advertiser 41, 246, 247, 302
Brown, John 32–33
Brown, Stuart 67–68
Brundrett, Ross 12–14, 22–23, 36, 67–68, 106, 170–71, 204, 284
Buchanan, Rachel 2
The Bulletin 100, 114, 159, 170
Bunte 288
Burge, Glenn 72–73
Bush, George W. 119
business and finance journalism 57–59, 146
Business Review Weekly 58, 187, 259, 300
Buthelezi, Mangosuthu 159
Butterly, Nick 301
BuzzFeed 208

cadetships 29–30, 32, 33–36, 40–41, 46–50, 56
 grading 35–36
 rounds system 48
 training 50–51, 54–55
The Cairns Post 59, 293
Canberra Times 31–32, 61, 89–90, 95, 96, 100, 194, 202, 205, 230–31, 254, 262, 284, 286, 288, 297
Cape Argus 66
Carroll, Vic 160
cartoonists 16–17, 58, 61, 64, 70, 173–74, 203–204, 215–19, 221, 233–34, 259, 288, 306
Catalano, Antony 266
Central Western Daily 40, 273, 307
Challender, Stuart 111
Chandler, Jo 53, 95–96, 99, 119, 145–46, 151–52, 178, 179–80, 189–90, 233, 256–57, 285
The Chronicle 289, 310
Chubb, Philip 98–99
Clemson Text and Media 266–67
Coastal Telegraph 297
Colac Herald 290
Colebatch, Tim 150, 197, 285
Colvin, Marie 137–38
Colvin, Mark 84
Community & Public Sector Union (CPSU) 207
Connor, Louise 207
Conroy, Paul 138

Index

Cooney, Campbell 23, 41–42, 222, 232–33, 268, 271, 286
Cooper, Jay 265
Cooper, Nick 265
Copas, Chris 98
The Copy Collective 264–65
Corby, Stephen 21–22, 31–32, 50, 68–69, 71–72, 115–16, 125–26, 135, 205, 210, 235–36, 237, 238–39, 286
Coslovich, Gabriella 270
The Courier 297
The Courier-Mail 19, 98, 168, 177, 261, 289, 298
Courtney, Michael 33–34
Covid-19 3, 4, 191, 281
Crikey 44, 85, 235, 295
Crisp, Lyndall 100
cross-media ownership rules *see* media ownership rules
Cumberland Group 226, 257, 258, 287, 297

Daily Express 290, 305
Daily Mail (London) 284, 286
The Daily Telegraph 59, 68–70, 78, 122, 152, 157, 181, 205, 264, 286, 287, 297, 304, 307
Daley, Paul 114
Dart Center for Journalism and Trauma 143, 144
Das, Sushi 233
Davidson, Gay 95
Davies, Anne 53–54, 57, 150–51, 193, 258–59, 287
Deane, Joel 4
defamation laws 120
De La Rue, Andrew 174
Denton, Andrew 86
Dexter, Nancy 95
digital disruption of media 3–4, 83–84, 168, 277–78
  digital advertising 180–82, 186
  innovation, lack of 171–72
  interviewees and 278
  job implications 175
  newspaper page layout 178
  online reporting before paper issue 170
  photojournalism 174
  positive aspects to 279–80
  quality concerns 175–77, 178–80
  redundancies due to *see* redundancies
  revenue declines 180
  slowness of managerial response 171–74, 182
  technical support 171–72
  training, lack of 171–74
  websites 171–72
Digital Platforms Inquiry Report 280
Diver, Stuart 114
Doncaster-Templestowe News 303
Duncan, Julie 30
Duncan, Peter 30
Dwyer, Lynne 39, 271, 287
Dyer, Glenn 54

Earl of Harewood 24
Easdown, Geoff 44
Eastern Suburbs Newspapers (ESN) 287
Edinburgh Evening News 291
Elder, Bruce 110, 288
environmental journalism 89–90
Evening Standard (London) 286
The Examiner 20, 33, 34, 51, 52, 98, 260, 293, 309

Fagan, David 168
Fairfax Media 1–2, 74, 185–86
  cost-cutting 186–87, 195
  digital disruption 178–79, 185–86
  editors, role of 195–96
  House Committee 74, 192, 196, 200, 204, 208, 218
  The Journalist's Craft 67
  Nine Entertainment Company acquisition by 1, 11
  redundancies 6–7, 191–93, 195–97
  redundancy payouts 200
  Rural Press merger 185
  standards of reporting 193–95
  sub-editing outsource 176, 192
Falls, Caroline 101
Farr, Bill 266
Faulkner, Brett 12
Fazzari, Rocco 16–17, 61, 64, 70, 173–74, 203–204, 215–17, 288

The Financial Times 136, 137, 308
Finkelstein Inquiry 83, 187
Finkelstein, Ray 6, 83
Fisher, Caroline 188
Forbes, Mark 225
foreign correspondents 20, 126–27, 136–43, 147–50
   personal and professional lives, balance 148
   post-traumatic stress disorder (PTSD) 137, 142–43
   women 95, 100, 137–38, 143
Franklin Dam blockade 174
Franklin, Matthew 19, 121, 136, 147, 187–89, 238, 259, 273–74, 276, 289
Fraser, Malcolm 161
Fray, Peter 166, 224–25

Gee, Margaret 93–94
Geelong Advertiser 46, 53, 95, 290, 297
gender discrimination *see* sexual harassment and discrimination; women journalists
Gillard government 6
Gold Coast Bulletin 97, 171, 175, 177, 182, 209, 236, 306
Golden Mail 302
Gordon, Bob 209
Gordon, Michael 238
Gourmet Traveller 287
Graham, Louise 50, 92–93, 94–95, 97, 129, 130, 134, 174, 211, 239, 266–67, 289
Graham, Vern 39
Grasty, Charles H 280–81
Grattan, Michelle 94, 100, 150
Grech, Godwin 122–23
Greiner, Nick 122
Greste, Peter 138
Griffith Review 257, 285
GroundCover 310
The Guardian 80–81, 257, 285, 290
Guardian Australia 75, 79, 86–88, 167, 170, 208, 258, 287, 298, 299
Gulia, Ugo 220
Gunn, Michelle 100
Gurrumul (Geoffrey Gurrumul Yunupingu) 110

Guthrie-Jones, David 50

Hammond, Jane 27, 32, 57, 97, 171, 193–94, 267–68, 289–90
Hancock, Lang 42
Hanlon, Peter 195–96, 231, 268, 272, 290
Hanson, Pauline 166
Hargreaves, Wendy 46–47, 53, 95, 204, 230, 290–91
Harris, Samela 37, 64, 91, 97–98, 152, 172, 206, 212, 291–92
Harris, Steve 129, 220
Haupt, Robert 95
Hawke, Bob 18, 35, 106
Hawke government 200
health journalism 151–52, 153
Heath, Sally 153
The Herald 5, 14, 15, 20, 35, 41, 47, 60, 67, 73, 79, 80, 84, 91, 92, 94, 101, 150, 174, 187, 193, 219, 271, 284, 287, 289, 293, 294, 299, 301, 302, 303, 305 *see also* The Herald and Weekly Times
The Herald and Weekly Times 4, 47, 59–60, 67, 176, 219, 255, 291, 298 *see also* The Herald; The Weekly Times
   Reporting for Work 67
   TV Scene 302
Herald Sun 12–13, 81, 113, 128, 129, 134, 176, 204, 228, 246, 284, 289, 290, 291, 293, 304 *see also The Sun News-Pictorial*
House Committee 204
Hickie, David 160
Hinton, Pat 73–74
Holden, Andrew 225, 233
Holmes à Court, Robert 57–58
Horin, Adele 101
Howard government 2
Howard, John 108, 110
Hunt, Linda 240–41, 292
Hutchison, Tracee 112, 154–55, 207, 238, 292–93
Hyland, Tom 20, 25, 55–56, 59, 104–105, 126–27, 139–40, 147–48, 155, 172, 179, 207–208, 217–18, 229–30, 233, 293
Hywood, Greg 179

The Independent 42–43
The Independent (London) 297

Index

Independent Inquiry into the Media and Media Regulation 83
Indigenous issues 108–109, 127–29
internet 168–69
Investor Weekly 300
<issimo.io> 265
<issimomag.com> 265

Jean Hailes for Women's Health 270
Jenkins, Kate 100
Jonathan Cape 162–63
Jones, Hugh 33–34, 51, 52, 98, 152, 174–75, 176–77, 178, 205, 219–20, 228–29, 230, 235, 255–56, 293–94
Jopson, Debra 25, 51, 68, 94, 101, 108–109, 127–29, 150, 171, 182, 192, 195, 234–35, 259, 294
   Oliver of the Levant 259
Jorgensen, Christian 141
journalism *see also* journalists
   accuracy 46
   breaking stories 12–14, 53–54, 57
   business and finance 57–58
   business model collapse 3–4
   cadetships 29–30, 32, 33–36, 40–41, 46–51, 54–56
   careers for young people in 278–79
   copy kids 31–32, 43, 64–65
   copy tasters 66–67
   description of 4
   digital disruption 3–4, 168–9 *see also* digital disruption of media
   editorial assistants 49
   editorial decisions and values 193–94
   entry into profession 29–45
   eyewitness accounts, power of 14
   gotcha questions 18
   grading of cadets 35–36
   importance of 279, 281–82
   interview skills 60
   inverted pyramid writing style 36
   job training 46–61
   male domination of 150
   mobility in media forms 60
   municipal politics 56–57
   News Limited scholarships 37
   opportunities in 59
   overseas bureaus 59–06
   phone interviews 51
   political developments 280
   potential of 279, 281
   redundancies *see* redundancies
   skills in, developing 51
   social media guidelines 171
   studies in 31–32, 36
   sub-editors 8, 39, 46, 52–53, 62, 64–68, 176–78, 192, 277, 280
   travel 59–60
   university programs/qualifications 38–39, 41, 48–49, 278–79
   women in *see* women journalists
   work experience 30–31
journalists 8
   book-length journalism 190–91
   drinking with contacts 123
   early careers 46–61
   emotional impact of stories 126–30
   family connections 33–34
   family influences 16, 17–20
   feedback 55
   first bylines 52–53
   freelancing 203
   front-page debuts 53–54
   hero models 25
   industry wisdom 8
   internships 38
   job interviews 32–35
   manipulation of 124–25
   missing the story fears 46–7
   mistakes *see* mistakes
   motivations 27–28
   personal and professional lives, juggling 146–55
   post-traumatic stress disorder (PTSD) 137 *see also* trauma, reporting on
   production roles 50
   public relations and 123–24
   reader and colleague relationships 47
   redundancies *see* redundancies
   regional newspapers as training grounds 39–40
   resilience and reinvention post-redundancy *see* reinvention
   school/teacher influences 21–23
   student newspapers 37, 283, 291

technology, relationship with 168–83
trauma, reporting on *see* trauma, reporting on
triggers for becoming 14–28, 78–79, 158–59, 245–49
women *see* women journalists

Kafcaloudes, Phil 131–32, 143, 294
Kalgoorlie Miner 247, 302
Keating, Paul 2, 44, 79
Kelly, Hugo 53
Kelly, Paul 191
   The Unmaking of Gough 191
Kennedy, Trevor 159
Kennett, Jeff 44
Kerr, Christian 43–44, 295
Kirk, David 192
Kirkpatrick, Rod 40
Kosovo 140–42
Kosovo Liberation Army (KLA) 141
Kyneton Guardian 285
Kyodo News 298

The Land 38, 55, 70, 211–12, 307, 310
Lattouf, Antoinette 22, 149, 202, 231–32, 295–96
Lawnham, Patrick 49
Lee, Elaine 78
Lettini, Isabella 143, 175, 220–21, 226, 257, 272, 296
Leunig, Michael 218
Lewis, Steve 54, 71, 107–108, 122–23, 268–69, 296–97
Lock the Gate Alliance 267–68
Lord, Gillian 57, 66, 202, 254–55, 297
Lyall, Kimina 144

McArthur, Ian 98, 260–61, 298
McCann, Mike 33–34
McClymont, Kate 287
McColl, Gina 218–19
McDonald, Willa 101
McGill, Linda 118
McGowan, Cathy 273
McGuinness, Jan 5
McKendrick, Brian 34
The Mail 67, 284
Mann, Simon 6, 29–30, 44–45, 56, 58, 74–76, 140–43, 148–49, 175–76, 233, 297–98
Marr, David 2, 11, 26, 62–63, 75, 82, 122, 170, 213, 224–25, 298
   editorship 160–61
   Fairfax 164–65
   first interview 159
   growing up 156–57
   journalism, choosing 158–59
   law, career in 157–58
   life after Fairfax 166–67
   Media Watch 165, 298
   Patrick White biography 161–64, 298
   writing influences 157–58, 163
Martin, Peter 197
Maxwell, Robert 189–90
May, Ken 37
Mayne, Stephen 43–44
Meade, Amanda 11, 77–88, 225, 235, 299
   The Australian 80
   cadetship at *Sydney Morning Herald* 79–80
   digital world 83–84
   Finkelstein inquiry coverage 83
   growing up 77–78
   Guardian Australia, joining 86
   journalism, breaking into 78–79
   media reporting 80–81, 299
   News Corp enemies 82–83
   News Corp, leaving 84–85
Meanjin 4
Media Diversity Australia 295
Media, Entertainment and Arts Alliance (MEAA) 101, 199–203, 206–207, 210, 211, 213, 272
The Media Gang 266
Media House 2–3
media ownership rules 1, 200
   cross-media ownership 2–3
MediaXpress 267, 272
Medical Journal of Australia 307
Megalogenis, George 19–20, 49–50, 52, 109–10, 190–91, 299–300
   The Australian Moment 191
Mellor, Dean 172, 184–85, 210, 217, 239, 269, 300
The Mercury 20, 34, 260

Index

Merredin Telegraph 33, 57, 289
Merrigan, Ken 266
The Messenger 284
Metherell, Terry 38
#MeToo movement 101
Metro Media Publishing 266
Millar, Lisa 139
Miller, Tony 66
Mills, Kate 171–72, 187, 259, 300
Minus Children 145
misprints 117
mistakes 117
   accuracy, importance of 118–19, 130
   defamation laws 120
   dubious sources 120–21
   freezing 126–27
   honesty about errors 120
   inaccurate leaks 122–23
   insufficient background knowledge 118
   loss of judgment 123
   manipulation 123–25
   misprints 117
   not writing particular story 117, 118, 120–21
   trauma and grief cases 132–34
   unproven allegations 119
   wrong names 118, 120
Mitchell, Chris 80, 83, 84, 187, 193
The Monthly 166, 257, 285
Moor, Keith 13
Moore, Lord Mayor Clover 276
Moore, Matthew 34–35, 74, 118, 120, 122, 125, 138, 192, 205–206, 234, 240, 276, 301
Morris, Sophie 23–24, 107, 223–24, 301
Moss, Irene 128
Muir, Ricky 107
Munro, Craig 161
Murdoch, Lachlan 71–72, 80–81
Murdoch, Rupert 7, 70, 81, 84, 152, 173, 205
Murphy, Paul 200

Nation Review 288
National Library of Australia (NLA) 9
National Press Club 269, 296

The National Times 68, 101, 159, 160–61, 170, 294, 306
Newcastle Herald 173, 199, 201, 209, 309
Newcastle and Lake Macquarie Post 309
Newgate Communications 268
News Corporation Australia 72, 165, 166, 185
   ABC and 82–83, 165
   culture 80–81
   digital world and 83–84
   enemies 82–83
   family friendliness 152
   Finkelstein inquiry and 83, 188
   House Committee 204, 205
   perspective and focus 187–88
   redundancies 9, 204–205, 209
   redundancy payouts 200
   scholarships for student newspaper editors 37
   sub-editing 176–77
   unions, hostility to 204–206
News Limited *see* News Corporation Australia
news media
   advertising revenue 7, 180–82, 186
   corruption of system 122
   digital disruption 3–4, 7, 169
   journalist mobility 60
   print business model 185–86
   support for transition 6
   20th century 4–5
News Media Bargaining Code 280
newspapers
   entertainment role 20–21
   independent publications 42
   regional 30, 40, 42, 44, 48, 53, 54–55, 191, 210, 246–48, 273, 280
   role in community 15–16, 40
   sport 20–21
   student 37
   suburban 16, 54, 57, 67, 96, 176
   20th century 5–6, 15
newsrooms 1–3, 62–63
   centralisation 176–77
   changes in 75, 170–83, 189–195
   copy kids 31–32, 43, 64–65
   copy tasters 66
   culture 4–5, 62–76, 79–80

deadline pressures 69, 74–75
descriptions 5
drinking 72–73, 99
editorial integrity 74
Fairfax versus News Corp 74
hierarchy 63–64
machismo 140, 148
power dynamics 69–70
rivalries 73–74
sexual harassment and discrimination 89–101
smaller, training in 54–57
sub-editors 8, 39, 46, 52–53, 62, 64–68, 75, 176–78, 192, 277, 280
unions in *see* unions
variations in culture of 63
New York Times 112, 126, 285
Nguyen, Van 139
Nine Entertainment Company 1, 11 *see also* Fairfax Media
Noonan, Gerard 71
Northam Telegraph 289–90
Northern Territory News 165
The North West Star 55, 207, 293, 302

Oakes, Laurie 94
O'Brien, Kerry 82
O'Donoghue, Lowitja 128
O'Dowd, Jeni 71–72, 100, 115
Orr, Aleisha 133–34, 193, 237, 267, 302
Osmond, Warren 79
Overlander 4WD 184, 300
Oxford Star 293

Packer family 159
Packer, James 184
Packer, Kerry 70, 159, 184
Packer, Sir Frank 70, 184
Pagemasters 176, 192, 287, 298
Palmer, Tim 82
Panama Papers 279
Patching, Roger 39
Pearson, Christopher 43
Pell, George 166
Pelosi, Nancy 281
Pence, Mike 281

Perkin, Graham 1–2, 94
photojournalism 50, 92, 94–95, 220–21
  digital technology 174–75
Piper, Tim 33
Pirrie, Michael 129
political journalism 122, 147, 238
  'drops' 122
  leaks 122–23
post-redundancy period
  adjustments 258
  anxiety 255
  confidence, loss of 258
  counselling 256
  doubt 255–57
  families, impact on 260–61
  financial and psychological blow 260–61
  freelancing 256–57
  grief 255, 256, 258, 263
  identity, loss of 10, 154, 188, 229, 260
  preparation for new life 254
  uncertainty 255
  variety of experiences 258–62
post-traumatic stress disorder (PTSD) 137, 142–44
Prerauer, Maria 111
Printing and Kindred Industries Union 199
printing presses 2, 173
Prior, Flip 11, 41, 69, 125, 134–35, 243–53, 302
  growing up 243–44
  journalism, beyond 249–53
  journalism, breaking into 245–49
  school, after 244–45
Progress Press 303
Pryor, Geoff 61
public relations 123–24

Qantas Magazine 307
Quarterly Essays 166, 298, 299
Queensland Country Life 310

radio 2, 5
Ramadge, Paul 195
redundancies
  ABC 221–22

Index

acknowledgement of service, lack of 230–31
betrayal, feeling of 154–55
Covid-19 191
days following *see* post-redundancy period
digital disruption, through 181, 217
downsizing 216–17
experience, loss of 188–89, 226–27
Fairfax Media 6, 9, 173, 191, 192–93, 195–97
farewell parties 239–40
future work opportunities 237–38
Hunger Games 222–23
impact 10, 88, 229
last days at work 228–42
lessons from last days 241–42
loss of professional identity 10, 154, 188, 229, 260
management and 208–209, 230
mass meetings 217
media coverage of job losses 312–26
mergers and acquisitions, impact 184–85
News Corp 9, 204–205, 209
pre-2012 192
printing ritual of farewell 234
process of 215–27
resilience and reinvention following *see* reinvention
secrecy 235
timeline of 312–26
2012 round 188–91, 192–95, 200–202
union negotiations 200–203
voluntary versus involuntary 201–202, 218, 223–26, 240
warnings 217–18
women 154–55
regional newspapers 40–41
Reid, Campbell 68
reinvention
    activism 267–68
    advocacy and fundraising 270
    chief at staff at newspaper 271–72
    climate change advocacy 270
    content marketing 269
    copy marketing 264–65

creativity 269
digital start-ups 265, 274
end-to-end publishing company 266–67
freelancing 269–70
independent media publishing 274–75
job variety 272
journalism skills 272–73
journalistic ethos 273
layout design 271
media recruitment agencies 266
mentoring 267
online businesses 267
personal and professional challenges 271
politics, in 273–74
professional 268
resilience 275–76
volunteering 267
websites 262–63
'repetitive strain injury' 169
Ridge, Veronica 91–92, 94, 101, 118, 130, 153, 265–66, 302–303
Ringwood-Croydon Mail 303
Roberts, Jo 15–16, 151, 259, 269–70, 303
Robinson, Russell 47, 59–60, 65, 73–74, 134, 303–304
Robinson, Walter 119
Rolling Stone 288
Rudd, Kevin 123, 166, 273–74
Ryan, Colleen 100

Sainsbury, Michael 18–19, 304
Sainsbury, Murray 18
Sales, Leigh 84
Saltau, Chloe 231
Sangston, Ray 42
Sara, Sally 143
    Stop Girl 143
Sargeant, Gary 36
The Saturday Age 164, 290, 292, 303, 306
Save the Children Australia 270
SBS 87, 202
    Insight 295
    World News 292
The Scotsman 300
Scott, Mark 122, 207

sexual harassment and discrimination 48, 89–101, 146–47
   abusive emails 89–90
   bullying 91
   cases 99
   gender discrimination 90–96
   men's views on culture 98–99
   photojournalists 94–95
Shapiro, Bruce 144
Shelley, Maureen 43, 74, 152, 172–73, 180–81, 264–65, 304–305
Shmith, Michael 24, 47, 60, 111, 205
Shmith, Patricia 'Bambi' (née Tuckwell) 24
Shorten, Bill 166
Simons, Margaret 99
Simons, Paul 124
Sinclair, Bart 168, 177, 182, 261–62, 305–306
Skase, Christopher 57
Slipper, Peter 107
Smith, Mike 75
social media 84, 85
   'bounce rates' 171
   guidelines 171
   training in 171
Solomon Star 302
South China Morning Post 303
Southern Cross 2
The Spectator Australia 295
Spooner, John 58, 218–19, 221, 233–34, 259, 306
sports journalism 20–21, 52, 95, 168, 195
Standard News 283
Stephens, Michael 89–90
Stephens, Mitchell 186
Stephensen, Inky 161
Stevens, Leigh 44–45
Stolen Generations 127–28
stories 12–14, 102–3
   access to 107
   airplane disasters 102–104, 134
   breaking 12–14, 53–54, 57
   buzz of 104
   capture and production of 112–14
   chasing and catching 103–104
   climate change 111–12
   cooperation across mastheads 110–11
   corruption 160–61
   deadlines and 114–15
   editorial demands 115–16
   grief, of *see* trauma, reporting on
   Hoddle Street massacre 104–105
   identification of 109–10
   'Lego-set' approach 115–16
   luck and initiative 106
   'Moomba Monarchs' 112–14
   negotiation for interviews 107
   1987 federal election 106–107
   'not sexy' 111–12
   not writing 118
   political 106–110
   power of 105–106
   sources 108
   Thredbo landslide 114–15
   trust 107–109
   violence and *see* trauma, reporting on
Storyteller Services 267
student newspapers 37
Suich, Max 159
The Sun News-Pictorial 4, 5, 15, 21, 52, 73, 133, 284, 290, 297, 299, 303, 308 *see also Herald Sun*
   'The Subs' Club' 99
The Sunday Age 114, 218, 289, 290, 293, 303, 305, 308
The Sunday Australian 51, 94, 294
Sunday Herald Sun 111, 176, 230, 291, 303–304
The Sunday Independent 304
Sunday Press 106, 284, 306
The Sunday Telegraph 64, 71, 81, 100, 125, 126, 286, 287, 307
The Sunday Times 43
Suzman, Janet 159
Swannell, Cate 97, 118, 120–21, 169–70, 171, 175, 177, 182, 209–10, 236–37, 256, 306–307
The Sydney Morning Herald 6, 16, 34, 35, 40–41, 78, 101, 110, 118, 123, 128, 138, 157, 170, 195, 258, 271, 287, 288, 294, 297, 298, 299, 301, 308, 309, 310
   cost cutting measures 186–87
   first woman editor 100
   gender inequality 150–51
   Good Weekend 166, 285

Index

Hunger Games 222–23
newsroom culture 72–73, 75, 79–80, 164–65, 167
redundancies 192–93, 203, 215, 224, 234–35, 240 *see also* redundancies
technology and 171, 173, 182
'women's pages' 95
Sydney Review 295

Tandberg, Ron 218
Taylor, Lenore 87
Tedmanson, Sophie 17–18, 30, 49, 50, 63–64, 69–70, 102–104, 307
television 5
Temple, Peter 39
Thomas, Di 40–41, 210, 235, 240, 273, 307–308
3AW 2, 3
The Times 102, 117, 290, 293, 307
Tippet, Gary 73, 114–15, 118, 132–33, 136, 143, 308
Today 293
Toowoomba Telegraph 310
Top Gear 126
Top Gear Australia 21, 126, 210, 286
Torney, Kate 222
Toseland, Martin 117
  A Steroid Hit the Earth 117
Townsville Bulletin 289
trauma, reporting on 131–44
  coping strategies 140
  court cases 131–32
  death knocks 132–36
  foreign correspondents 126–27, 136–43
  impact on journalists 131–32
  'knocking on grass' 135
  Malaysian Airlines Flight 17 134
  massacres 140–41
  mental health claims 144
  natural disasters 138–39
  post-traumatic stress disorder (PTSD) 137, 142–44
  stories of grief, sharing 133
  war zones 140–42
Trump, Donald 279, 281, 282
Turnbull government 3, 273
Turnbull, Malcolm 123, 273
The Twin Cities Post 308

Twitter 83, 84, 85, 171, 249, 251–52, 262, 265
typographical errors 117

Uhlmann, Chris 269, 296
unions
  declining membership 202, 212–13
  disillusionment with 204–205, 207, 210–11
  editors and 210–11
  employer-worker relations 206, 207–208
  Fairfax 74, 192, 196, 200, 204, 208, 218
  House Committees 74, 192, 196, 199–201, 205, 208, 210, 213, 218
  News Corp hostility to 204–206
  redundancy package negotiations 200–204, 213–14
  strikes 207
  weakened state of 212–13
Universal Magazines 300
University of Melbourne student paper *Farrago* 283
'Utegate' 122–23

Victoria Police rigged court cases 146
Victorian land scandals 145
Vincent, Graeme 95
Viner, Katherine 167
Vogue Australia 307

Walker, Tony 20–21, 60–61, 136–37, 308–309
Walkley Awards 82, 140, 189, 265
Warren, Chris 200
Washington Post 126
Waterhouse, Charles 34, 260, 309
WAtoday 302
Watson, Alysson 173, 199–201, 206, 209, 309–10
The Weekend Australian 17, 100
The Weekly Times 176, 293 *see also* The Herald and Weekly Times
Wells, Liz 38–39, 55, 70, 211–12, 310
Wendt, Jana 78
The West Australian 43, 134–35, 193–94, 197, 246, 249, 267, 290, 301, 302
Western Times 284

West Gate Bridge collapse (Melbourne) 13–14
West, Michael 25–26, 35, 72–73, 123–24, 186–87, 222–23, 259, 274–75, 310–11
Wheeler, Barry 147
Wheels 21, 126, 235, 237, 238–39, 286
White, Dick 161
White, Patrick 161–64, 298
White, Ruth 161
Whitlam, Gough 60, 157
Whitlam government 21
Whitsunday Times 306
Wiedermann, Rod 266
Wilkinson, Marian 298
Willesee, Mike 78, 107
Williams, Kim 84
Wilson, Amanda 100, 195
Wilson, Bruce 14
Wilson, David 146
Woman's Day 303
Women in Media (WiM) 101, 206, 212
women journalists 37
    abusive emails 89–90
    child-rearing 146–47, 150–54
    discrimination 146–47
    editorships 100
    foreign postings 95, 100
    gender discrimination 90–91, 152–53, 212 *see also* sexual harassment and discrimination
    'glass ceiling' 150–51
    harassment 89–92 *see also* sexual harassment and discrimination
    human interest stories 94
    1970s 95
    1980s 96
    numbers, increase in 100
    online abuse 100
    pay gap 90–91, 153–54, 212
    'the pregnancy round' 152
    redundancies 154–55
    sexist attitudes to 93–94, 211
    underestimation of 96
Woolcott, Richard 54
Wright, Peter 42

www.ingramcontent.com/pod-product-compliance
Lightning Source LLC
Chambersburg PA
CBHW031425230426
43668CB00007B/438